Additional Praise for
The Savage Way

Frank's story is not just his story but *our* story: how a whole generation of African-Americans that came of age and were educated in an era of racial segregation, went on to become captains of industry. Shattering glass ceilings, we many times carried both the burden and the opportunity of being "the first". . . . What is particularly remarkable about Frank's narrative is his meteoric assent at a time when there were no role models in the global financial arena, and little appreciation for the importance of globalization.

—A. Barry Rand, Chairman of Howard University Board of Trustees, and CEO of AARP

One of the most difficult things in life is to overcome adversity. Frank Savage demonstrates how to navigate disturbed waters in times of peril. Integrity is a core value in life. Frank's experience of restoring his reputation after the Enron debacle is inspiring.

—Gary Jobson, America's Cup Hall of Fame and President of U.S. Sailing, the national governing body of sailing

Frank Savage has written a wonderful book that tells the story of personal determination and career achievement. . . . [*The Savage Way*] is also an insightful window into global business.

—Vali R. Nasr, Dean of The Johns Hopkins University's Paul H. Nitze School of Advanced International Affairs

A page-turner of a memoir! *The Savage Way* is the winning way. Bravo, Frank!

—Loida Lewis, businesswoman, philanthropist, civic leader, and author

Frank is a special person – professionally and personally. His ever-present smile, pride in family and friends, and business and sailing accomplishments all combine to make him a role model and a wonderful friend and colleague. This is a compelling life story worth telling."

—Pamela P. Flaherty, Chairwoman of the Board of Trustees, Johns Hopkins University

The Savage Way teaches us that no dream is unattainable and that in the face of adversity, especially in uncharted waters, we must draw upon our core beliefs and values to right the ship of our own journey. *The Savage Way* is filled with heartfelt and candid reflections on personal and business experiences with lessons learned that both instruct and inspire.

—Sidney A. Ribeau, President of Howard University

Despite pursuing a demanding international business career, Frank Savage always responded when called upon to help his home community. As chairman of the Harlem-based Freedom National Bank during its troubled times, and as an investor of much needed capital in fledgling black businesses, Frank Savage as founder and CEO of the Equitable minority business investment initiative, never forgot his roots. *The Savage Way* is a testament to his commitment.

—David N. Dinkins, the 106th Mayor of New York City and Professor in the Practice of Public Affairs, Columbia University

I have known Frank almost 45 years and I've come to have a deep appreciation for his professionalism, his desire to be the best, and his business acumen. He is one of the one unsung heroes with respect to the success of *Essence* magazine. As a member of its board of directors, his judgment, his leadership, his commitment to the empowerment for African-American women was all deeply appreciated by me.

—Edward Lewis, Founder of *Essence* magazine

Frank's honesty and courage in writing about some of his darkest days and sailing's magical healing powers, presents a moving look at the shape of his humanity as well as his enduring survival instincts.

—Shahara Ahmad-Llewellyn, Commissioner of New York City Commission on Women's Issues

The Savage Way is an inspirational story of finding joy and achieving success in unexpected places.

—H. Carl McCall, Chairman of the Board of Trustees, The State University of New York

I met Frank Savage when I was a 20-year-old undergraduate student serving on the board of trustees for Howard University. Since that time, he has been a mentor, a counselor, and a friend whose advice helped me become the 59th mayor of the city of Atlanta by the time I was 40 years old. *The Savage Way* includes so much of the guidance I received on so many late-night and early-morning calls. I could not be more pleased that he has made the decision to share it.

—Kasim Reed, Mayor of Atlanta, Georgia

The Savage Way

Successfully Navigating the Waves of Business and Life

Frank Savage

WILEY

John Wiley & Sons, Inc.

Cover image: Kimberlee Holcombe
Cover design: Paul McCarthy

Published by John Wiley & Sons, Inc., Hoboken, New Jersey.
Published simultaneously in Canada.

Limit of Liability/Disclaimer of Warranty: While the publisher and author have used their best efforts in preparing this book, they make no representations or warranties with respect to the accuracy or completeness of the contents of this book and specifically disclaim any implied warranties of merchantability or fitness for a particular purpose. No warranty may be created or extended by sales representatives or written sales materials. The advice and strategies contained herein may not be suitable for your situation. You should consult with a professional where appropriate. Neither the publisher nor author shall be liable for any loss of profit or any other commercial damages, including but not limited to special, incidental, consequential, or other damages.

For general information on our other products and services or for technical support, please contact our Customer Care Department within the United States at (800) 762-2974, outside the United States at (317) 572-3993 or fax (317) 572-4002.

Wiley publishes in a variety of print and electronic formats and by print-on-demand. Some material included with standard print versions of this book may not be included in e-books or in print-on-demand. If this book refers to media such as a CD or DVD that is not included in the version you purchased, you may download this material at http://booksupport.wiley.com. For more information about Wiley products, visit www.wiley.com.

Library of Congress Cataloging-in-Publication Data:

Savage, Frank.
    The Savage way : successfully navigating the waves of business and life / Frank Savage.
       p.   cm.
    Includes index.
    ISBN 978-1-118-49460-8 (cloth); ISBN 978-1-118-51376-7 (ebk);
    ISBN 978-1-118-51377-4 (ebk); ISBN 978-1-118-51366-8 (ebk)
      1. Savage, Frank. 2. Capitalists and financiers—United States—Biography.
    3. Businessmen—United States—Biography. I. Title.
  HG172.S35A3 2013
  332.1092—dc23
                                                2012033922

Printed in the United States of America

10 9 8 7 6 5 4 3 2 1

The origin of my memoir is a story in and of itself. It started years ago, when Cynthia Winston, the youngest tenured professor of psychology at my alma mater, Howard University, asked me to sit for an interview. Dr. Winston was eager to apply a new approach to oral history she was developing to chronicle my tenure as chairman of the university's board of trustees. I was happy to comply.

This history was destined to be filed away in Howard's Moorland-Spingarn Research Center, along with the archives of all of the university's rich history. But along the way, something else happened, something I would have never anticipated.

Cynthia happened to be the daughter of one of my Howard classmates, Michael Winston, a former vice president of academic affairs at Howard and a Phi Beta Kappa. And this, perhaps, gave her the comfort to probe my experiences a little bit deeper than most might. At some point, during Cynthia's questions regarding my background in the international business, philanthropic, and sailing worlds, she stopped almost mid-sentence and remarked, "Frank, you have a psychology of success that is unique. And your life is different from not only any previous Howard chairman, but any other African American I know. Your story needs to be told and disseminated around the world."

I was taken aback, yet intrigued by her observation, and suggestion. With that, Cindy guided me on a journey of self-discovery which lasted five years. She has been with me all the way, and I could not have written this memoir without her insight and inspiration.

On the eve of the publication of this book, I was saddened by the untimely and quite serious illness of my colleague and partner in this effort, Cynthia Winston.

I dedicate this book to her.

—Frank Savage

Contents

Foreword

Frank Savage. Yes, sir!

Did I tell you that Frank is a generous man?

To know Frank Savage is a good thing because Frank is a man who has some credit cards. *Ahhh, sukie.* When Frank calls and says, "Let's go out to dinner," "Let's do something," I know I don't have to bring *my* credit cards. One of the greatest men on the face of this earth, a long and very dear friend of mine (and I better keep his name to myself if I want to keep it that way), taught me the trick. Yes, don't bring your credit cards, but also make sure you have good posture. You don't slink away. Understand? No sir.

But time and decades of experience have taught me another golden part of that formula: Make sure my man Frank Savage is there.

Not only is he generous, Frank Savage is the kind of man who has a deep respect for how things are supposed to be done. He has great respect for his race and his culture. He would be embarrassed to be in a fine restaurant, these two men, Frank Savage and Bill Cosby, sitting there when the check arrives—Uh-Oh—and neither one of us has credit cards to pay for the meal after running up a great bill. That sort of just leaving things to fate, "oh well," is not the Frank Savage way, it hasn't been the way the man has lived his life and made himself into such a first-class success.

Before Frank shared this book with me, he told me all about what he had planned to write in it. He told me at dinners and business meetings, how he wanted this memoir to inspire every reader, young and not so young—like Frank—to find what is best in them. He said he wanted them to be inspired to reach higher than they ever thought they could. Stretch for excellence, no matter what color you are or where you're from. And that's more true, he says to me, for people not born with a famous name tacked on the back of theirs, or a leg up in the race to the top.

When Frank asked me if I would write this foreword, I was thinking I could write a sketch of the man and try not to give too much away, so you can have almost as much fun as I have had getting to know Frank Savage. Then there it was. This foreword popped into my brain. It was written and ready to go. This thing has made a home in my head and was just waiting for Frank to finish his book so it could hop on these pages.

There is so much of Frank's story here. We see how his teen-age mother got on a train leaving her home in North Carolina and headed for a better life in Washington, DC. She got on that train with her infant twins, Frank and Frances, and just two bottles of milk. When she got to DC the milk was spoiled but, hey, her children weren't. Frank shows us how this mother, a master chef of a beautician, reinvented herself into a kind of DC business legend, Madame La Savage. Everybody called her that, even little Frank and his sister. Then we see Frank getting his education, going to Howard University, and Johns Hopkins University, and how his world goes international. Before anybody can say Saudi Arabia, Frank and his young family are living there as he sinks his teeth into global finance as a young, African-American banker.

Then he's in Africa, where he always dreamed of working. And then he's back in America, raising money to help black businesses get a start. Has anyone heard of Essence magazine? Hello. My man Frank was there to help finance the single largest and most influential black woman's magazine in history. And then he's back to Africa, fighting apartheid in South Africa with smart money and a daring plan to use it.

Then Frank Savage went on to travel the world raising millions of dollars in one place, and I think even billions in another, as an international financial wizard, a major player with a pocket of shiny credit cards. An office in Japan. Meeting and holding high-finance dinners in Switzerland.

Once, Frank told me that there is no real secret to his life. He says he conducts his life and business the same way he sails—and races—his beautiful sailboats. All of them named for his lovely wife, Lolita. Smart man. I think there is a metaphor here: the man and his boat navigating through rough waters. Everybody can conjure up a picture of sailing, being out there on those waters even when there are sheep grazing on the sea.

I'm not joking.

You don't know about the sheep? That's sailing talk. It means when the winds are blowing so hard that you get these foamy tops on the water. From an airplane, it looks like sheep out there grazing on the ocean. With sailboating, most of us have two pictures in our heads: one, where people are just sitting there; and, two, everything is upright or you can read the small print on the bottom of the sail—yes!—because the wind is whipping all around you.

But when Frank sails, when he does anything, it is all about confidence and leadership. Confidence. And. Leadership. He says his magic to winning sailboat races is that, "I always know how to put my crew together, and get it to work beautifully together. That's why I win, Bill."

When he's racing, he has to get a crew of sixteen, seventeen, people working like one. This is a man who knows that every person has to be held accountable. He knows that every person on that boat is going, for him, above and beyond his, and her, job, while making sure their two arms and two legs are magically working to somehow keep this boat out of danger and heading to the finish line.

I told him to please don't tell too many other people because these are the very qualities everybody wants to have in their leaders. He'd get snatched up. These are all the great qualities that people remember in human beings, period. He just smiled at me the way he does with that warmth of his. If you know Frank Savage you have to know that smile. Here it is smack across this book's cover. There are few people I know who quite have Frank's smile, his warmth.

You take one look at the man and you know he's comfortable with life. And that feeling, it's very, very contagious. At times, one could almost become depressed when thinking of oneself when sitting next to Frank Savage; one might say to oneself, "Why am I not like this?"

When I told him this, Frank just smiled and reached for his credit card. Isn't that marvelous?

That's why I love Frank.

BILL COSBY

Prologue

Her name was *Lolita*. And not every port she carried me to over the years was charted in degrees of latitudes and longitudes. On a flat sea her keel sat deeper in the water than twice the height of most men. From her teak deck, which flared with her hull like a dancer's hips, her mast towered nearly 80 feet. And her length, from the stem to the stern, was an inch shy of 57 feet. With the wind bold in her sails, *Lolita*, the third and last vessel of that name that I have owned, was exhilarating as she knifed through the waves, leaving a foamy wake and a stinging, salty spray.

But like most things that matter, my gleaming sailboat, named for my dear wife, was much more than the sum of her parts, much more than could ever be suggested in her simple specifications. I trusted her to not only win sailboat races around the globe for me and my crew, I trusted her to sail me out of the storms of earthly preoccupations and into the places where serenity meets fulfillment as snugly as the sky meets the sea.

Not so long ago, drifting in this ephemeral place of open sea and open mind, I found myself contemplating what had brought me to this marvelous moment in my life. I had logged more than 70 years, a life that began in uncertain waters to find sweet swells of an enchanting childhood shared with my twin sister, Frances, then early success in international banking. It has been a life marked, sometimes painfully public, by dead seas and heady trade winds, too. It has been a life that has bestowed on me a beautiful and loving family, a devoted wife who has never left my side, even in the most difficult of times, and my children and grandchildren who mean more to me than life itself. And friends, such good friends.

I was blessed, I reminded myself, that afternoon at the helm, as I glided along a breathtaking waterscape with my heart light and soul brimming with gratitude, alone in my thoughts. I had literally journeyed so far beyond my birthplace of Mount Rocky, from the tobacco fields of North Carolina. I had sailed so far beyond the limited expectations too often the burden of black boys like me who grew up between the wake of the Great Depression of the late 1930s and the first promising ripples of the civil rights movement of the early 1960s. I was a kid, not too unlike black kids growing up today, who dared to dream larger than those who dared to doubt my capacity to make those dreams real.

So many of those dreams did materialize in my waking life; very few, but some, by way of luck or accident. Most came from being psychologically and emotionally prepared for opportunities.

I had learned at the feet of my incredible mother, watching her reinventing herself in our adopted hometown of Washington, DC, and becoming an icon of self-determination, an independent businesswoman long before such things were fashionable and profitable for black women. She would come to be known and addressed by just about everyone, as Madame La Savage.

As I steadied by boat's helm through the sharpening wind that afternoon, lost in the wispy clouds of memory, I saw myself as a young man again, married to my first wife and expecting my first child. I saw myself heading to Africa for the first time as part of Operation Crossroads Africa, a brainchild of a visionary, Presbyterian minister based in Harlem.

I will never forget joining my fellow Crossroaders gathered at a special White House ceremony in the Rose Garden. President John F. Kennedy himself greeted us and told us that we represented the future of a rapidly changing world, one in which the old boundaries and provincial thinking was dissolving before our eyes. Of course, he was right as doors once shut began to loosen on their hinges just as my hard work gave me sturdy legs to walk through them.

Racing *Lolita* with Frank at the helm of his Swan 56, becoming overall winner of Around Block Island Race 2000.

After more than 30 years of thriving in two major Fortune 500 financial companies, I set up my own. Since August 2001, I have been the chief executive officer of Savage Holdings LLC, a global financial services company I founded and based in New York. Savage Holdings was to serve as a platform for me to give advice and guidance to global companies such as Hinduja Group, a family-owned conglomerate based in India.

My years in finance have afforded me a life even I could not have imagined 50 years ago. There are days when I sit in my mid-Manhattan office overlooking the storied corridors of America's still formidable financial might and ponder the odds I beat to get here.

I wonder how much my resume reflects the man I am. Yes, it reveals some signposts of a life thoroughly lived: serving on the boards of numerous corporations and not-for-profit organizations, including Bloomberg, L.P., Lockheed Martin and the New York Philharmonic. It will indicate that I am chairman emeritus of the Board of Trustees of Howard University and trustee emeritus of Johns Hopkins University, my alma maters.

I have been a major contributor to political causes and candidates with whom I share a passion for making positive change in a country that has given me so much. I have also donated millions of dollars to Howard, where it all started for me. I also, and with great pride, set up one of the largest scholarships of its kind at Johns Hopkins Nitze School of Advanced International Studies, also known as SAIS, in Washington, DC.

On completing my graduate studies at SAIS, I was recruited by Citibank. I became the first African-American officer of Citibank and member of its international division. From my office on 54th and Madison Avenue, I can actually see the old Citibank building where my career began.

My first assignment: Jeddah, Saudi Arabia. It was a challenging experience and one that came as a surprise because I had expected to go to Africa. Eventually, after two years of proving myself, I was dispatched to Africa where I had long wanted to return since my Crossroads days there.

There is a picture of me that I cherish. It freezes me at an intersection of time—mid-1970s—and place—the Ivory Coast—and ambition—boundless. I am young, trim, and athletic, standing in an African marketplace dressed in an open-collared khaki shirt and matching pants. My hands are in my pockets as I pose, head slightly tilted, among African women who hover and mill about as if I were some lost son now found. My skin is the same luminous, rich, smooth brownness as theirs. I'm smiling in a kind of satisfaction only the photograph can do justice. My eyes are shaded behind dark brown sunglasses, yet there is a sense in my gaze that I was looking at my future. I have always loved Africa. Even as I traveled throughout the globe pursuing my financial career, Africa is still in my heart.

For some 50 years, I dedicated myself to international banking, corporate finance, and global investment management. And, as a black man, even as a part of the Great Mobility of the 1960s and 1970s when new generations of well-educated and well-prepared African Americans entered professions previously denied them, I often found myself a minority of one as I climbed to the top of my field and interacted with heads of commerce and state.

Race was always an unpredictable and potentially dangerous current. But I never let that stop or slow me in going as far as my talents and determination could take me.

Once, when I returned from a business trip to my Tokyo office, an African-American friend innocently asked me, "Frank, how does it feel working with Japanese, in Japan, knowing they are racist?"

"I have never experienced any racial prejudice in Japan," I responded. "They know I am the chairman of a $35 billion American company and I am in charge of our business around the world."

At that time, I was senior vice president of the Equitable Life Assurance Society of the United States, and vice chairman of Equitable Capital Management.

In 1993 I was named chairman of Alliance Capital Management International, a division of Alliance Capital Management Corporation. This move came as a result of the merger of Alliance Capital and Equitable Capital management Corporation. Whether to stay with the merged companies or to follow other pursuits, like some of my colleagues did, was a crucial decision point in my life.

At the time of the merger, Alliance was the largest publicly traded asset manager in the United States, with more than $800 billion under management.

After deciding to join Alliance Capital, I and a colleague, Norman Bergel—with the support of Dave Williams, who was Alliance's CEO—raised more than $100 million to invest in the "new" South Africa. When Nelson Mandela was released from prison in February 1990, Thabo Mbeki, Mandela's successor as president of that nation, asked me (largely based on our already bold investment efforts there) to join his International Investment Advisory Council to help the nation attract foreign investors.

At this point in my life, I was serving on the boards of corporations as diverse as Lockheed-Martin, Essence Communications, and, yes, Enron.

At home, I had served, pro bono, as the chairman of Freedom National Bank in Harlem, which had been started there by Jackie Robinson, the legendary black baseball player who desegregated major league baseball in 1949. The bank had fallen on hard times, principally because of management mistakes. A number of other African Americans in the financial community, including my friend Hughlyn Fierce of Chase Bank, had been asked to help out. I volunteered and soon became chairman of Freedom.

I had seen the world many times over and became as comfortable in the nerve centers of power and wealth, whether they be in New York, L.A., in Europe, Asia, the Middle East, and Africa, as I am in my summer home in Italy; as comfortable as I am with the softer touch of power commanding my record-winning crew as we raced my *Lolitas* on the waters off Newport, of the Caribbean, of the Mediterranean, and beyond. In recent years, my love for and devotion to all things sailing earned me a seat on the honorary board of directors of the National Sailing Hall of Fame.

In April 2003, my wife and I mounted the steps to the awards ceremony to accept the prestigious Lord Nelson Award as the overall winner of the annual Antigua Classic Yacht Regatta, one of the world's premier yachting events. For a quarter of a century it has attracted some of the best yachts and crews from the United States, Europe, Australia, and the Caribbean islands.

On that afternoon, Lolita and I stood on the winners platform under a clear, azure sky on Falmouth Harbor. We were greeted by a palpable, momentary hush among the assembled competitors. Although they knew that my Swan 56 cruiser/racer, *Lolita*, had won the regatta;

they could not help but notice the graceful lines of my sailboat, her wind-swept sails and rigging, her magnificent crew working like a single organism bent on winning, when *Lolita* bested her competition.

But what many apparently had not noticed, had not known, was that her co-helmsman and owner was African American, was me, Frank Savage, Grace Savage's boy from Rocky Mount, North Carolina.

This was the first time in the history of this prestigious race that a black man and a cruising boat had won the Overall Winner trophy, a large silver bowl that graces my living room today. The local Antiguans who had always crewed for the boats and worked to get them perfect for the race, were absolutely ecstatic. It was a moment of great pride for them that a "brother" had beaten all of the "big boats."

Winning the overall Winners Trophy at Antigua was the crowning jewel of my sailboat racing career, a decades-long love of mine, a passion that began in the most unlikely way when I glanced at a sailing magazine on a flight home from St. Thomas with my wife. I was fortunate to have had the time and the resources to buy, for instance, a million-plus-dollar sailboat, and to afford another half-million dollars to equip her to sail and compete.

I was even more fortunate to have assembled and befriended an international crew, including two people of color, a Harvard-educated New York lawyer and an experienced Antiguan sailboat racer who knew the Antigua waters as well as the fish bred and born in them.

This victory was built on years of preparation with my first *Lolita*, a 46-foot Swan, and our victories in our class in the 2001 and 2002 Antigua regattas. Sailing well, like living well, is not a casual affair. It comes down to self-confidence, preparation, tenacity, and leadership, all qualities my mother instilled in me at the earliest age I can remember. In a very real way, my passion for sailing is the personification of my philosophy of life.

Nothing is accomplished alone. Nothing worthwhile is achieved strictly by chance. And nothing can be truly known unless it is understood by your heart as much as by your head.

This sense of me is what enabled me to break new ground in business, to live in a beautiful home overlooking Central Park where I have entertained world leaders and bounced each of my four grandchildren on my knee; this sense has helped me be the best husband and father and friend I can possibly be.

This is what I have endeavored to bring to this book, a sharing of my values. These pages are not so much a story of one man's life, but a chart, a compendium of my successes, and, yes, failures, too, to assist you, any reader, in navigating your own course to success and fulfillment. That means even in the darkest of days and through the most treacherous of seas, whether you have the wind at your back and your destination in sight.

In either case, we must always be the helmsmen of our own destiny.

Chapter 1

Too Much Money

The most dangerous thing is illusion.

—*Ralph Waldo Emerson*

It was late summer 2001. I was 63 years old and on top of the world; and I very much liked the view. It felt like the zenith of my life as a man of business and investment, as a husband and father who had lived his life exceedingly well. And yet, I was convinced that there was more successes ahead for me.

I wasn't interested in taking it easy any time soon.

I had recently retired from Alliance Capital where I began as its chairman of the international division in 1993. That post, in the heady and rarefied universe of global finance, came after rising through the upper ranks of its parent company, Equitable Life Assurance Society of the United States, the third largest life insurance company in America and its wholly owned investment subsidiary, Equitable Capital Management Corporation. I was also thrilled to be launching the Africa Millennium Fund, my own operation. With it, I was seeking to realize my life's dream of creating a Western-style investment fund to drive much needed capital to a continent practically starving for development capital.

After all, I had created investment funds to invest in India, South Africa, and Egypt while at Alliance, so I was confident that I could accomplish this most ambitious continent-wide achievement.

Africa was important to me. Africa *is* me. I *am* Africa. *I am an African man.* That is one of the things that defines Frank Savage. Everyone will tell you that. I'm a lover of Africa. One way or the other, that's where we all come from; that's where humanity began. In terms of my heart and my soul, I have been in Africa since I was a kid. My mother planted that seed of the international deep within my imagination long, long ago. It never stopped growing.

In that late summer in 2001, I was serving on several prestigious boards overseeing major corporations and institutions of higher education. I believed, and still do, that part of the obligation of business leaders, men and women who have amassed a lifetime of skills, insights, and influential relationships, should share all what and who they know by sitting on the boards of various corporations and institutions. I must admit that I took pride in this, especially being, for instance, an active member of the board of trustees at Johns Hopkins University and the chairman of the board of trustees at Howard University, institutions that had helped to prepare me for my career.

I cannot tell you how pleased I was to be able to pledge $5 million to Howard; and at Johns Hopkins I set up one of the largest scholarships of its kind for African-American and African students in need of financial assistance to attend that university's premiere Nitze School of Advanced International Studies. My career in international finance owes a great debt to that school. And through the Frank and Lolita Savage Boost Fellowship, 50 other well-deserving students of color have gotten the same chance I did when I attended this incredible institution in the 1960s.

During that late summer, I sat on the boards of Lockheed Martin, Qualcomm, and Bloomberg LLC. I was also a member of the board of directors of Enron Corporation in what I had imagined would be a sort of crowning glory on an outstanding and fulfilling career.

These were good times. Or so I thought. I had experienced half a century of unrelenting success. And believe me, I never for one moment took that for granted. I remember cruising in Martha's Vineyard during the summer of 2001. It was so beautiful. I was below deck in my custom-crafted, air-conditioned skipper's cabin. I just sat there and took it all in. *Jesus Christ*, I thought, *I'm so lucky.*

I was making a lot of money. I was very successful in business, very successful when I was at Equitable where my job was to bring in what this multibillion-dollar concern did not have—international clients. I was able to attract more than $3 billion to Equitable Capital, which was unheard of. My early success there also marked the first time I was paid $1 million in a single year. And that was just a bonus. I went on to have tremendous success, *tremendous*. I could do whatever I wanted.

Frank and Lolita with Bill and Camille Cosby at New York gala.

But one of the faults of that period was that people like me had so much success; we had too much money. We used it to buy things. I never thought that I would get into a period where I would ever have to ask questions like, should I buy this or should I buy that? Should I want to? For so long, I could always get whatever I wanted. And I had amassed enough wealth to guarantee a comfortable retirement, although actually retiring never really dawned on me.

Personally, life with my wife, Lolita, could not have been better. We always supported each other. I had my global financial work; she had her international career as a fine painter; together, we had our family, our lovely homes in Italy and another overlooking New York's Central Park. My family was proud of me, too. Many of my six children had settled into families of their own. Every year I made time to steal away with them and their children to the Vineyard when autumn and summer begin to blend like cool cream in hot coffee.

Lolita and I traveled the world on Alliance business. We'd fly off to South Africa, for instance; we jetted throughout Europe and Asia, all over. We attended some of the most prestigious business conferences in the world, like Davos in Switzerland, World Bank and the Institute of International Finance. It was a deeply enriching experience for us. And it certainly didn't hurt that Lolita is fluent in six languages and remarkably comfortable in the dizzying whirl of high finance in high places. There were times during these trips in which I happily felt much the way a young President John F. Kennedy said he felt when he was the man "who accompanied Jacqueline Kennedy to Paris."

Together, my wife and I cultivated friends from all parts of the world, of many cultures and religions. We were at ease in this environment and luxuriated in the silent solace of setting suns while living lives as bright and vibrant as high noon.

And there were my plans of adventure, sailing *Lolita* and racing her competitively, which posed just enough dash of danger to make it all the more enticing. And rewarding. My newest sailboat was showing great potential, having won virtually every race she had completed in the early summer races on Long Island Sound, New York.

Lolita had been delivered to me only months earlier. I had her built by the Swan factory in Pietarsaari, Finland, one of the finest shipyards in the world. I was planning to sail her around the world. And why not?

This vessel, made by the ancestors of Vikings, practically arrived winning races. Call it a victory lap.

■ ■ ■

Then months seemed to pass like hours, and it was September 11, 2001. I was in South Africa at my partner's office with the Africa Millennium Fund team on business when terrorists infamously crashed jet airliners into the World Trade Center towers in Lower Manhattan, then shortly later, another passenger jet into the Pentagon; and finally, another one crashed into a Pennsylvania field, killing all aboard. I was devastated by the sheer idea of it, the awful loss of 2,977 victims, innocent lives, the insult to morality and to my country. I worried about my family and was relieved to finally learn by phone that they were unharmed.

I tried to leave the next day, but the U.S. air space was totally shut down. I was stuck in Johannesburg for three days. I'll tell you one thing. That period made me better appreciate how refugees separated from their families feel. I felt so helpless. Luckily, my business partner in South Africa, Leonard Fine, moved me into his house. He and his wife, Zel, took care of me, and, for that, I will always love them.

In the early aftermath of that horrible time for Americans everywhere, I didn't immediately realize that the attack would have tremendous impact on the viability of my Africa fund. I struggled mightily for three years to keep the fund alive but eventually, it toppled, too, into a pile of unfulfilled opportunities and broken promises, and millions of my own dollars lost in its dust. But more about that later.

Suddenly, the year was practically over, and there was a headline in the *New York Times*: Enron Admits to Overstating Profits by About $600 Million.

The 1,565-word article by Richard A. Oppel Jr. and Andrew Ross Sorkin appeared on November 9, 2001, and for me, it was the beginning of the single greatest crisis of my life, one that all these years later still reverberates in waves of disbelief, loss, and, yes, some lingering hurt.

■ ■ ■

Enron Corporation, if you don't remember, was a Houston-based energy, commodities, and services company with operations as far-flung as India. The company was co-founded in Omaha, Nebraska, in 1985 by Kenneth Lay, a conservative man by nature who held a doctorate in economics from the University of Houston. Initially, Enron was a natural gas pipeline company, selling, just what you might expect— natural gas. But Ken Lay had more in mind. He was driven by a vision of an unregulated energy industry.

When that day finally came in the 1990s, Lay's Enron quickly rose from a modest conservative concern into one of the world's most powerful companies. Lay transformed Enron into an energy and commodity trading company, buying and selling energy and power like stocks and bonds. He aspired to produce returns rivaling the Wall Street investment bank, Goldman Sachs, his model. He was not satisfied with producing only the stable, while less risky, pipeline returns. This opened the way for Enron to become heavily involved in electricity, natural gas, communications, and even pulp and paper products. Before the *New York Times* article appeared, Enron's balance sheet indicated that it had revenues of almost $101 billion and was employing some 22,000 people.

For years, Enron's reputation was stellar. *Fortune* magazine named Enron "America's Most Innovative Company" for six consecutive years. At one time, the company's stock price stood around $90 a share. Its gleaming headquarters, the Enron Complex in downtown Houston, was a postmodernist cathedral of commerce. And its cross was the giant black "E"—tilted, for no reason I knew of, to the left, and lit in red, green, and blue neon. It was planted near the building's entrance.

In December 2001, Enron, with $25 billion in assets, filed for bankruptcy and subsequently disappeared in one of the single, largest flameouts in U.S. corporate history. Its bankruptcy shook the foundations and confidence of U.S. capitalism itself. (WorldCom's bankruptcy would eclipse Enron's, to be followed in even more recent history by the bankruptcies of Lehman Brothers and Washington Mutual.)

So many lost so much. Retirement funds were lost. Life savings were lost. Careers were lost. Lives, and reputations—including my own—were lost, too. I still get chills when people mention the name Enron. Yes, to this day. I still look at people and wonder if they are looking at me through the lens of that failed company. Deep inside, and it hacks at me like a butcher's cleaver, I hurt over this. To put this pain in perspective, I also understand that the people most damaged, those with vastly fewer resources than I have had, can look at me and say that in Enron's wake you've still done all the things that you have always done. They can look at me and say that you've still sailed, still traveled the world; you still were able to send your children to the finest schools and universities. You did not lose any of your beautiful homes.

Even though I say to them that I am sorry, I know it doesn't mean anything to people because on a relative basis they have suffered more than I have. How can I express my sorrow for the damage that has been done to lives? Nothing I can say will ever be adequate. That hurt and damage to so many people as the result of Enron's demise is what troubles and pains me the most. I acknowledge that as a director of that company, I have to take some responsibility for that—not a legal responsibility, but a moral, an ethical, responsibility.

The pain that Enron inflicted on people is something I wish I could correct. Unfortunately, I can't correct it. As people go through life, I've noticed, they often take a more balanced view of things. That is what I would like people to do regarding my role as a director of Enron, take a more balanced view.

The collapse began with a loss of confidence among Enron's investors. That largely began with Jeff Skilling, Enron's chief executive officer, losing his composure on an analyst conference call in June 2001. Yes, this was the one in which he famously called Richard Grubman, an analyst with Highfields Capital who was pressing for more details regarding Enron's finances, an "asshole." As a director, I called Skilling about this. I asked, "Jeff, is this correct, did you call a guy an asshole?" He said he did and immediately realized that it was the worst thing he could have done. The call had been recorded and was soon widely disseminated.

One day in mid-August, Ken called to inform me that Skilling had tendered his resignation.

Skilling said he was, at the time, having a terrible time with a son who was suffering from a severe handicap and he felt he had to resign to give his son the attention he required. I was shocked. But my concerns were greatly alleviated when Ken told me that although he never intended to do so, he was willing to step back in as CEO because these were extraordinary times and he was committed to restoring confidence in the company. Boy, was I relieved to hear that because Ken was the reason I had joined the Enron board and I had full confidence in his ability to navigate us through any crisis. That said, I was greatly disappointed in Skilling.

As to be expected, when Ken announced to the world that he was resuming the CEO position in light of Skilling stepping away, all hell broke loose. Wall Street did not buy Skilling's explanation. Skilling was perceived as the consummate Type-A, fiercely ambitious man who often talked about where he was going to take Enron and how he was going to make it the best company in the world. The financial world could not believe that such a driven CEO would leave for "personal reasons." Enron's critics became even more suspicious, and the problems at Enron swirled like insatiable flies at a picnic.

At the time, Ken told the *Houston Business Journal* that, "We regret Jeff's decision to resign, as he has been a big part of our success for over 11 years. But, we have the strongest and deepest talent we have ever had in the organization, our business is extremely strong, and our growth prospects have never been better."

I agreed with Ken. From my perspective as a director, Enron appeared to be in a strong position and I had confidence in its future. Quite frankly, as damaging as Skilling's abrupt departure was, I always had confidence in Ken, too, and was pleased by his return to the CEO position. At the very least, it would calm market fears that Enron would be rudderless during these challenging times. Unfortunately, despite all that Ken did to restore confidence in Enron's future his efforts did not stop the continuing decline of Enron stock, nor the rumors of its pending acquisition or even bankruptcy.

Skilling's faux pas and sudden departure was followed by the CFO, Andy Fastow, showing a side of him that I had not previously seen. It emerged in the wake of the 9/11 terrorists attacks on New York and Washington, DC.

The impact on the financial markets was swift and devastating. The stock market closed—the third prolonged shutdown of the New York Stock Exchange in its history (the first was the stock market crash in March 1933, and the second, months after the United States entered

World War II in December 1941). As the market plunged after 9/11, investors fled to U.S. Treasury securities. Virtually all lending declined sharply, cutting off liquidity to big companies, a choking off of cash that was just as life-threatening to corporate America as cutting off the escape for the poor souls who had been trapped in the burning World Trade towers. The Bush administration tried to restore confidence and the Federal Reserve Board felt it was necessary to pump more funds into the banking system to restore liquidity.

Enron, along with all financial institutions, including investment and merchant banks, was directly impacted by this crisis. The company was heavily involved in taking trading positions in various commodities, letters of credit and other financial instruments that were critical to its trading and market-making operations. All of that was thrown into jeopardy. Without adequate liquidity, in other words access to great sums of money, Enron would go out of business.

Ken presided over a meeting to inform the board that the company was undergoing a liquidity crisis, like so many other corporations in the immediate aftermath of 9/11. This took place while I was still stranded in South Africa. I participated by way of a conference call from the Johannesburg International Airport. I heard Ken explain that he wanted to review our strategy to cope with the problem. "We feel we have the situation under control," he said, "and I have asked Andy to outline our situation and strategy."

Fastow began his presentation, first reviewing the state of the financial markets in the United States and around the world, focusing on the liquidity of markets in the world. The situation was dire; only a few days had passed since 9/11 and everybody was still in a state of panic. Consequently, there was very little trading going on.

Everyone, at least all the major financial institutions, were being extremely conservative. Among other things, that meant not taking on new risks. In some cases, margin calls—brokers' demands that assets that have lost value at a certain point either be sold or more money be put up to back the asset—were being made as banks tightened their lending standards. Liquidity was incredibly tight.

Fastow detailed our current situation. He addressed that among others, our lines of credit availability with banks and the overall risk profile of the company. He gave us the bottom line: although this was a difficult time, we were in close contact with all of our banks and felt that we had the adequate liquidity to survive this crisis. Yet, we still weren't out of the high grass. The Federal Reserve Board had, like I said, stepped in to provide more liquidity to the banks to relieve some of the pressure and it looked like the markets might be coming out of this crisis, but it was still very much touch-and-go.

Fastow was staying in close contact with all our banks and customers to ensure that we were able to meet any obligations.

After the presentation, the board felt a greater sense of comfort that Enron would come through this crisis. Ken resumed control of the meeting and asked Fastow to excuse himself.

"There's one other important decision that we have to make today," he said. "It's about Andy. Andy has come to us with a proposition. He thinks he can lead us out of the crisis, and quite frankly I think he can also. I feel very comfortable with him being in the CFO position during this challenging time. All of our financial partners and banks have confidence in him."

Good news so far, I thought to myself.

"But he has two conditions."

Conditions?

"He's asked to be promoted from executive vice president to deputy president. That's the first one. Secondly, he wants to have assurance that he can only be fired by the board of directors."

There was dead silence from the board members. Fastow did not report to us. He reported to Ken Lay. I was the first one who spoke up.

"Ken, wait a minute. Who the hell does he think he is? He's essentially saying that he wants to go around you. I can't agree to that."

Ken tried to put a good face on it. "I don't think that he's trying to go around us. He just wants to know that he has the board's support."

I thought to myself again, *here we are in a crisis. It looks like he's trying to take advantage of this situation to move himself closer to the CEO position. How dare he do this!*

Of course, all the directors chimed in as well, with exactly the same view, and refused to meet Fastow's terms. We instructed Ken to tell him that the board did not think this was an appropriate position to take and that it deferred to Ken to make recommendations regarding the people that reported to him.

Ken, a bit embarrassed, agreed. From my standpoint, I was quite surprised that Fastow would make such a request. But I was even more shocked that Ken would bring this to the board.

My God, Ken must really be concerned about the impact of 9/11, I thought. He wants to make sure that Fastow is always in place to deal with the banks, because he's the man who has their confidence.

Maybe Fastow had put Ken in a bind by threatening to leave if he didn't get what he was asking for? Internally, I started questioning Fastow, especially his poor judgment and selfishness in bringing this up at such a critical time for the company. I was now convinced that he was trying to take advantage of the situation, including Skilling's resignation. I didn't know what had transpired between him and Ken or what was behind Fastow's proposition. But I never forgot it, and it negatively affected my opinion of him.

Any thought of my supporting Fastow if he were in line for CEO disappeared. Had he successfully navigated the company through this financial crisis, of course his standing in my mind would have been enhanced. Perhaps I would have been ready to support any reasonable promotion recommended by Ken. But to jump the gun and try to advance himself amid the crisis seemed very unwise on his part and forever changed my opinion of his qualifications to be the CEO. In fact, we did weather the 9/11 storm, but the issue of giving Fastow a promotion never came up again. What we later learned about his terrible, selfish deeds went far beyond anything I ever imagined.

■ ■ ■

During and after 9/11, financial analysts and researchers on both the buy and sell side started assessing all financial companies to determine their ability to withstand unexpected fiscal crises. In the process, questions began emerging in the perceived cracks in Enron's financial strength and accounting practices. As a result, Enron's stock came under selling pressure. In plain language, it lost value.

Any chance of Enron's survival evaporated when it was discovered that Fastow, as Enron's chief financial officer, had been running a conspiracy inside the company and secretly skimming money for himself—totally without the knowledge of the board.

These revelations, along with the restatement of years of financial statements that wiped out previously declared profits, were Enron's death knells heard around the financial world.

The company's stock would slide to 25 cents a share as the shadow of bankruptcy fell on the "E" on December 2, 2001.

Enron's demise was definitely the first, big corporate scandal of that era. People are still talking about it to this day. It's amazing. It will be with me for the rest of my life.

On reflection, the heart of the Enron scandal was a pattern of corporate deceit, some by commission and some by omission. All of it occurred without the board's awareness and under the guise of standard operating procedures, all with no red flags raised by Enron's accountants, auditors, or lawyers that I was ever aware of.

The Securities and Exchange Commission had sent us what is called a *Wells Notice*. That is an official SEC notification that the agency is seriously considering taking action against a company. In response, our board decided to initiate our own investigation and formed a special board committee, which I briefly chaired, to review the financials. We hired a new accounting firm to assist us in this effort. It carefully reviewed several years of Enron financial statements. Ultimately, the Powers Committee—named after my successor as chair of the committee, a new and independent director—assigned this accounting firm to fully review Enron's audited financial statements over a number of years. The firm issued a report to the committee, which disagreed with how Arthur Andersen had regarded a number of these transactions between Enron and certain Special Purpose Vehicles (SPV), which are basically off-balance sheet companies. In the words of Enron critics, they were "shell companies" expressly created to hide some of the company's assets and transactions.

Essentially, the firm asserted that Enron's revenues over a number of years had been overstated by $600 million because Enron had classified the sale of assets to these SPVs as sales, whereas, according to their findings, Enron had agreed to buy back the assets. As a result, these transactions were not actually sales and Arthur Andersen, Enron's auditors, had erred, in the firm's opinion, in permitting Enron to reflect them as such in their audited financial statements. Consequently, five to six years of Enron financial results had to be revised downward to reflect this accounting mistake.

The board was shocked, to say the least. Arthur Andersen had been the company's outside auditor for many years. It had never, at least in my brief two years of service on the board, given any of us on the board a reason to question its audited and certified financial statements. We immediately terminated Arthur Andersen, and reported the committee findings to the SEC and the press. When news of the required restatement became public, all hell broke loose—again.

Investors who thought they had enjoyed gains on the Enron stock now realized they actually had overpaid for the stock if they adjusted for the restatement. The Enron stock dropped like an anchor as even more questions about goings on at Enron began to surface.

Further investigations into the SPV unearthed that Fastow—apparently unbeknownst to Ken Lay or Jeff Skilling when he was still aboard, the men who were bosses and who had been responsible for his compensation—had skimmed more than $30 million from the SPV transactions. As difficult as it was to accept this, we, the board, did, and immediately fired Andy.

But, again, it was too late to stem the rupture of Enron's reputation. No prudent investor or company would acquire a company with this many skeletons jangling in the closet and outright wrongdoings among the company's top executives. Bankruptcy was the only available course of action.

How could this giant, successful company have sunk so deep so fast?

Enron became a popular symbol of corporate fraud and corruption, and the poster child for an era when other major corporate frauds were discovered. It was a factor in the creation of the Sarbanes–Oxley Act of 2002. That congressional response to the scandal, if you recall, mandated a number of measures to greatly discourage the destruction of financial records (which Andersen did) while a company is under investigation, as well as to discourage lapses in corporate morality.

Although more laws and regulations to prevent such Enron-like situations are definitely needed, laws by themselves cannot prevent dishonesty. The key remedy is not so much about what rules and regulations are put into place. Solutions should be more about infusing in people who assume these positions of responsibility a sense of moral obligations. Values. More on that subject later.

The Enron situation was not a self-contained disaster. It went on to batter at the business world at large by, for instance, basically destroying the Arthur Andersen accounting firm. It was founded in 1913 and was one of the most respected companies in its field.

The Powers committee we set up concluded that Andersen, "did not fulfill its professional responsibilities in connection with its audits of Enron's financial statements, or its obligation to bring to the attention of the Enron's Board (or the Audit and Compliance Committee) concerns about Enron's internal contracts over the related-party transactions." In the early waves of the scandal, Andersen went from 28,000 employees in the United States and 85,000 overseas to around 200 based primarily in Chicago, fending off swarms of civil lawsuits and carefully dismantling itself.

At the same time, Enron's complete and utter collapse raised questions like stage whispers. Among them were: What was the role of management, and the directors of Enron, including myself, in its financial calamity? Who knew what? And when? Who benefited financially, and by how much?

I was caught between a rock and a very hard place. When the first indicators of trouble began to show themselves, I couldn't believe it— and nobody else could believe it either. In the not-so-distant past, several Fortune 500 companies had experienced temporary earnings, operational or even management problems. Yet, these companies maintained a solid business, and this, in the early stages of Enron's fall, seemed to be the case for us. Enron appeared to be one of the so-called fallen angels, troubled, but solid companies that could be reinvented, even through bankruptcy, to continue operating and to be highly successful once again. At one point, I actually thought the company was going to be purchased. I was ready for that. Don't forget, Enron was, before the fall, the seventh largest company in the world.

Several companies and Warren Buffett were looking at Enron. Dynegy Inc., a much smaller company and cross-town rival, was ready to acquire Enron for a bargain basement price of $8 billion in stock. A year earlier, Enron was valued at $70 billion. But Dynegy walked away. Do you know why? When its executives learned that Fastow was at the center of what appeared to be massive corruption, the deal was dead. Dynegy then had to ask itself, what else is there? You don't touch a company if it has those kinds of problems.

I understood that. Still, Enron was a nightmare within a nightmare for me. In the aftermath of the collapse, during the many investigations and hearings on Enron, I was summoned to Houston in what would be one of the most critical moments of my life. I would be the first Enron director to appear before the lawyers representing the biggest banks in the world—JPMorgan Chase and others—who wanted to absolve themselves by making allegations that we, as directors, had been remiss in our duties and should be held accountable. I knew that this was going to be it for me. I would either come out of there the winner, or . . . I hated to think about the alternative.

■ ■ ■

After spending a good period of time sailing and clearing my head, I was rested and ready when I walked into that deposition room with my lawyers. Above all, I had a clean and clear conscience. I knew that there was nothing that those lawyers could reveal to implicate me in any collusion or dereliction of duty, because there was none. I was very confident. But yes, I was scared. I would have been stupid not to carry any fear in my gut about this days-long encounter. My life and the lives of all the board members were, like they say in spy movies, hanging in the balance.

It turned out to be a very tough deposition. The room was full of lawyers—20 of them—representing each bank with others plugged in via conference. One after another, they came at me like a wrestling tag team, many asking the same questions over and over again. It seemed as if the rapidly fired questions would never end on that opening day. One question, then a second question, then another. And the same question all over again, over and over as if the answer would magically change with another asking of the same question.

"Mr. Savage, you are a very, sophisticated businessman. You've worked all over the world. You've been on several boards. . . ." As the pinstriped, silver-haired lawyer went on, I willed my spine straighter, more upright. I could hear Madame La Savage's voice.

"Frank," she whispered only to me, "you just sit up. Tell those lawyers whatever they need to know. Be confident. Answer their questions. Tell them the truth. You have nothing to hide."

There she was again, always there when I most needed her, unencumbered by the absence of a physical body. She was pure, ever-present spiritually on those days in Houston. For me, she was just as alive then as she had been when warm flesh and blood.

"Didn't you recognize that this Andy Fastow was a criminal?" the lawyer continued.

Speaking very deliberately, I responded, "Sir, let me tell you something. You're right. I have had a long and very successful career. You're also right that I have been on many boards and have worked with a lot of really talented people. But you know something? I have never worked with criminals in my entire life. I never had the experience of dealing with people who, basically in their DNA, were criminals."

I could hear myself repeating this word, "never," but I wanted to make the point. And then reemphasize that point: never.

"I've *never* been around that element in my entire life. I didn't grow up around criminals. I didn't go to school with criminals. I've always worked with people who were upstanding, honest, and of the highest character. I may have agreed to disagree with them many times. I may have called them to task for various business and other decisions.

"But criminals? No, sir. Most of those people come from some of the best schools in the country. They've already had successful careers. They may have come from good families. They may be icons in their communities. So why would I expect that they would be criminals? Normally, companies do background checks on senior employees before hiring them to confirm their character, so why would I, as a director, expect they may be criminals?

"No, I didn't expect it. You can judge me any way you want, but I never suspected that Andy Fastow had criminal intentions."

That day in the courtroom, I saw my life played back to me like a slowly unspooling film. I knew I had to face, eye-to-eye, so to speak, the meaning of the Enron episode in my personal and professional life.

I was accustomed to being the "first," as I was on this day. Sitting in that stiff chair facing the gray sea of seasoned, high-priced lawyers, I knew my life would never be the same.

This was not just a deposition. This was a fight for my life, for my reputation, for my family, for my friends, and for the next generation of young, aspiring businesspeople, especially those of color. I knew that I could not let them down, and I came to that deposition determined to redeem myself over those next four days. I could feel the full weight of this on my shoulders.

It was very lonely. I couldn't have my wife with me. I couldn't have my kids with me. I couldn't have friends with me. It was just me, Frank Savage (along with my lawyers) in that room, in that chair, surrounded by people who wanted to bring me down.

But I had something they lacked: confidence and a totally clear conscience. So I knew that, in the end, I would win. But the deposition was extremely difficult and I could not let my guard down, not for one single second, as the questioning continued day after day.

"What do you know about Enron? When did you know? What else do you know? Didn't you know . . . ? Shouldn't you have known . . . ?" On the third day of being bombarded by what were essentially the same questions, just phrased differently, I blurted out, "Now two other lawyers have come to me, and they've asked me the same, exact question." Sitting up straight as my mother had insisted, I continued. "Now, I'm prepared to answer it, but I'm going to tell you right now, I'm going to give you the same answer that I gave about what I knew, because it's the only answer.

"So if you think that by sending different lawyers to me and asking me the same questions in different ways you're going to get another answer and trip me up, it's not going to happen, because there's only one truth that I can tell you about what I knew."

On the third day, the tide began to turn in my favor. The lawyers were less aggressive than they had been before. Coming to a question that was previously asked, the lawyers would say, "That's already been covered." I could sense that they had finally come to understand that, no matter how they posed their questions, they would find nothing because there was nothing to find.

Questioning ended early on the third day. That night, I sat by myself at the hotel bar and ordered a Scotch. Neat. It wasn't my usual drink of choice in those days, but I wanted one. I sat there and said under my breath, "Wow, Frank, you've done it. You have come through this challenge."

As I had hoped, the next day, the fourth one, was easy and we broke up early.

I went home and immediately hugged my wife. "Lolita, I think I've come through. I think that this was the absolute height of the challenge, and we're on a downhill slope now."

Later on, my prediction was confirmed when the banks' lawyers made a very telling decision on future depositions: They didn't want to question all of the other directors and they shortened the deposition time. Clearly, anticipating depositions from my co-board members that would confirm my testimony they knew that they would not be able to incriminate the board. So why waste their time? This was a monumental crossroads, a critical juncture in the Enron debacle.

Ultimately, all the civil cases against the Enron directors, me included, were either settled or dismissed and, more important, the SEC never took any action against the directors. Finally, the legal battles were over.

■ ■ ■

As I reflect on what caused the failure of Enron, I find it hard to really pin any one, single thing down. But at the core, I believe it was facilitated by the significant character flaws of the trio who basically ran Enron at the time: Ken Lay, chairman, Jeff Skilling, CEO, and Andy Fastow, its chief financial officer. What were the flaws in their characters? And was it the flaws themselves or instead a confluence of events that created an environment for these aberrations to manifest, resulting in the company's destruction? I don't think we'll ever really know: Skilling is still in jail and not talking, Fastow is out of jail and not talking. Kenneth Lee Lay, who was convicted of 10 counts of securities fraud and related infractions, died on the day after the 4th of July 2006 of an apparent heart attack. He was vacationing in Colorado while awaiting sentencing. He was 64 years old.

Nevertheless, I do have some thoughts to share.

Fastow was found guilty of fraud and sentenced to six years in prison. He knew exactly what he was doing, all for his own personal gain. He lied to the board. He manipulated the financial information. He concocted a scheme to place himself into a dual position as CFO and manager of the Enron-sponsored private equity funds to enrich himself. He bribed other Enron employees to collude with him. He conspired with a lead bank employee to defraud the Enron shareholders. The case against him is clear.

But I am always puzzled as to why Fastow, already a wealthy man from a prominent Houston family, would resort to lying, cheating, and stealing from a company that had rewarded him handsomely and afforded him an excellent reputation among his peers and in the financial industry.

In my estimation, Jeff Skilling, convicted of fraud and sentenced to 20-plus years in prison, was motivated by raw, unbridled ambition. Was he so ambitious that he lost his sense of judgment and turned a blind eye to Andy's wrongdoings? Did he abruptly resign in August 2001 because he discovered some of Andy's activities, which would inevitability result in the collapse of Enron? Did he withhold this information from Lay and the board? Can this ever really be known?

What we *do* know is that as things really turned bad, Skilling jumped ship. But as CEO, he had been too deeply involved in Enron to escape responsibility, so he is paying a price in jail right now. Did he know about the conspiracy? Was he a party to it? These questions remain unanswered.

Ken Lay seemed to be a man with it all. He was wealthy, admired by many, and a close friend of President George W. Bush. The president fondly called Ken "Kenny Boy." Lay engineered Enron's conversion from a sleepy pipeline company into a world-renowned diversified energy conglomerate. Why did he let these things happen at Enron? Did he, too, turn a blind eye to Andy's illicit activities or was it that he just placed his total trust in Andy out of naiveté? What did he think when Skilling abruptly resigned? More questions that may never find answers.

At the end of the day, Kenneth Lay, in life and in death, will be held ultimately responsible for the Enron scandal because he was the CEO, a founder, and the visionary of the company.

Although I can only speak for myself, I do not believe that *any* of the outside board members were party to the nefarious activities that contributed to the downfall of Enron. And I can honestly say to the whole world, today, what I said at that Houston deposition in 2004: I did not have even an inkling of an idea that there was any wrongdoing at Enron until the investigations and revelation of Fastow's stealing and lying. I admit to being totally blindsided. And that has cost me dearly. No, I'm not asking anyone to feel sorry for me.

Should I have known? I did everything I could within my role and power to fully carry out my directorship duties. I did so in the exact manner that I have served as a director for 20 years at Lockheed, 10 years at Qualcomm, another 10 years at Bloomberg and during my few years at ARCO and Lyondell Chemical. I have always carried out my board duties in a conscientious, diligent, and prudent manner, as each of these companies would attest.

It is unfortunate, in my estimation, that the senior management and board of directors of a corporation like Enron could not have operated with the synchronicity you'd commonly find on a racing sailboat. There, we, the directors, would be found in what we would call in sailboat parlance, the afterguard of the vessel. This is in the rear of the boat and where the decision makers of a sailboat's racing team do their jobs. The CEO would be the helmsman or driver with his or her hand on the wheel, or close by it. The board of directors would be comparable to the boat's navigator, mapping out the course and making sure the helmsman and his team, including the tactician, sail the vessel along the right course.

The difference, though, in running a corporation and racing a sailboat is that in sailing everything happens in real time. We all move in tandem. The vessel's tactician is not telling you to go in one direction and the navigator is saying go in another. Everyone has to collaborate, talk it out among ourselves, and agree as we race ahead.

But in corporations, boards are not there for the day to day. We meet seven or eight times a year, and we have to rely on so many others to execute and understand the winds and currents acting on the ship of commerce.

You never know what's going to happen in life. I never, ever dreamed that I would face an Enron situation. It was nowhere in my thinking pattern, anywhere. Therefore, even when it happened, I still didn't fully accept or appreciate the potential impact on my business plans. I continued to push my Africa fund. I even sunk about $3 million of my own money in it, money that I wish I had right now.

To me, failure was not something I even contemplated. My whole psyche has been built around success and throughout my business career I had always made certain to associate myself with sound and respected people and companies. I thought Enron fit that description. But obviously I was mistaken. A colleague and friend, Cindy Winston, calls my sort of thinking "the psychology of success."

But that sort of mind-set carries a liability. The problem with it is that when you face adversity sometimes you are not psychologically ready for it. I was not ready for Enron. As a result, I didn't take any defensive, self-protective steps.

Before the scandal, I had just set up my new office for Savage Holdings. I had taken my longtime executive assistant, Eva Evgenis, and Leonard Murray, a trusted investment professional, and my most respected senior investment executive from Equitable and Alliance, Jim Wilson, with me. They are with me today. They all left their nice, comfortable corporate homes and came with me. I could have said to them, "Hey guys, I'm sorry. I'm stuck. Here's six months pay." I could have said that I'm not going to do the African Millennium Fund.

I would have been more than justified in terminating my efforts to launch my fund. No one would have blamed me if I had sold my sailboat, and hunkered down for the legal fights and terrible publicity that were to follow. But no, not Frank Savage. I was still absolutely confident that this situation would quickly pass and I could continue materializing my dreams: running the African fund and sailing *Lolita* around the world.

But reality has a way of imposing itself. I was on the board of Qualcomm when Enron self-destructed. I had to resign from that board to comply with the Department of Labor Consent decree that forbade me, and all Enron board members, from serving on a board that oversaw an Employment Retirement Insurance Security Act or ERISA pension account, as was the case at Qualcomm. This was a tremendous professional blow. I loved Qualcomm. When I first went to the company, it was very small, no one knew much about it then. But I thought those people had something and I joined that board. And, boy, that was a fantastic move for me.

The scandal put a cloud over me, basically. That's what killed me, the cloud. Institutions have to deal with people who have good reputations. It wasn't that I had been found guilty of anything. It was just a question of being under a cloud. That cloud also put my Lockheed Martin board seat in serious jeopardy.

Again, it came down to pension funds. Part of the Enron settlement with the Department of Labor (DOL) required each Enron board member to sign the agreement that none of us would sit on boards that handled pension funds guaranteed by the DOL.

This is how the DOL agreement came about. It looked at us on the Enron board to see whether we had done our jobs, our fiduciary responsibility, as a board. It is important to point out that contrary to Lockheed and other companies that have legally structured separate companies to oversee and manage the company's ERISA assets, Enron had a similar structure to Qualcomm. In both cases the ERISA assets were overseen by the board itself, although a management group actually oversaw the pension funds.

Therefore, legally, the board was accountable for the assets although the board was not involved in the day-to-day allocation and investment strategy of those funds. When Enron crashed, even though the management committee managed the pension funds, the board was legally responsible and held accountable.

Initially, when the labor department evaluated us and our role in overseeing the ERISA pension funds, it acknowledged that the board was not the entity that recommended investing in Enron stock, which accounted for the huge employee losses. But as the national election season approached, all of a sudden, the DOL became a lot more aggressive. It said, look, because you were legally responsible, even though you had nothing to do with it, we are holding you accountable. We want to send a message to people like you that no one should ever put themselves in this kind of position again.

Consequently, DOL imposed a heavy penalty on the Enron board that effectively barred any of us from managing any ERISA pension or savings funds without their explicit approval for five years, from 2002 through 2007.

Most of the members of the board of Enron were not investment professionals like I was. They could pretty much go about their business lives as usual. But for me, and another member, Pug Winoker, our lives *were* managing such funds. We were professional investment and money managers. This move deprived us from pursuing our lifelong businesses. I could not get involved in any money management. That, in effect, took away every business opportunity for me. I couldn't work. This was devastating to my career.

Thankfully, Lockheed Martin had a different setup. In fact, it had a totally separate company to manage and to oversee its pension and retirement funds. I had nothing to say about its investment strategy or anything, so I didn't have to get off that board.

Yet this issue would haunt me on Howard University's board of trustees, eventually forcing me to step down and surrender my chairmanship of it. That hurt. This was Howard, where my college career started. My twin sister, Frances, and my cousin, Janice, attended Howard. My mother's business had been right down the street from Howard. This was personal and it cut me deeply because I was a role model at Howard. I was so embarrassed by the Enron case.

Around this time, another test awaited me. My third grandchild had just been diagnosed with Down Syndrome. The news, while very difficult to absorb and process, stirred powerful thoughts in me. And those thoughts led, quite on their own, to reflections that evoked the lessons of my mother's life, reflections about how Grace Savage, a poor black girl from the country, had turned her own tragedies into triumphs in Washington, DC.

I could again hear the voice of La Savage, who had passed away 20 years earlier, speaking to me.

"This too shall pass" she whispered as if waving away my troubles as if they had been little more than stale air.

I knew I had inherited my mother's grit, knew that La Savage had raised me to be just as determined and calm under fire as she was. I realized more than ever at that moment that my mother would want me to collect the best of myself and fight through this crisis. And you know what? I never let her down in life; I was damn sure I wasn't going to start then. I could feel her spirit with me throughout the toughest days of the Enron's collapse and immediate aftermath—through every crisis, professional or personal.

■ ■ ■

I set on a mission to set the record straight. People had to know what the professional, personal, and financial toll of the Enron scandal had been on me as one of its directors.

For decades, I had stood proudly among the world's most successful businesspeople in international banking, corporate finance, and global investment management. And I had stood practically alone as an African American in this international arena of megawealth and power. For a long time, I had to be silent to the outside world. There were legal mandates to consider, alliances and confidences that are part of any corporate life that had to be kept.

A troubling consequence of this during the collapse and its fallout was that it forced me to witness my reputation being gnawed and chewed in public hearings, in the press, in circles of influence that were awash with baseless posturing and speculation that poured from numerous civil lawsuits aimed at Enron. I was a collateral casualty. And, there were the direct attacks on my character, blatant and subtle. At shareholder meetings of Lockheed Martin I had to endure baseless assaults.

One such shareholder, a black woman, protested my presence on the Lockheed Martin's board; she loudly advocated that I step down in view of "my role" in the Enron scandal. In an article published by the *American Prospect*, Joshua Green, a journalist, referred to me as "an authentic bad apple" because of my membership on Enron's board.

As recently as August 2, 2011, while I was writing this book, another article appeared in the *New York Times*: "Ex-Directors of Failed Firms Have Little to Fear."

It insinuated that I, and my fellow former Enron board members, had hardly been harmed by that company's implosion. What this story clearly failed to appreciate was the damage Enron did to the reputations of its board members. Our integrity was wrongly thrown into question in board rooms and living rooms, in news rooms and in televised congressional hearing rooms.

It took me 30-odd years to build my reputation. I was only on the Enron board for two years, from 1999 to 2002. Nevertheless, one of the things I valued the most, my good reputation—priceless in business, as well as in life—was tarnished by Enron in ways I find difficult to fully express. I didn't benefit financially—almost nothing at all—from

Enron. Maybe pennies. Everything I had at the time, I had before
Enron. My association with Enron was only negative for me, negative
in terms of my self-confidence, negative in preventing me from
working to help people who I was committed to helping, like creating
my Africa fund.

I would have loved to have worked more closely with people like
Barack Obama. But all of those things, and more, were totally shut off
to me following Enron. I came to the realization that everything I had
done, all the success and trailblazing and helping hands to others, was
nothing compared to the colossal collapse of Enron. This is one of my
greatest sources of pain.

Through it all, I have been expected to suffer quietly and with
dignity. For the most part I did, while quietly rebuilding what I could,
and turning to my wife and family, and truly personal friends for support. I escaped, whenever I got the chance, into the rush of wind, the
taunt muscularity of *Lolita*'s sails, the invisible drive that has driven
mariners for thousands of years. It was its own glory to have that wind,
that yacht of mine, carry me and my 17-man crew to victory over some
deep, blue perfection.

What I love about sailing is what I love about the challenge of
business. In business, the situation, its environment, is ever-challenging
and changing every day. You have to be flexible; you have to focus, and
you have to know how to move, when to move, and when not to
move. In sailing, it's the same way.

It is no accident that powerful businesspeople like Ted Turner,
Barry Diller, and Oracle's co-founder and CEO, Larry Ellison, love to
sail. For businesspeople like us, it's all of that together that moves us so,
literally and figuratively. And with sailing, you're in nature. You can test
your skills against the elemental natural element. It's the ultimate test.

When I went through the Enron thing, my boat really was my
sanctuary. It wasn't just a boat. I became an avid racer. My wife said to
me at the time, "You know, Frank, what happened with Enron was
something you couldn't control; you were innocent. You hadn't
done anything; you were being attacked and you couldn't do anything
about it.

"But when you're sailing, when you're racing . . . you seem to find
peace and control over your destiny. . . ."

I knew what Lolita was telling me. Racing my yacht took on a greater importance for me in those dark days. It wasn't just racing for racing's sake. I buried myself into this competitive environment. It was the only place where I could find that kind of thing. Why? Because when I was on my boat, when I was racing, that's all I thought about.

By the way, when I was sailing, nobody ever, ever, *ever* said anything to me about Enron, not during the whole time I was going through that period. You know the only thing they cared about? "This damn Frank Savage is a sailing son of a. . . ."

In the end, I realized that I went head to head with the head winds of the Enron scandal, and I survived to sail another day.

Chapter 2

Getting In, Struggling Out, Getting Right

You have to risk going too far to discover just how far you can really go.

—*T.S. Eliot*

A decade has passed since Enron disappeared into a sea of red ink, bitter tears, and spilled blood, and I still ask myself how in the world did I get myself tied to the mast of such a sinking ship? Let me further express myself in some of my favorite nautical terms. Before I agreed to board Enron, I had done my due diligence in long, detailed talks with its captain, its first mate, and its financial navigator. I inspected the strength of its hull, the sureness of the tiller, the timber of its boom, and the fabric of its great sails.

I found nothing, nothing, to raise a moment's alarm. Then again, that's so often how a voyage of the damned begins.

It started in 1995 when my friend, Ron Brown, then Secretary of Commerce, invited me to join him on a business trip to India. I was chairman of Alliance Capital Management International, which raised funds from investors all around the world. We had billions of dollars under management.

I was 57 years old. But I felt and acted 20 years younger; some even said I looked the part, too.

"Frank," Ron said to me in the spring of 1995, "I'm taking a business delegation to India to try to promote business with the United States. Would you be interested in going?"

As luck would have it, I was on the verge of launching Alliance's first India mutual fund, called Alliance 95. The prospect of going to India with a top-level U.S. business delegation to announce the launch of this fund presented a great opportunity. I quickly said, "Ron, I'd love to go."

A few weeks later, I, along with several other prominent U.S. business leaders and representatives from the Commerce Department, State Department, and the Overseas Private Investment Corporation, to name a few, went to the Department of Commerce for our briefing on the objectives and itinerary for the trip. As I scanned the list of people who were coming, I saw the names of Ken Lay, chairman of Enron, Irwin Jacobs, the chairman and chief executive officer of Qualcomm, and several other CEOs.

I thought to myself, *this is a high-powered delegation*. Besides launching the fund, this would be a great time to meet with several of the Indian businessmen whom I had previously met at the World Economic Forum in Davos, Switzerland. They included P.P. Hinduja of the Hinduja Group, a company I would subsequently join as a consultant. This was not just a great opportunity, but a *fantastic* one.

The trip to India was out of this world, at least any world I had previously known. And I had known many. Most of us flew on an official U.S. government jumbo jet with Secretary Brown, who was one of the most visible of Bill Clinton's presidential cabinet appointments. Before he was named Secretary of Commerce, the first African American to hold that post, he had been the highly effective chairman of the National Democratic Committee. There is no question that in that position, Ron Brown provided a sure hand in Clinton's successful 1992 run for the White House. Some say he was vital to engineering that victory, and I wouldn't disagree with that assessment.

Our flight to India that spring, long and untroubled, gave us all time to get to know one another and further brief the Secretary on our separate Indian businesses. When I briefed Ron, he and I shared a private moment. It was extremely satisfying that two African Americans like us, one the head of Commerce and the other the chair of a major financial company, were actually on this all important trip. We could hardly believe it. And in a nod and glance, and maybe even a wink, we silently applauded a feat unimaginable just a single generation ago.

Frank with U.S. Secretary of Commerce, Ron Brown (seated) en route to India on official U.S. mission in 1995 to advance U.S./India business and commercial relationships. On this trip Frank meets Ken Lay, CEO of Enron.

The following year on April 3, Ron lost his life during a similar flight on a similar official trade mission; this time set in Croatia. The military version of a Boeing 737 crashed into a mountainside on its approach to Dubrovnik Airport, killing Ron and all 34 people aboard. He was 54. A terrible, terrible loss.

Before he left on what turned out to be his last mission, Ron called me and asked me if I would join him on it. I said, "Ron, I love to go on these missions but it has to be something that makes business sense for me. It makes sense for me to go to Europe. It makes sense for us to go to the places we've been. But we're not doing business in Croatia. Quite frankly, the way it is—it's still in the middle of a war there—I don't think we'll do business there for some time.

"Thanks a lot," I told him, "but I can't go on this one."

He sounded like he understood. Then I added that around the time of the Croatia mission I was scheduled to be at another business conference in Abu Dhabi. He told me that he was supposed to be at the same Middle Eastern conference but the Croatia initiative had been deemed more pressing by the White House.

"Send my regards," Ron told me.

"I will," I replied.

Those were the last words of our last conversation.

I went on to Abu Dhabi and had a fabulous time there in its glittering opulence of a nation-state so clearly on the rise. I stopped briefly in Italy to pick up Lolita and we returned to New York together. When we landed, we were met by my driver.

"Mr. Savage," he said as we made our way to the car, "I have some bad news for you."

At first I thought it was one of my kids. But he didn't let the pause linger.

"Secretary Brown's plane went down in Croatia and everyone on board was killed," he said without further hesitation. Something deep inside me fell, like books from a high shelf.

"What? My God!" was all I could manage. I was devastated. I felt terrible. He was a good friend and had created for me, in some important respects, a launching pad into some key markets around the world. When Ron got into his position at Commerce he was working very closely with the Clinton administration and he was bringing as many African Americans he could into the mix of power, influence, and business. He brought me in and I began to get very involved with the administration. Lolita and I were even able to spend a night in the White House during the early Clinton years there.

Luck is very important to any course steering for success. But preparation is very important, too, because if you are prepared you can take advantage of luck when it floats your way. After my years overseas with Citibank, my years in international finance with Equitable, and then Alliance, which included setting up major investment funds in South Africa, Egypt, and India, I was prepared to make full use of the opportunities Ron opened for me.

Shortly before his death, Ron and I had been talking about doing business together. The thought of working with him was very, very appealing. And, yes, I knew he was under investigation for corruption. But I also knew there was nothing there, and I had so much confidence in Ron.

I recall 1990, when Nelson Mandela was released after serving 27 years of political imprisonment in South Africa. Years later, President Clinton sent a delegation to demonstrate to the South African people that we were behind them, that we supported their leader, Mandela, who was elected that nation's first black president in 1994. He asked Ron Brown to lead that delegation. I went on that trip with Ron. It was huge. And it was one of the greatest honors I have ever had.

Ron was a remarkable man. And as a black man, we haven't had anyone since him to get to the position that he did. Of course, Barrack Obama has gone to another, higher level. He has opened up new ground. But even Obama would acknowledge that people like Ron Brown laid the groundwork.

■ ■ ■

For our India trade mission in 1995, we started off the week-long trip by meeting with several of the Indian government officials, giving each one of us the chance to describe our business activities. The interesting thing about the new Alliance Capital mutual fund was that it would be the first in India to daily publish the net asset value, basically what it was worth. Although this may sound strangely routine in the United States, where all mutual funds are required to do so, this was not the case in India, hence its promised transparency was a big issue, an asset on its own.

Indian investors were excited at the prospect of investing in the Alliance fund and actually knowing the value of their investment on a daily basis. This was in stark contrast to the only existing mutual fund in India at that time, called UTI, which published the net asset value once a week. The Indian press had a very enthusiastic reaction to the fund. One accurately quoted me as saying that "We are very happy with the progress of the economic reforms in the country and are optimistic about the economy."

This was true. I was part of Ron's Presidential Business Development Mission and I could clearly see how my Alliance fund could attract more foreign capital to India and its burgeoning companies. You could feel the real beginnings of India's ascendency all around you, something now so evident that it is practically taken for granted.

We visited the Indian Institute of Technology in Mumbai, one of the best graduate schools in the world. Secretary Brown made a major speech there on U.S.–Indian business and political issues.

Overall, we received a warm reception from the Indian business community. And it turned out to be exactly the great opportunity I had hoped for: meeting with major Indian business leaders on their own turf. Some of these leaders I had known from our world financial meetings at Davos. And having the United States Secretary of Commerce at my side certainly enhanced my reputation and profile in India.

Near the close of the trade mission, Secretary Brown told the Chicago Tribune that he and 25 U.S. business leaders had managed to secure $5.5 billion in transactions in four days. And the delegation, according to a "senior official," anticipated another $1.5 billion worth of deals before the mission ended in Mumbai, the commercial and entertainment capital of India.

Ron asked me to participate in a panel discussion on how American business viewed opportunities in India. The discussion was packed with Indian businesspeople. The panel included Irwin Jacobs, Ken Lay, and me. I welcomed the chance. The discussion went extremely well. I explained Alliance's reasons for entering the Indian market, our positive outlook at the growth potential of India; I described how our fund would increase transparency in the mutual fund market, and described Alliance, which was then the largest publicly traded asset management company in the United States. Some of my comments were rushed into the Indian business press.

One remark that echoed throughout the mission was when I told Indian reporters that "India is a very important market for us." It reverberated like a clarion call in a virgin valley.

I also felt that I held my own with these two major chief executives, and I was feeling especially proud of myself. At the end of the panel discussion, I told Lay and Jacobs what a pleasure it had been for me to participate with them. I told them that I looked forward to seeing them throughout the rest of the trip.

It may have sounded pro forma, but I was sincere. Honest.

Jacobs stayed for the entire trip, but Lay left early so I hardly saw him again. But I never forgot that first impression of him. This son of a preacher who held a doctorate in economics, struck me as polished, professional, and personable—and warm, which is not something you can always say about a chief executive, especially after a first meeting.

As it turned out, that panel discussion led to my joining two boards. About six months after I returned to New York Jacobs invited me to join the board of Qualcomm. I immediately accepted because I believed the company was going to be a leader in high-technology communications and digital networking. Qualcomm already had a very impressive Code Division Multiple Access (CDMA) technology, then an innovation that significantly increased the capacity of voice and data communications over the Internet, which at the time was still in its relative infancy. As it has turned out, Qualcomm became one of the most successful companies in the world.

Joining the board of a public company, depending, of course, on the company, can be very prestigious, empowering and lucrative. Again, depending on the company, a board member is usually paid a fee for serving. That could mean annual compensation of $250,000. Part of that is usually in cash and another part is in company stock, which you are obligated to hold for a period of time. It is important for directors to own stock in the companies they guide. It aligns the interest of the directors with those of the company's shareholders. It is, as we say, having "skin the game."

Soon after my Indian trip with Ron Brown, there was a slew of requests for me to join the boards of various public companies.

■ ■ ■

One of the requests, from an energy company, prompted me to mention all of this interest to Lod Cook, CEO of ARCO Chemical Company and a fellow board member of Lockheed Martin. I just happened to share with him that some headhunter was calling me in hopes that I would join the board of a major energy company. At the time that's all I knew about the company. I was turning to Lod for a little advice.

Instead, he quickly pivoted, asking me, "Are you interested, Frank, in joining the board of an oil or energy company?"

I said, "A matter of fact, Lod, I haven't thought about it."

He said, "Let me talk to you about joining the board of our company."

This guy moved fast. He dispatched a corporate jet to pick me up in New York and then fly me to an ARCO facility in Texas. It was impressive. Very impressive. The next thing I knew, I was a member of the board of directors of ARCO Corp., a subsidiary of ARCO Chemical. Two years later, in 1998, Lyondell, another major energy company based in Texas, acquired ARCO Chemical in a $5.6 billion deal. I had to be persuaded by the Lyondell's chairman to stay on as a member of the Lyondell board. I agreed to a transitional period of six months to a year. I had no intentions of staying on that board beyond that. Staying any longer, I informed the chairman, was not in my plan.

Requests for me to join other boards kept coming until finally I got a call from Spencer Stuart, a well-known search firm.

"Frank, we have a very interesting client who has asked us to contact you to see if you'd be interested in considering joining the company's board. It's a Fortune 100 company," one of the first calls went.

I responded to the voice on the phone. "I really appreciate your call, but right now, I'm not in a position to accept any public boards. I'm on the board of Lockheed Martin, Qualcomm, and Lyondell Chemical. I have an agreement with my company that three public boards is the limit. I have very demanding responsibilities here at the company."

I asked Spencer Stuart to identify the company, but the voice preferred not to do so, because I could not entertain the offer anyway.

"Fine," I said. "Well, you know, let's talk six months from now. Things do change."

And that was the end of the conversation. It didn't matter what the company was. I could not accept that board seat at that time. About six months later, Stuart did call me again about this mysterious company.

"Do you remember that we talked? I just wanted to follow up with you to see where you stood, Frank."

"Well, quite frankly, nothing has really changed between now and then. I still have the same situation." But I said, "Please tell me, what is the company that we're talking about? You know, give me some more information."

"Well," he said, "I've been authorized to identify the company. It's Enron."

Enron? That's interesting that Enron is calling me because when I ran the energy portfolio at Equitable Life, we invested in its predecessor, a very conservatively run gas pipeline company. I had been struck by how it had been transformed into a really dynamic, highly diversified energy company. I also recounted that I had been on a panel with Ken Lay during the Ron Brown mission to India. Spencer Stuart was aware of the chance meeting.

"Very interesting," I went on. "That does put another light on it. But, again, like I said, I can't do it now. But, let's keep in touch."

Then he told me that Ken Lay, the chairman, would like to "have the opportunity to talk" to me directly.

"Sure," I said. "Okay, I would love to talk to him. I haven't seen him since we were in India together with Secretary Ron Brown. Have him call me."

Lay did call. He explained to me that Enron was growing fast and the company needed to strengthen the board by adding financial and international experience, both of which I had. India was a major target for the company and, as he knew from our aforementioned trip, I was familiar with India's business community, and Alliance had a similar commitment to the country. All of this made me an ideal board candidate and Lay expressed his hope that I could join its board. I must admit, I was impressed with Lay's warm demeanor and his convincing case. He was charming.

I had to give this serious consideration. This was Enron. The company was viewed by the entire financial and business community as one of the most dynamic companies in the world, and part of that sense of Enron was rooted in what appeared to be a kind of stunning, rapidly mounting success that makes Wall Street—and people like me—take close notice.

We ended the call agreeing that we would talk again. I was certainly interested. In the meantime, I did some homework on the company and discussed the offer with some associates. Down to the person, almost everyone thought that being on the Enron's board would be an impressive feather in my already heavily plumed cap.

Then one day, at a Lyondell board meeting, in reviewing a routine report of the largest shareholders, I was surprised to see that Alliance, my company, had bought a significant amount of Lyondell shares. I mentioned it to Lyondell's compliance officer and asked him to keep me informed if the holdings breached the 5 percent level, which would require Lyondell and Alliance to file with the SEC, in addition to probably requiring me, as an Alliance officer, to resign from the Lyondell board. I kept this knowledge to myself.

A couple of months later at another Lyondell board meeting, the compliance officer advised me that Alliance had accumulated more than 5 percent of Lyondell shares, probably because the share price of Lyondell had declined. The percentage of Alliance's holdings in that company had increased as a function of simple arithmetic. It didn't matter how, only that the Alliance shares in Lyondell crossed a threshold that could present an appearance of a conflict of interest.

"So we have to report this," the Lyondell compliance officer said, "and you may want to raise this with your compliance officer at Alliance."

I did just that. I explained that Alliance had acquired more than 5 percent of Lyondell Chemical's shares, and that I was very concerned because I didn't want to end up in a situation where it may be perceived that my membership on that board represented a potential conflict of interest. And, yes, I had a pristine reputation that I cherished. I did not want even the slightest shadow of possible impropriety darkening my name.

Mind you, as an employee of Alliance, I did not know the full extent of Alliance's holdings in Lyondell because of the existence of what we call a "Chinese wall" at Alliance. The strict separation of me as a board member of Lyondell and any contact with Alliance's investment division regarding the Lyondell holdings was standard operating procedure in corporate America. Such things matter quite a bit. Besides, no one at Alliance would have listened to my investment advice anyway. If I had suggested "buy" Alliance would have sold. This was not my end of the operation.

Less than an hour later, the Alliance compliance officer called me. "Frank, you have to immediately resign from the board of Lyondell Chemical," he told me. "We are at an SEC reporting level, so you have to resign."

I called the Lyondell CEO and advised him of the situation. He understood.

■ ■ ■

As a result of the Lyondell resignation, I was now in a position to consider the Enron board offer. I called up Ken Lay and explained the turn of events. He was delighted and officially offered me the Enron board seat right then and there over the telephone. It was September 1999.

"Frank, we're very happy that you'll be able to join the Enron Board, and we know you're going to make a tremendous contribution," Lay told me, his charm just as persuasive over the phone as it had been in person. "So let's get underway."

He said that according to Enron's schedule, I would be elected at the board of director's October meeting. But he said he wanted me to come down to Houston before the election to meet some of the board members before I was officially made a director.

"Ken, that sounds fine."

Enron was at the absolute top. I kept doing my homework and there still was not one person who I spoke to about Enron who didn't agree. Reviews of the company in various leading newspapers and business journals were glowing. Lay was a close personal friend of President George H. W. Bush, and his son, George W. Bush who would nickname Ken "Kenny Boy." Jeff Skilling, Lay's right hand, was seen as the miracle-working one-day successor to Lay, and the architect of Enron's transformation into a firm comparable to Goldman Sachs.

To be asked to join Enron's board was widely seen as an incredible accomplishment on my part, particularly as I approached my retirement years. I was enthusiastic about my lineup of directorships, which would consume my time in retirement. I had Qualcomm, Lockheed Martin, and now, Enron. That's a great group of boards.

My family brimmed with pride, too. I felt that I had really accomplished a lot in my career and being elected to this board was the final imprimatur that I had, in fact, succeeded. I was convinced that joining the board of Enron in 1999 would be universally seen as a great honor. And it was! For a while. . . .

Alliance approved my joining the Enron board and, as planned, Ken Lay presented me to the full board in October 1999. At Lay's request, I observed a board committee meeting prior to a full board meeting, thus having the chance to meet some committee members and staff. I was going to be assigned to the finance committee.

Ken Lay called me one day and said, "Frank, I'd like you to meet with Jeff Skilling, my executive vice president who is ultimately going to succeed me."

Without hesitation, I agreed that we should arrange something. Meeting with Skilling made perfect sense, because I was joining the board and Skilling would be assuming the CEO position at Enron. Naturally, Lay wanted to make sure that there was good chemistry between Skilling and me.

A few days later, Skilling flew up to New York, and we had an interesting meeting over dinner. He talked at great length about his bold vision and aspirations for Enron. I don't even remember what I ate that evening. Skilling's background as one of the youngest partners in the history of the top global consulting firm, McKinsey & Company, shone through. He clearly had a big ego and was running over with self-confidence. It practically dripped and pooled under the dinner table.

Perhaps as a result, I cannot say he seemed that interested in me, or getting to know me, my work, or my ideas. Our meeting was mostly about *his* relationship to Enron, rather than mine to come. As I sat there in the cheerful churn of a busy Manhattan restaurant, I did my best to be a good listener. It was obvious that this guy was extremely bright. He had a concise plan about where he wanted to take Enron. It appeared, based on his experience, Harvard education, and time at McKinsey, that he, in fact, had the ability to realize his aspirations. In contrast to Lay's warmth, Skilling struck me as more of a type-A corporate executive— you know, a workaholic shark. He seemed to be highly motivated, always swimming, always in search of the next kill.

I think he was determined to prove that he could build the best company in the world, and that he perceived Enron as much more than just an energy company. Indeed, it was far beyond the old pipeline company that I had known. Skilling wanted to build an entity that rivaled Goldman Sachs, the preeminent Wall Street investment banking firm.

When you get right down to it, Enron operated more like a merchant investment bank rather than a pure energy company.

Enron was not only producing energy, but also creating markets in energy and other commodities, which was very important to Skilling. He was excited by the potential to substantially increase the return on capital and return on investment by taking market risk positions. For example, Enron seemed up to bet on almost anything it believed it could commoditize—even the weather. It was a remarkable time with tens of millions of dollars riding on such bets. But for an incredible run of bets, Enron appeared to win far more than it lost.

This was definitely not your grandfather's energy company. It was exciting and you could feel all of this enterprising electricity in Enron's huge trading floor in its gleaming headquarters building.

I must say that after talking to Skilling, I, too, could feel that excitement. I believed that this man could greatly move this company forward, particularly if he worked closely with Lay. Furthermore, Skilling seemed to hold Ken Lay, who happened to be one of his fraternity brothers, in high regard, which was important to me because the man I was betting on was Lay. I thought that if you paired Lay's experience, background, interpersonal and leadership skills with Skilling's intelligence and vision, then this company would continue to thrive. I think that's what most people on Wall Street and in corporate boardrooms around the world believed, too.

I didn't get the feeling at that meeting, or any others for that matter, that Skilling was the kind of person that I could get close to. But that wasn't my requirement. The question was: Did he have the skills to run the company? I definitely sensed that I had more in common with Ken Lay, even a level of trust with him. It was important to me that Lay remain at Enron. He struck me as the soul and conscience of the company. And to this day, I am not saying a bad word about Ken Lay; I can't in my heart. Ultimately, he had the responsibility for Enron's failure because the buck stopped at his desk because he was the man in charge.

After my dinner meeting with Skilling, Ken called me. "Frank, Jeff got in touch with me and said that he feels very, very good about you, and he's looking forward to working with you on the board."

With that, we had closed the last loop that was required for a board seat, and I was ready to join the company. I looked forward to an exceptionally meaningful experience.

■ ■ ■

December 1999 marked the first full board meeting that I attended as a director. Coincidentally, this was the last meeting of the year in which management had all of the various divisions present an annual report to the board. Early on, I had the chance to hear presentations from some of the management that worked directly under the top executive vice presidents. I was extremely impressed with the depth of talent. I came away from that meeting feeling, again, that Enron was in very good shape because, in addition to having Lay, Skilling, and Andy Fastow as the chief financial officer, the division heads were extremely strong. There were some exciting younger people who hailed from the country's best schools.

The company seemed to have a firm grasp on its business. That, at the time, was comforting. I was particularly impressed by Enron's risk management control, a fundamental element in the trading business. This reinforced my sentiment that this company had management depth and leadership that would sustain its forward motion. If we were to lose any of the top people, it seemed to me that there were plenty of people qualified to easily move into positions of greater responsibility.

Looking back, I have to acknowledge some memorable events in my brief Enron tenure that didn't involve financial disaster. One was a Christmas party given by Ken and Linda Lay in 1999 at their high-rise condo overlooking Houston in stunning 360 degrees. Walking proudly along the hallway to Lay's 33rd-floor home that some have called a castle retreat in the sky, I was accompanied by Lolita. So beautiful. She moved with the grace of a dancer in an emerald green dress that fit her like the princess she was that night. And as we approached the double, carved front doors that stood from floor to ceiling, I began to release Lolita's hand to knock. But before my hand fully left hers, a man dressed in a tuxedo and wearing pearl-white gloves, opened the door and greeted us.

"Good evening," said the handsome, African-American greeter. "Welcome to the Lay residence."

We stepped in the doorway of one of the most exquisite apartments I've ever seen. And I have seen many beautiful homes in my years and travels. Ken and Linda came directly over to welcome us. With her hand outstretched, Linda Lay shook mine as Ken offered his introduction.

"Honey, this is Frank Savage, our newest director from New York." And without hesitation, he continued, "And this must be the very lovely Mrs. Savage."

"Lolita," I injected with a beaming smile.

"It is so nice to meet you, Lolita," said Ken. "I'm so glad you could join Linda and me at our house tonight."

With that, Linda smiled and embraced Lolita in a gracious hug before she and Ken led us deeper into their home.

"Please come join the party," Linda said. "Have some champagne or a cocktail. We have some wonderful food, too. Meet some of our friends from Houston."

We scanned the party and noted without comment or alarm that I was the only African-American guest, and Lolita, who is a native of the Philippines, did not see anyone at the party who looked like her, either. This was hardly unusual for us. The fact was that few people of color existed on the higher rungs of the U.S. corporate ladder. Lolita and I never let that make us feel uneasy or unsure. We belonged there, and we knew it. It never troubled my wife, nor I. But this blatant fact also continually charged my commitment to see this change, to widen the opportunities for talented and driven people of all colors to enter and thrive in this world of deals, doers, and dollars where I thrived.

I'm not going to walk around carrying a racial cloud over my head. Why should I carry the race thing on my shoulder? First off, that's going to prevent me from seeing and taking on opportunities, from taking risks, because I'm not going to be as confident as I need to be. Second, that lack of confidence you harbor is projected onto others. When you're trying to be a leader, or you're in a competitive situation, you've got to stand tall. This is part of your negotiation strategy; this is part of your leadership strategy. If you are not confident, people will sense it and then you can't lead anymore.

I couldn't afford any of that. My mother, La Savage, taught me this to such an extent that it came as natural to me as breathing and winning. She gave me the confidence decades ago to realize my own gifts and understand that my only limits are those I impose on myself.

I walk right up to people, and declare, "Hello. I'm Frank Savage." (Just like my mother would walk up to people and say "Hello, darling, I'm Madame La Savage.") I look them in the eye and thrust out my hand for a firm handshake. The color of my hand should be, like Haile Selassie once said, no more important than the color of a person's eyes.

Ken and Linda led us into a huge living room, its walls adorned by world-class art that I remember very clearly. Lolita, an accomplished painter, was very much taken with their collection. Almost immediately on our entrance, Linda and Ken began to introduce us to the various people in attendance. Arm in arm, Lolita and I floated through the room exchanging friendly greetings with each of the guests, some known to us, many not. Although I had just recently met many of these people at a board meeting, I didn't really know them that well. So the Lays made sure that they introduced us to everyone.

After taking considerable time to welcome us and showing great kindness, which we could really feel, Ken and Linda excused themselves to converse with another cluster of guests. That night, Lolita and I observed that with us, as with all of their guests, Ken and Linda were able to sincerely make people feel good. I call that excellent interpersonal skills, akin to those of my mother who preferred to relate to people as individuals rather than en masse. La Savage had such a golden touch with people.

Prior to the Lay's party, I had asked Ken to join the Howard University board of trustees. "Ken, the reason I'm asking you is not only that I respect you so much, but we just launched a major campaign at Howard University to raise $250 million plus, and we're trying to attract corporate executives to the board who will appeal to other donors. I think that you would be a tremendous addition."

I took the opportunity of sharing my board invitation to Ken with Linda, who had once been Ken's secretary. She greeted the news with a smile. "Frank, I know," she told me. "Ken told me and he's going to join your board. He's happy and proud that you asked him. He's busy as heck, but he wants to support the great things you're doing for Howard and he knows that it is a great institution."

I was overjoyed with this news. She went on to explain that he was joining Howard's board because he thought it important, not because he felt obligated to do it. "He just thinks it's absolutely the right thing to do," Linda told me.

I was so touched by her words and sentiments. Ken's membership on the board would be of tremendous help to Howard University, still the leading African-American university in the country and a great treasure—until the approaching Enron scandal forced Ken's resignation as a Howard director. I will always love Ken for joining the Howard's board when I knew he didn't have the time and that he did that for me.

As we headed back to the hotel from the party, Lolita and I shared the warm feelings each of us had for Ken and Linda. They were the kind of people we were happy to be around and be associated with; these were good people. Ken was not only a great corporate executive, but he was a generous person who had a strong sense of civic responsibility. I likened him to Henry Smith and Coy Eklund of Equitable, the CEOs who initiated affirmative action at Equitable. That night, I was even more confident in my choice to join Enron. Not only was it a business success, but it was also led by a man I could respect, even like. Trust.

Lolita's impression of Jeff Skilling was not as positive. Perhaps it was woman's intuition. The occasion of Lolita's full assessment of the man came during an Enron board meeting in early 2000. It was held in West Palm Beach, Florida, and spouses were invited. The first evening there was a board dinner in a glorious setting. I was glad to have Lolita with me for so many reasons, one of which is that I tremendously value her judgment of people.

During the cocktail hour, she and I were engaged in a private moment when Skilling, who had only recently been appointed as Enron's CEO, and his fiancée, an Enron staffer, approached us.

We exchanged pleasantries and introductions, quite superficial and quick; Skilling said hello to Lolita, and his fiancée said hello to her, too. Lolita returned the greetings. The interchange, unlike our experience with the Lays, was quite formal, maybe even reflexive.

It felt like Skilling did what he felt obligated to do, to come over and say hello to me, before he and his fiancée moved on, as briskly as they had appeared. Right away, Lolita turned to me with a skeptical look on her face.

"Frank, I don't have a good feeling about this guy, Jeff," she said, still following him with her eyes. She searched my face for a reaction then asked, "What do you think?" But before I could respond, she said, "He seems to be sort of condescending, in a skilled way. Didn't you get that feeling, Frank?"

"Well, why do you think that?"

She just looked at me, and said all too knowingly, "Trust me."

I filed the whole thing away in a corner of my mind, and left it there. Actually, I hadn't come to a judgment on Skilling one way or the other. Of course, looking back, her initial impression turned out to be concretely correct.

■ ■ ■

During the ensuing year or so, I had the opportunity to observe Jeff Skilling in his role as CEO, and Andy Fastow in his role as chief financial officer. Ken had begun to take a little bit of a backseat; he was really looking to Skilling, and he didn't want to interfere with his leadership. Skilling was an interesting character because he would come to board meetings in jeans with his shirt sleeves rolled up, several drawers below office casual chic. It was clear that he wanted to adopt a relaxed style at board meetings. For some of the seasoned board members, like me, it was hard to adjust to Skilling's almost codeless dress code. To us, casual chic meant a blue blazer, gray or khaki pants, and a white or blue shirt, usually with a tie.

I never will forget when I flew down to Houston early for one of my first board meetings. I went to Brooks Brothers and told the salesman, "I just joined a board, and they have adopted a dress code called corporate casual. I don't know what that means. Please tell me what I should wear."

The salesman, looking at me slightly amused, pulled a pair of khaki pants and a nice blue blazer from a nearby clothes rack. "Now you don't have to wear a tie with your shirt," he advised. At first, the thought of not wearing a tie to a boardroom was one that I just couldn't get accustomed to. But I finally got it, and at the next board meeting I was corporate casual to a Texas tee. My conversion was not universal. Some of my fellow board members never could get used to attending board meetings without wearing a blue suit, white shirt, a blue or red tie and black dress shoes.

Dress code aside, I would say that Enron board meetings over those next several months were similar to what I was accustomed to on other major corporate boards. They were run in a formal manner; they had the appropriate business and committee reports, with lawyers and accountants present, should their expertise be needed. Business as usual.

And that was comforting. Beyond that, the Enron board was quite engaging, and asked numerous questions when an issue demanded discussion.

I was particularly outspoken when Skilling laid out his strategy to de-emphasize our international business, a key, lifelong concentration of mine. He wanted Enron to pull out of the international power plant business, and instead, focus on activities that would enhance shareholder value in the short term, such as commodity trading. He did not want to tie up capital in long-gestation power plant projects, which had attendant political ramifications. Although I supported his strategy of promoting businesses that could enhance shareholder value, I opposed pulling out of global energy markets, especially the emerging markets, like in India. Such energy markets were widely expected to grow faster than the developed ones, thus requiring more power to be sold to them.

Moreover, I was concerned that if we pulled out of these markets abruptly it would prove difficult to reenter. Skilling knew that I had a strong professional affinity to the emerging markets. However, he strenuously argued that it was in the shareholders' interest to reallocate resources to other activities. After lengthy debates among the board members, Skilling's strategy was approved, but my concerns had been registered. And they lingered.

Other than Ken Lay and Jeff Skilling, the executive Enron officer whom I probably saw most frequently in meetings was CFO Andy Fastow. My first exposure to Fastow was in October 1999 when, prior to officially joining the board, I visited Enron to meet the current board members and observe committee deliberations, namely the finance committee. After sitting in and listening to the various members, I came away impressed by Fastow and his team. He appeared well-versed on the entire business and he had command of the financials.

Previously, he had obtained board approval to serve simultaneously as CFO of the company and as the manager of a few Enron-sponsored private equity funds, which had several non-Enron affiliated institutional investors. He and Skilling spent a great deal of time, supported by outside counsel and accountants, detailing how the proper checks and balances had been put in place to avoid any conflicts of interest.

The board concluded that it was in the best interest of the company and shareholders to permit Fastow to play the dual roles. Obviously, at that point, the directors were unaware that Fastow had already launched his conspiracy to defraud the company. To hear him speak and make board presentations, one could only be impressed by his business knowledge, and he was an important contributor to the executive management team. He was clearly an ambitious person, as are most high-level corporate executives. As I took a measure of the man, I certainly saw an executive who aspired to be CEO, but I saw nothing that suggested what he ultimately proved capable of doing.

Fastow had self-confidence and independence, qualities desirable in a CFO, who often has to challenge operating division heads on their financial performance.

As I attended more board and committee meetings, I noticed that Fastow would, on occasion, take issue with the business heads. It was unclear to me whether he did this to make himself look good or to genuinely raise questions. This tension was, again, not unusual for a CFO who is not necessarily supposed to agree with the operating heads. His mission was to make sure that those heads were putting forth financially sound plans. Fastow appeared to be a strong CFO and the other members of the management team respected him. At least, that was my impression at the time.

But we know, as hindsight has brutally shown us, this was not the case at the.

Fastow, along with Skilling (who famously jumped ship) turned out to be criminals. They drove Enron aground, nearly drowning me and all the board of directors in his corruption.

At some point in November 2001, and unknown to the board of directors, a young Enron staffer—Sharon Watkins—had written a letter to Ken Lay voicing her concerns about the company's accounting practices, and asserting that Jeff Skilling's resignation suggested that something was seriously wrong at Enron. She also raised concerns about Fastow's conflicting positions as CFO and manager of some Enron-sponsored private equity funds. Ken turned the letter over to the company's outside counsel to investigate the charges, but unfortunately, he did not advise the board of the employee letter until a couple of months later. What's more, because this employee worked in Enron's financial department, Ken's handling of this situation would prove especially damaging to the company.

As previously mentioned, there were additional revelations about the $600 million accounting restatements and Andy Fastow's conspiracies that led to his firing in the Watkins letter. Even though the board's investigations revealed these transgressions, it was too late.

So many incidents and revelations were happening simultaneously, including wild speculation. Enron was taking on water—fast. The *New York Times* described this period as a "surreal spectacle." On December 2, 2001, Enron declared bankruptcy. On a Wednesday evening January 23, 2002, Ken Lay resigned from Enron and "his baby" capsized and slipped below the waves, beyond resuscitation or resurrection. All I and the other board members could do at that point was to watch in shock and amazement.

■ ■ ■

This was an especially taxing time. My wife and family suffered quietly and stood by me without reservation. I'm sure they were puzzled by all of the innuendos about my role at the company, which they knew were groundless. But how could this "dream directorship" have so quickly turned into a nightmare for me, husband and father? I could see the question in my family's eyes. I was so very concerned about the impact on them. Had this Enron mess cast a shadow over them as well? Would I now be defined by Enron, and by extension, the whole Savage family? Just the prospect of this ate me up inside. People could pick up the newspaper and see my picture implicating me in this mess or read unflattering articles about me. Most were fully aware of the severity of Enron's collapse, even if they did not know me personally.

Some even held me, and other board members, somehow responsible for the billions of dollars the Enron collapse cost employees, shareholders, and institutions. They drew their own conclusions, contrary to the facts, about my role. This was abundantly clear in some of the coverage in the *New York Times*, which seemed to relish groundless speculation about the role Enron's board played in the corporate shipwreck.

On the other hand, in the darkest hours of the Enron coverage, there were some encouraging moments. One such time was in November

2001 at a charity event in Stamford, Connecticut, our hometown at the time. My name and face were all over the newspapers there.

A group of young African Americans came up to me and said, "Mr. Savage, we wanted to meet you. We have so much respect for you and your many accomplishments. We know you're going through a tough time with this Enron thing now, but we know that you're going to come through it because of your track record and reputation. So, hang tough! We believe in you!"

Boy, did that touch me. These people didn't know me. They only knew *of* me and their sentiments were very heartening. Standing beside me, Lolita simply turned to me and smiled. She knew I needed that support in that moment.

I had another restorative experience at the same event. Despite Enron, which was falling apart like a cheap suit, I was elected as an honoree. My friends Darwin Davis, Duane Hill, the Mayor, Dan Malloy, and many more of my Stamford neighbors gave me a standing ovation when I was presented the award to let me know they were behind me. I saw some light at the end of the tunnel and finally perceived that my reputation and my support of worthy organizations and activities throughout my professional life were beginning to take precedence over this singular bad business event in my life. This recognition gave me further fortitude to press on in reversing the damage that it had done.

Throughout my entire life, following La Savage's example, I had established a practice of doing good deeds for people and various organizations without ever asking for anything in return. Regardless of my success, I never forgot about those less fortunate than me, whether it was the $5 million that I pledged to Howard University, the work that I did with Claude Brown on *Manchild in the Promised Land*, visiting poor areas of Washington to bring aid, going on Crossroads Africa to help the African people improve their way of life. My unforeseen reward came when I most needed it, during the dark days of Enron, in the form of support and confidence from many people. This is an important lesson to learn in life: doing good can never be bad for you. And you never know when your good deeds may come back to you.

Regardless of the innuendos my relatively brief association with Enron engendered in some, I continued to be a hero to those who knew me. Much the same remained true regarding my relationships with institutions and organizations, such as the Boys Choir of Harlem, which had benefited from my support, and to the black businesses I had supported at Equitable and to the young people at Howard and Johns Hopkins. This was so comforting to me.

But I must admit that inside of me, the toxic ghost of Enron was burning me up. I had to endure a number of painful experiences, especially one that occurred at the Lockheed Martin 2002 Annual Shareholder's meeting. Many labor unions, were, of course, exceptionally upset over the losses Enron union employees had suffered by holding basically worthless Enron stock in their pension and savings plans. They held the directors responsible for those losses, regardless of the fact that the directors were not responsible for allocating those savings to the Enron stock.

The labor unions were out for blood. They argued that my service as an Enron director deemed me unfit to serve on the Lockheed Martin board and mounted a "war room" effort to get me ousted. Thankfully, I always prevailed at those meetings and got reelected.

Nonetheless, at this particular meeting, a woman representing two unions as a shareholder, stood up and started berating me. She asserted that I was unfit to serve on Lockheed Martin's board. She blamed me for losing the money of all those people at Enron and accused me of failing to carry out my fiduciary role as an Enron director. Worse still, she hinted that I may have been part of the Enron conspiracy by virtue of my affiliation with Alliance Capital Management, a large holder of Enron stock. She went over the top. What troubled me about this was that she was an African American, and I sensed that, because of her race, she was being used as a pawn to take down another person who shared her race. Her speech got so bad that the directors sitting on either side of me in the first row, nestled up to me and whispered, "Frank, just be calm. Just be calm. You'll get through this. You'll get through this."

It was excruciating for me to sit there and take that. And then she called for my resignation. Vance Coffman, then CEO of Lockheed Martin, thanked her for her comments, expressed his sorrow at the union members' loss and then added, as I remember it, We hear your allegations about Frank Savage. As far as I know, we still live in America and people are innocent until proven guilty. Frank has been a director of Lockheed and now Lockheed Martin since 1991. He's been a great director. We trust him. We know his strengths. We know he is a man of character because he has proven it to us over the years of his board service. We don't believe that Frank is capable of being involved in the type of conspiracies and crimes that were committed at Enron. However, the future investigations and court hearings will make that determination. But it is totally out of character with the Frank Savage that we have known for all these years. If we find otherwise, we will deal with it. So we're going to stick by Frank until we get the final judgment.

Now, that was trust. And that trust was justified by subsequent court rulings.

In addition to the support and love of my family that sustained me through the Enron crisis, I received encouragement and strength from friends and colleagues as well. This held great significance, as we all respected opinion makers who had worked with me professionally over the years. Their thoughts and comments about me counted enormously in my financial world. People like my friend and former Mayor of New York, David N. Dinkins, and current New York Mayor, Michael R. Bloomberg, my longtime co-trustee at Johns Hopkins University who asked me to become a trustee of his company in 2001; this was prior to his first successful run for the city's top job in 2001.

As I went through those tough Enron times, never once did Mike ever even suggest that I should step aside from the Bloomberg board of directors. He had known and trusted me for almost 30 years. Bill McDonough, former president of the New York Federal Reserve, a former trustee, and a friend of mine on the board of the Council on Foreign Relations and the Institute of International Finance, also never flinched in his support of me. There were so many others who stood by me, among them: Paul Guenther, the chairman of the New York Philharmonic Board on which I sat for almost 20 years; Bill Brody, the former president of Johns Hopkins University, and Pat Swygert, president emeritus of Howard University. Cliff Wharton Jr., the former Deputy Secretary of State and CEO of TIAA-CREF and the first African-American graduate of Johns Hopkins University, SAIS. I will never forget the steady support of Irwin Jacobs, the former CEO of Qualcomm who, in spite of the fact that I had to leave the board as a consequence of a Department of Labor order, he always stood with me.

And there was Thabo Mbeki who, as president of South Africa, continued to value my economic advice throughout the whole Enron period; First Lady of Bermuda and my dear friend, Wanda Henton Brown, intervened on my behalf with the labor unions; Dave Williams, founder, CEO, and my partner in the African Millennium Fund, quietly but firmly let everybody know that he believed in Frank Savage; my dear friends, among them, H. Carl McCall, former comptroller of New York and his wife Joyce also lent me great support. In the political arena, Hillary Clinton and Congressman Charlie Rangel, to name a few, never expressed a moment's doubt in me. Their votes of confidence were invaluable to my professional standing as I felt as if I were being assailed from almost every side.

And, of course, there was Vernon E. Jordan Jr., the inimitable lawyer, businessman, power broker, and longtime friend since my Howard University days, who virtually held my hand, so to speak, as he helped me through my bleakest days, days when my name was being smeared in the newspapers. One morning, when I felt as if I was about to crumble, I called Vernon, the one person I knew I could talk to and who would understand what it was to be subject to such attacks in the media. He had weathered his own trial by printed and televised innuendos following his shooting in May 1980 after he, a black man who was the president of the National Urban League at the time, dropped off by a young white woman at his Fort Wayne, Indiana hotel.

I was beginning to more thoroughly explore why I was fast becoming such an ugly poster child for everything wrong in Enron. Was it because I was the only black person on its board? It certainly would not have been the first time a black man who had risen to unprecedented heights in business or politics had been unduly singled out—because of race—for especially harsh criticism when troubles occurred. Although I had tried to avoid attributing any racial motives for my treatment in the press, I was not naive about the role that race continues to play in the United States. I had grown up in a racially divided Washington, DC, and attended separate and yet unequal black schools until I entered graduate school. Race was, and still is, a reality shifter in the United States.

"Vernon, I need your help," I started. "The onslaught I'm getting is about to kill me."

Without hesitation, he said, "Frank, come on over."

I went to his elegant fortress of an office in New York, where he coached me on how to conduct myself during this firestorm of criticism. I will never forget what he did for me and how he stuck with me.

■ ■ ■

The period 2001 to 2005 was extremely difficult for me. However, I knew I had come through when I received more than 91 percent of the shareholders votes for reelection at the 2009 Lockheed Martin annual shareholders' meeting. What sweet vindication. I couldn't dwell on self-pity or look for motives or people to blame for my predicament. I moved forward with my life. I was confident that, in the end, my innocence would win the day, win the race. I just had to hold my head high and move on to the next phase of my life.

For more than a decade, really, I lived with the burden of Enron every day. Mind you, I did not let this stop me. I fought hard for three years to launch my Africa fund with the support of the Overseas Private Investment Corporation, and Dave Williams, former CEO of Alliance Capital, and my African brothers, like Yusif Ibrahim, a prominent Ghanaian businessman who knew the importance of the fund. But, to my great disappointment, I was forced to terminate my capital raising efforts.

In the summer of 2004, a fortuitous occurrence which would have a major bearing on my future . . . just happened.

P.P. Hinduja, my longtime friend from my more than a decade and a half of attending the World Economic Forum, and one of the powerful Hinduja brothers, invited me to lunch at his Trump Tower home. He never missed calling me when he was in New York. I had always looked forward to enjoying his hospitality and talking about global economic and political issues. But, as I entered his beautiful, Manhattan penthouse, I immediately sensed that there was something different about this meeting. There was a new sort of seriousness in the air.

Also in attendance were two New York-based Hinduja Group executives: Ken Petersen, a former U.S. Navy nuclear submarine captain and former Bechtel executive along with Ali Ganjaei, the Group's trusted legal counsel. After pleasantries, P.P. got right to the point.

He wanted to talk to me about joining the Hinduja Group in New York to assist it in expanding its presence in the financial industry in the Americas. I was surprised, but honored that the vast Hinduja Group with more than 30,000 employees worldwide, would offer me this opportunity when they could have gone to any major Wall Street financial or legal firm that would delight to have Hinduja as a client.

Why me? I wondered.

P.P. was quick to respond as if he read my mind. "Frank, you know the U.S. market, you are global like us. But most important, we know you and trust you." He added, his eyes smiling, "My son Remi, a graduate of the Wharton School, is planning on moving to New York to launch this initiative. I think the two of you would make a good team."

At that moment, P.P. called Remi into the room. We talked and it was clear that the chemistry between us was excellent. Remi and I subsequently spent many hours together getting to know each other and discussing the Groups' Americas strategy. I felt good about our conversations.

Apparently, Remi felt good as well because he asked me to go to London to meet with S.P. Hinduja, the Group's Chairman. The time I spent with S.P. in the Group's London offices convinced me that this was the type of organization in which I could flourish. S.P. exuded both warmth and wisdom. Most interesting was his stated desire to advance the economic well-being of minorities and less fortunate people around the world. Of course, this point resonated with me. It was totally consistent with my personal philosophy of combining success in business with helping others. The guiding principle of the Group's founder, "WORK TO GIVE," is prominently emblazoned on all the Group's offices.

This was a company where I could pursue the rest of my international career, I told my wife Lolita that night as I walked in front of stately embrace of Buckingham Palace. In addition to being a successful global enterprise, the Hinduja Group shared the same principles I hold most dear: integrity, concern for others, respect for family and co workers. I felt right at home. I joined the Group as Chairman of Hinduja Capital Advisors. I brought along my two trusted colleagues, Eva Evgenis, who is my executive assistant, and Jim Wilson, a former longtime head of fixed income investments at AXA Equitable and Alliance Capital.

I could feel the deck beginning to run smooth and sure beneath my feet, again.

In fact, my passion for world-class sailboat racing was a tremendous comfort to me during the terrible aftermath of Enron. The ocean was a vast, new world devoid of Enron. Sailing became essential to my peace of mind and my survival. During the early post scandal years, from 2001 to 2004, my heart would stutter a beat or two at the mere mention of *Enron*. I couldn't bear to hear it, bear to feel my stomach clench at the sound of its name that dampened my brow with a kind of poisonous perspiration. I never watched any of the movies about it. In fact, it wasn't until recently, in May 2010, that I watched *The Smartest Guys in the Room*, an exceptionally solid documentary of the scandal. Even then, after all these years, it was so painful to me that I could hardly keep my eyes on the screen.

Most people would be happy with the plate of plenty that I had in the years following Enron. I served as a member of South African President Thabo Mbeki's International Advisory Council, on the board of Lockheed Martin, and I still serve on the board of Bloomberg and am chairman of the Nile Growth Company, a mutual fund that I started in 1997 at Alliance Capital. But I still smart under the knowledge that the Enron debacle hindered me from making my Africa Millennium Fund a reality and being able to become more helpfully engaged in politics and not-for-profit activities.

I do, however, constantly remind myself to keep my Enron problems in perspective. I don't want anyone to feel sorry for me. When I think about all the other people in the world who are less fortunate than I am, who cannot feed their families, are sick with AIDS and other debilitating diseases, who have lost their jobs or their homes because of this economic downturn, or have children who are on drugs or in jail . . . I consider myself lucky and blessed. I have none of these problems and my family is doing very well. That is what really counts.

Although business positions, boards, and the like are important, they pale in comparison to the importance of family, loved ones, and personal health. I am blessed to have all three. The Enron scandal tested me to show what I was made of and I discovered that I am pretty strong inside. I have my mother to thank for instilling in me such internal fortitude and a compass that always guides me toward true north.

My whole life had been premised on working hard, providing aid to those less fortunate, and setting an example for young people who would follow in my footsteps. As chairman of Howard University's board, that trail of footsteps ahead could not be obscured by a corporate scandal, by the greed and criminality that wrecked that company. More than any other point in my life, I knew that I had to triumph over Enron's legacy. I could not let this Enron experience become my own living personal and professional nightmare.

That was not an option. I refused to have the next generation of business students and professionals, who I so much want to inspire, look at me through a cracked lens of disappointment and doubt. I could not, would not, let them down. I had to persevere.

I knew I had to reclaim the Savage name. It was a family's reputation as much as it was my own that I had to save. Such insight inspires me.

The downfall of Enron brought to light one crucial fact: in business, trust is everything. In this particular case, Ken Lay and his entire senior management team were not only trusted but also highly respected around the world, even by then President of the United States. But beneath the facade of the managerial dream team that Ken assembled hid some deep, personal flaws, which led to the destruction of Enron.

But for me, the Enron disaster is no reason to cease to ever trust again.

■ ■ ■

Looking back, I see how misplaced trust reared one of its deceiving heads in Bernard Madoff's $65-billion Ponzi scheme. Madoff's victims trusted him. Yet, it is critically important for the next generation to recognize that while a person cannot live his or her life in suspicion of everyone, one should not overly trust either. You can trust people, but you need to actively seek out some verification of their character. And test it to your satisfaction. Sometimes I wonder if the many savvy investors in the Madoff Ponzi scheme ever wondered how in the world could Madoff produce such steady returns, even while the markets could not. Or did they just decide to take the money and run, so to speak, and just leave well enough alone?

I have often revisited my willingness to trust Enron's management when I joined its board. With cheap 20/20 hindsight I see how my hubris may have dimmed my judgment. Remember, it was a time in my life when I felt like I was standing sure-footed on the peak of the world.

But it was my ambition, coupled with La Savage's encouragement to always strive to excel, that drove my decision to accept Ken Lay's offer back in 1999. I know that now. Enron was one of the most respected and admired Fortune 500 corporations in the world. I was extremely successful and had the added distinction of being widely considered to be the preeminent African American in global finance.

Joining that board seemed like a natural progression in my professional life, one that I viewed as a reward, an honor that I deserved. I also knew that the splendid Alliance analysts held Enron in the highest regard. So, if the company was good enough to pass their rigid investment screen, it had to be a good company. This bore out and confirmed all the positive analyst reports that I had read during my independent research on the company. The Enron experience taught me that sometimes it is important to hold ambition in check and not be so eager to gallop off where it wants to take you. It might be over a cliff. It was out of ambition that I decided to join the board of Enron. But, frankly, at that point in my life, I did not need more prestige by joining another board. I had nothing to prove. Yet, somehow I felt I did. One more prize. That impulse cost me greatly. Strictly in terms of dollars and cents, my Enron experience cost me millions in income and much, much more in terms of lost opportunity gains from my failed Africa Millennium Fund and Qualcomm board seat. I might likely be a billionaire today, rather than simply a millionaire. But, it was not about the money, just my drive and ambition—characteristics that are common in Type AAA businesspeople like me.

But, again, I don't want anyone to feel sorry for me. I don't.

My family stood by me like a rock to cling to in a troubled sea, in silent encouragement, but I know it pained them to watch me try to keep a stiff upper lip. Apart from the support of my loved ones, my knowledge, deep within myself, that I was totally innocent and had nothing to hide was the only other thing that sustained me over that period. Over the course of the Enron proceedings, in which this innocence was eventually revealed, I learned the value of taming ambition. It was a brutally difficult lesson, which I want younger generations to take to heart.

There is always risk in deciding to be a person who strives to impart lessons to the next generation as I am doing here. However, taking risks is a significant part of my identity. No person begets the experience of living without taking risks and few people have achieved phenomenal success without both taking risks and tasting failure. Consider the arc of the creative life of Steve Jobs, an innovator and visionary businessman who had his brightest years of success when he, in 1996, returned to Apple, the company he co-founded, after being ousted 1985.

In my life, I have always carefully weighed risks and opportunities, which have come in many forms such as success at Equitable Capital Management Corporation and a deeply disappointing business failure in Africa in the 1980s.

And I take, without hesitation, the risk of sharing important lessons with you, among you, I hope, the next generation of aspiring leaders. At the core of all of these lessons is the shinning significance of trust. Not blind trust, but instead a trust rooted in an analysis of a person, a company.

Trust must be earned by exhibiting integrity and honesty. If one violates these traits, trust will quickly be lost. A boyhood memory of my mother comes to mind. She would always walk as if she were 7 feet tall. She was actually barely more than 5 feet in height.

Observing her from my little boy perspective, she seemed monumental, not in stature per se, but in character. "Frank Jr., it is important that people trust you," she'd tell me. "That's the most important part to building a good reputation."

So, even as a young boy, the value of trust and verification was alive within me as I cultivated my own reputation in my mother's trustful shadow.

Reflections

The troubling aspect of the current corporate crisis, which famously started in 2007, is that the collapses of our economic system have become systematic versus being perpetrated by one person, like an Andy Fastow at Enron. This systematic character threatens the whole capitalistic system on which the United States has been built, and it jeopardizes the faith in the U.S. financial sector all around the world. As I travel the globe, I am dismayed by the disenchantment among foreigners about the U.S. financial sector. People have always looked to Wall Street and followed its lead. But the recent U.S.-led subprime mortgage losses that has ravaged much of the 99 percent the Occupy Wall Street protesters have coined, followed by the Madoff scandal, which attacked much more of the moneyed 1 percent, have together severely tarnished the United States' reputation. It has eroded the world's trust in us, in our way of doing business, of managing and investing capital.

It is important to always remember that all it takes is one well-placed rip in the hull of a ship to sink it. Remember the "unsinkable" Titanic? I discovered there was more than one bad hole in the leadership of Enron to sink the company. But they were the last people one might suspect to have been engaged in such devilment because of what they had at stake, had to lose, and because of what they had already gained. And yet, something inside of them, a fatal flaw in their personalities, their nature, caused them to go bad, to crack.

The same could be said of Madoff. He lied, cheated, and produced financial statements that reflected substantial, consistent, and dependable earnings. A person with a total lack of integrity, he took everybody down with him, people who trusted him with their futures. This was the clearest example of a failure of investors, both the sophisticated and unsophisticated, to adhere to the trust-but-verify principle. And Bernie Madoff didn't care whose life he destroyed along the way, be they family, friends, or even Jewish philanthropic organizations. It didn't matter. How do we explain that? His whole life was one big lie. Where does that fatal flaw come from? Did they have a bad example that they followed? Were they born with this deficiency? I don't know the answers, just in this case only the insight to ask the right questions.

I also believe I possess the insight and experience to urge the next generation of business leaders to join corporate boards despite the risks they carry. I think that the shareholders and companies would be the ultimate losers if qualified board candidates refused to join boards. Say yes if asked, but I advise new directors to do what they can to protect themselves.

As directors who only come to meetings perhaps a maximum of 10 times a year, there is a great deal of dependency on outside accountants and lawyers to verify and represent information provided by management. And this makes directors vulnerable to fraud and malfeasance committed by a top officer, like a CEO or CFO. That is especially the case if he or she is hell bent on defrauding the company and enlists the help of people in sensitive areas such as legal and accounting in the company to perpetrate the fraud.

Scary, isn't it?! So let there be no illusions, even by following the trust-but-verify mantra, directors are still vulnerable, just like I was on Enron's board. We have no choice but to depend on having CEOs and CFOs who have impeccably high integrity and honesty; in other words, trustworthy. That's the bottom line and why it is so important that our society focuses on generating future business leaders who have been taught by their parents and schools that "honesty is the best policy" and trust must be preciously developed and preserved. No amount of law, no amount of checking, will guarantee this. It must come from inside.

Board candidates must spend as much time as possible digging deep into a company before joining its board. And then, of course, again, you have to trust but verify. Yes, this puts a lot of pressure on directors because we have a day job.

For the next generation of business professionals who are aspiring to join boards it is important to remember that there used to be a time when a board seat was the ultimate reward for a career well done. A seat on a board of a major company showered the director with a lot of prestige. And I think it still does, but, more important, the flip side is that joining a big board brings risks that can undermine all of the good works you may have done throughout your career. I am a perfect example of that.

Does it mean I would never join another board? No. Does it mean that I will become an even tougher and questioning director? Yes, although I was equally probing as a director at Enron, but I never saw the fraud coming because it was perpetrated by the one person I relied on to protect the financial integrity of the company. But, I have notched up my questioning to an even higher level on my boards, not to the point of asking frivolous questions, but to a place of asking probing questions that may reveal any inconsistencies that may deserve further investigation.

Unfortunately, in the U.S. financial community, we've gone through a very dark period. It may have seemed a golden era for the people who have used it to make rivers of money—and there's nothing wrong with making money; that's part of capitalism. But the question looms: What price did we have to pay to make all this money? Was all that money made by creating products for clients that were in their best interests, or was it motivated by greed? Simple greed?

Special, structured products—like derivatives Special Purpose Vehicles, feeder funds, and securitized vehicles, which have been in existence for years and are quite legitimate—have been used by irresponsible and greedy financial professionals. They have simply lined their pockets, taking advantage of unsuspecting investors and, in some cases, committed outright fraud. Worse still, these products have been sold all over the world to unsuspecting investors and institutions, sometimes with the collusion of marketers. As a result, the financial soundness of the whole world has been thrown into peril.

At some business schools and the educational system more generally, as well as some families, have forgotten to teach ethics. We forgot to emphasize the commitment to both clients and ethics. All we've taught to our next generation of business professionals is how to make money, lots of money, and scramble to the top at all costs to make more money. We must get back to square one to train young people the need to think about the customer, the client first, and think about profitability and then sales second. If the next generation understands this, in the long run, we will all end up doing better. The clients will trust you, they will bring their business to you, whereas if you are not trustworthy, you probably will be able to treat them badly once, maybe twice, maybe even three times, but over the long run, you're undermining the very system that has enabled you to do well and enabled us to do well as a country, not 1 percent or 99 percent, but opportunities for 100 percent of the United States.

So, we have a real challenge on our hands. President Obama has set a refreshing tone of putting the common man first because he's a man who came up in humble, ethical surroundings with responsible grandparents and a devoted mother who taught him about the importance of being trustworthy. He witnessed poverty in Hawaii, Indonesia, Chicago, and Kenya. Money has never been his motivation, although he thoroughly believes in the U.S. capitalist and market systems that have helped to make the United States a country where anyone can create a good life for their family. He has consistently been 100 percent determined to restore ethics in business so we can regain the trust in our financial leadership. I am as certain of this.

The next generation will have a burden and an opportunity. It will have to lead the country and world in going back to emphasizing the importance of morality in business, the obligations of CEOs to their shareholders, and resisting the temptation to only be guided by how much money can be made in the shortest period of time.

I know today that I am one of the luckiest men alive. I have survived the greatest challenge to my professional life and regained my reputation. Most important, it is such a rare opportunity to be able to reflect and share the lessons of life's challenges with those stepping up to their first substantial challenges, or those getting up from the burdens of challenges too heavy to bear.

With no regret, I understand there comes a point in life that the actions of yesterday have to be transformed into the lessons for tomorrow.

No matter how old we become, we are always tomorrow's people.

Chapter 3

La Savage, the Source and Inspiration

To describe my mother would be to write about a hurricane in its perfect power.

—*Maya Angelou*

My mother drove a pink and black Pontiac Bonneville, a long cool drink of a car that was first introduced by General Motors in 1957. Slightly reclined in its sofa of a front seat, she, often alone, would glide along the streets of Washington, DC. She liked to drive with her window down, her sparkling brown eyes straight ahead and her hair—dark and cooperative in a sophisticated swirl with her trademark, frosted streak—daring any breeze to undo a hairdo that only she could do.

She wore gloves and silken scarves that spoke of her ease with elegance. Her makeup, on a face that was as soft and pleasingly warm as a ripe morning sun, was always just so. Okay, she was a little over the top, and I loved her for it.

This was the late 1950s. It was a time in much of the United States, even in the North, when most black people had so little to show for their hard work, and those who did tended to display it only to their own. This was a time when Jim Crow laws sharpened the unforgiving edges of black life. Black dreams tended to be meager, close to the ground, or were so big and up in the clouds many of its dreamers had a tough time imagining stairways to reach their visions. Remember, back then we were only a handful of generations out of slavery. This was a time when the civil rights movement was still young and Martin Luther King Jr. was a boyish-faced preacher making a name for himself as a honey-tongued soldier for social justice.

Yet this was the time when my mother, Grace Savage, had transformed herself from a humble, colored girl from North Carolina, into a portrait of well-deserved pride and success in the nation's capital. She knew that driving her pretty car was less about transportation but more about transconfiguration, evidence really, of her triumph as an independent businesswoman.

My mother christened herself *Madame La Savage International*, a self-made brand. Her evolution from Hattie and Thomas Pitt's little girl to an internationally renowned beautician was so deep and profound that even my twin sister and I stopped calling her mother. By the time Frances and I were in junior high school, we lovingly called her *La Savage* (pronounced La Sau Varge). And that's the way she wanted it.

What my mother was called and how she represented herself came as the result of a series of transitions. The first was from "Mother Dear" to "Madame La Savage" when she operated her beauty shop; the next transition came when she went for the first time to the International Beauty Show in New York and she took me and my sister with her. She came back and labeled herself "Madame La Savage, International."

When I was going to Benjamin Banneker Junior High School in Washington, lots of my friends called me "La Savage"—in jest. Of course, I knew I was Frank Savage. My mother's renaming of herself was business; it was all commercialization, marketing herself. It's remarkable, thinking back on it. She didn't go to business school or have any background for any of this. And I still wonder how she knew what she apparently knew.

To say that my mother in those years had become bigger than life underestimates the gravity of her carefully crafted professional persona, as well as the woman she had become by way of it. La Savage, a single mother and relentlessly her own woman, became, in my earliest memory, the single greatest source, my shining source, of strength and inspiration.

At her feet, I learned the life lessons regarding the value of hard work, good character, and high self-esteem; each contributed to my own success at practically every stage of my life. In today's got-to-have-it-yesterday, instant-gratification world, cultivating good character and maintaining positive self-esteem are often overshadowed by the pressure to just "get it done" and "by any means necessary." That's a mistake.

Growing up with my mother, having her teach me, largely by example, I discovered that there was much more to a well-lived life than the obvious. I came to realize, at a fairly early age, that there were higher obtainments to be had, like the things you couldn't hold in your hands, but in your heart.

For instance, I learned to love the pursuit of excellence for the very sake of it. I found a thrill in learning not just for a grade or a teacher's approval, but for the sheer pleasure of replacing ignorance with knowledge.

As I've gotten older, and hopefully wiser, I have come to realize that I am a true reflection of my mother.

La Savage gave me my love for the business world. I watched her enroll in the Madame C. J. Walker Beauty School in Washington to refine her skills as a beautician that seemed to have come naturally to her. My mother adored and admired Madame Walker, a black woman who knew something about personal transformation.

Walker was born Sarah Breedlove in Delta, Louisiana, two years after the close of the Civil War. Shortly after the turn of the twentieth century, Walker began experimenting with various products to attack the problem of hair loss, something many women suffered back then. This probably had a lot to do with the general bad plumbing of the times and other poor conditions that made it difficult for women, black and white, to wash their hair very much. Walker eventually developed a shampoo that encouraged hair growth, and then other ointments that led her and her third husband to establish a factory in Indianapolis to make and market her hair products.

After building a profitable beauty and real estate business—mostly alone after her last divorce in 1912, Walker established a school for aspiring beauticians like my mother.

When Walker died in 1919 at age 51, she was one of the richest African Americans of her time. Many considered her one of the first self-made women millionaires in America. She was certainly a tremendous role model for black beauticians. My mother modeled her entire beauty career on Walker's and to tremendous effect.

By the time I had grown old enough to understand such things my grasp of my mother's origin story seemed an unlikely one, nonetheless, true.

■ ■ ■

She grew up in hard scrabble surroundings in Rocky Mount in the 1920s, one of eight children. Her father, Thomas, was a strikingly handsome black man and was said to be very quick on his feet. Smart. Her mother, Hattie, was one of the first black women to graduate from college after slavery ended. She was a graduate of Shaw University in Raleigh, North Carolina, a college founded specifically for *Negroes* in 1865, the year slavery was abolished in the United States.

Two of Thomas's and Hattie's children died at a young age, one from an illness and another from burns when she opened a coal stove in her home to tend its fire. At the very instant she opened the stove a blaze shot forth; she literally inhaled the flame. There was only one boy, named after his father, and five surviving daughters, Hazel, Louise, Nancy, Naomi, and my mother, Grace.

There would be more tragedy. My grandfather was killed by a train while crossing the tracks in Rocky Mount. Very soon after that, one of his daughters, Nancy, came home from studying in Raleigh and discovered that her father had been killed. She was so upset, so stricken from grief, she died soon after that. This left my maternal grandmother with five teenage children to raise. Prospects in Rocky Mount looked grim.

My grandfather's death coincided with the Great Migration, the epic exodus of blacks escaping from the South by the millions to go north and west. So, Hattie Pitt and her kids fit right in as she left everything she knew seeking better economic opportunities and relief

Grace (Madame La Savage International) Savage, Frank's mother, inspiration, and guiding light.

from the heavy hand of Southern racism. They all—except my mother, a teenage bride back in Rocky Mount—landed in Washington, DC, and moved into a rented house at 3522 Center Street NW. It was a quiet, tree-lined neighborhood a few blocks east of 16th Street, near the Woodner Hotel. If you walked south long enough on 16th Street you would dead end on the White House.

But we lived in a rickety, old wooden house with a wooden front porch and wobbling railing. The house, two stories tall with a coal furnace, wasn't big, yet it had lots of places to sleep. It had to. For most of my childhood, I lived there with my Grandma Hattie, my mother, and most of her sisters, as well as my uncle, Thomas, and the son and daughter of my aunts Hazel and Naomi.

■ ■ ■

It was a happy house. Some of the happiest days of my life were living at 3522 Center in Upper Northwest Washington because we were all together. We had a matriarchal family because Hattie Pitt was the boss, but not a boss in that harsh sort of way. She kept everybody stable in that house just like government jobs would come to keep the family financially stable. And everyone was taught to be independent. I was trained how to wash my clothes; they trained me how to iron my clothes. I am one of the best ironers of shirts you will ever see—even to this day. Of course, I can afford to have somebody else take care of my shirts, but I like to iron my own shirts.

And I had chores. I was responsible—along with my uncle until I got old enough to do this myself—for getting up every morning in the winter and making the fire in the furnace. I always had a job. As a boy I was, like lots of boys, a paper boy. I delivered the *Washington Post* all over the neighborhood. The Woodner, the single largest air-conditioned building when it opened in 1952, was on my route. Once, feeling especially mischievous, I went to its top floor and peed over the side just for the experience of it.

I liked working, liked making my own money, but I didn't work because I had to.

We were never poor. I don't ever remember being hungry in that house. But I also remember eating—especially during the war years—chicken feet there, and neck bones and chitterlings, too. I still occasionally sit down to a plate of chitterlings, steaming hog intestines that don't taste quite like anything else in this world. I, and most of my family, were natural born Southerners living in a city just across the Potomac River from Virginia, the first of the colonies to have slaves.

Our family survived by taking on all sorts of odd jobs. As each of Hattie Pitt's children became 18, they were able to get jobs in the government. Thomas, especially resourceful—and taking advantage of being a man in a male-dominated society at the time—was able to get a job at the nearby Mexican Embassy. Functioning like sort of a cooperative, the family became economically stable by sharing costs and pooling incomes.

By 1938, my mother decided that it was time for her to leave Rocky Mount—and her husband. She was 16 when she married my father, Frank Savage, a handsome, brown-skinned man who eventually went into the military and served in World War II. I spent little time with my father. I do remember visiting him from time to time when I was a teenager and he was living in Philadelphia. He escaped the South soon after my mother left him. My sister, Frances, looks a lot like our father, and I look almost exactly like my mother. It's funny how genetics works out.

I never entirely knew the background that led to my mother's decision to leave my father. I know my mother loved him, but that was apparently not enough. I only know that she realized back then that their marriage wasn't going to work out. I believe she simply made a calculation that it was vastly better to join the rest of her family in Washington than to be unhappy in North Carolina stuck in a bad marriage. When my mother said she was ready to join the rest of the family in Washington, my Aunt Louise went down to North Carolina to accompany her on the train with "her two twins," as La Savage used to call us.

■ ■ ■

In 1938, when Frances and I were six weeks old, we were bundled up with a bottle of milk between us, and headed to Washington and my future.

My mother's immediate plan was not to follow the path of all of her sisters—all elegant, beautiful black women—who worked in government jobs. It wasn't that Grace Savage was averse to hard work. It was just working for someone else that was contrary to her natural entrepreneurial tendencies, which had already emerged in Rocky Mount.

My Aunt Naomi shared with me that La Savage was always entrepreneurial. She actually started "fixing hair," as they called it, when she was 13 years old. Aunt Naomi's eyes gleamed when she told me how the two of them would go house to house fixing women's hair for 5 cents a head. And my mother was good at it, exhibiting a flair for cosmetology that seemed to be in her blood.

But once she got to Washington, DC, a Southern town at heart but much larger and more cosmopolitan than Rocky Mount, my mother decided that she would make an effort to get a reliable, government job after all. She had two hungry mouths to feed.

One morning she got up early, dressed in her most business-like dress and made her way to the Civil Service Administration for a job interview. She prepared herself to take whatever entrance exam required of her.

The door closed behind her, as if on its own. It was an ominous sign, but my mother chose to ignore it, or at least she tried to. Unusually nervous, she walked into the dimly-lit office of the examiner, a non-descript space that had an almost overwhelming blandness.

Will this be the job . . . the one that I need to take care of my two twins? my mother wondered.

A tall, pudgy white man appeared, like out of thin air and shadows. He wore a grin without warmth and then asked in a way that made his every word feel like an order, starting with, "Please have a seat." He motioned my mother to a gray, steel chair sitting directly across from the large, mahogany desk where he was sat, oddly impish and imperial.

The questions and answers went quickly; the examiner's tone was flat and cold. My mother was all business, and her responses reflected all the information she carefully provided weeks earlier on an application form she had submitted. Grace Savage noticed that the form was resting on the top of the examiner's manila file folder. She also noticed that he never glanced at it, not once.

After what seemed like a rather routine interview, she was relieved to sense that it was coming to an end. The time had passed much slower than any clock indicated. The whole thing had been uncomfortable and draining. Yet, my mother gave herself a bubble of optimism. *"This is going fairly well. Maybe I will get this civil service job and then we will be on our way in establishing our new life here."*

Many years later, she told that at this point she let her thoughts drift to me, the need to find the right school, friends for me. She thought about Frances, too, and how her needs as a daughter would be different and somehow easier for her to tend to as a woman. My mother sat with her thoughts until she heard the examiner, a man who looked early middle-age, getting to his feet to dismiss her with a stern, matter-of-fact "that will be all."

My mother rose slowly, gathering herself and the last of her hopes for the job. She grabbed her purse, tugged on her gloves, and turned her back on the examiner, who, as far as she was concerned had receded back into the shadows from whence he had come. She took a step toward the office door, which was still closed. The examiner, in what seemed like a burst of pent up good intentions, quickly stepped forward, then pass her.

Oh, that is nice, she thought as he moved by her. *I like the way they do things up here in the North, opening doors for a colored lady. Folks were right. Moving from North Carolina was a good idea.*

A few steps and seconds later, both the examiner and my mother were at the door; the examiner reached across her path with one hand extended firmly for the tarnished door knob, and my mother took another step toward the door, her face brightening with satisfaction of knowing she did a good job in the interview. The officer door opened and with it my mother felt a breeze of fresher air. Then suddenly there was something else, something abrupt, crude, and dehumanizing.

The examiner, with one hand still on the door knob, reached down with his free hand and smacked Grace Savage, mother of two, the daughter of Thomas and Hattie Pitt from Rocky Mount, North Carolina, on her derriere.

With that single act of disrespect, our world wobbled and shifted. What should have been an easy walk into the valley of 9-to-5 and steady paychecks suddenly became an ice-capped mountain. Right there on the spot, my mother decided to take a different path, one that she would create. She vowed to never subject herself to a position that would compromise her dignity. She would be, from that moment forward, persistently determined to build a life of self-reliance and self-respect for herself and her children. No matter what it took, she told herself, she would succeed in finding a grand place in this world. And she was going to build it in such a way that dignity and respect would come to her as naturally as rain comes from clouds.

After completing beauty school, my mother launched her beauty business from my bedroom in the Center Street house. I could not go to sleep until she finished her last customer, normally after 9 P.M. Often, I would fall asleep on the living room couch, a scratchy, lumpy thing that really wasn't that comfortable to even sit on. When Grandma tried to wake me up after the last paying customer had left, she would gently squeeze a wet towel over my face and say, "Frank Jr., it's time to go to bed."

Grace Savage had a very powerful work ethic, and an infectious charm that enabled her to build a loyal clientele and ultimately open her own beauty shop at 2228 Georgia Avenue, the intersection of Barry Place NW and Georgia Avenue, the same Washington avenue where Howard University is located. This was an amazing achievement during the 1950s. Throughout my mother's life, I worked with her in her business. I was in her shop almost every day after school. I cleaned up, helped her put away her hairdressing irons, and when I became old enough, I would drive her home.

■ ■ ■

Over the years, from my days at Banneker Junior, then Dunbar High School, and, finally, Howard University, I would always stop by the shop when I wanted to see my mother, now Madame La Savage. I knew I could find her there because she was always working there. Though we called it "the shop," my mother proudly posted its name and motto on its front door: La Savage Beauty Clinic, "Beauty at its Best."

Watching my mother work so hard, making every dollar count, I came to internalize her sense of self-reliance. Besides my paper route, I washed cars, shoveled snow, delivered groceries, and prescriptions. And, yes, I did do windows, washing as many as I could for a buck. Well, I did draw a line at washing windows on the upper floors of a DC government office building in downtown Washington. In 1956 my friends Sonny and James asked me to hang out of the third floor of that building to wash windows. I said, "No way." I was about 17 years old and it was the first time I quit a job.

Even though La Savage could afford it, I paid my way through college by working nights in a hot and sweaty government Xerox reproduction office at the CIA, a job that my Aunt Louise, who worked there, arranged for me. Interestingly enough, Democratic Congressman Steny H. Hoyer, the present House Minority Whip, worked alongside me in that office. He and I obviously shared the same drive to work hard. Although I worked for many decades in major corporations, I never relinquished that entrepreneurial, independent streak that La Savage gifted my DNA.

I also never let go of my sense that I lived in a much larger world, not just some small corner of it where I happened to be born or where I had been raised. It was the capital, so people from practically every land lived and worked in Washington, but mostly as diplomats. As I've mentioned, my uncle worked at the nearby Mexican Embassy. Just about every nation had an embassy in Washington, many of them dotted along Massachusetts Avenue. Even nations, like the Soviet Union, the United States' chief adversary during the Cold War, were there, too.

But my deep-seated love of international affairs was planted in me by my mother. La Savage introduced Frances and me to a vibrant international world with an invitation to participate in the International Beauty Shows at New York Coliseum, a hulking, broad-shouldered building that once stood on Columbus Circle. It has long since been replaced by a twin-towered, crystal palace-shopping mall and hotel and office complex called the Time-Warner Center. Starting from before we were teenagers, my mother would take us each year to New York where we would stay in Harlem with a family friend named Alice. La Savage, the only black beautician in the show, was so proud of us and would show us off to all of the other beauticians at the show. We were typically twin-cute little boy and girl reflections of one another. I guess that makes it hard for people to resist patting our heads or pinching our cheeks that were as dark and sweet as milk chocolate.

Our mother was a one-woman Madison Avenue, launching campaign after campaign about how great we were in school, how we never gave her a moment's problem and how optimistic she was about what we would achieve in life. She never had enough good words to say about us. And she dreamed big dreams for us, prompting me in time to dream even bigger dreams for myself while I searched for the stairwell to make them all come true.

In those days, segregation was still very much a part of the land. As late as the early 1960s, motels and restaurants were famously barred to blacks along the corridor between Washington and Baltimore, for example. Just for my mother to travel to New York on her own was a very big deal.

At the New York beauty show, there were beauticians and stylists from all over the world. I was so proud to see my mother among them. It was at the show where she adopted her professional name: *Madame La Savage International*. The "International" was not because she had been abroad, because she hadn't. It was in recognition of her awards and success at the Show, and maybe reflective of her larger aspirations. Her own big dreams. I think bestowing herself with a title as much as a name was a badge of honor and a means to set herself apart from all the neighborhood practitioners of her art. It helped her to firmly establish a special identity in her industry.

Her sense of self-worth was extraordinary. And her unwavering belief in the power of her own talents was immeasurably important in cultivating a winning, "can-do" mind-set in me and Frances. My own success as a businessman, as a man in general, can be directly attributed to the example of my mother's vibrant spirit and invincible attitude.

La Savage's participation in the Beauty Show was not the only way that she introduced me to the international arena. She also ushered the larger world into my life when we moved to our second home, this one on Columbia Road in an area of the city known as Adams Morgan, an ethnic and racial melting pot on a low flame. We thought the house was beautiful and she made tasteful renovations to make it more than suitable for entertaining.

Her identity with the International Beauty Show prompted her to become involved in the diplomatic community in Washington. She would often bring Liberian and Ethiopian diplomats to our home, at that time the only African representatives in Washington. Their foreign accents echoed through our house as they switched back and forth between English and their native languages. Some wore brightly colored native garb; others dressed in business suits, white shirts, and narrow ties. I knew I wanted to see their countries, visit them, inhale the same air that my ancestors must have.

In time, I would travel to such places and many more that I could not imagine from our home on Columbia Road. I am, by any definition, well traveled, worldly.

It was this early exposure to foreign diplomats and foreign cultures that I attribute to laying the groundwork for my eventual ease with working with many kinds of people, in many parts of the world that helped me in my pioneering rise to the top levels of the global financial arena. Through my early experiences in Washington, I was introduced to Africa, and what they taught me is that the reality of Africans and Africa could not have been further than any notion of the "Dark Continent" popularized in juvenile jungle adventure books and Tarzan movies, Johnny Weissmuller in a loin cloth most of all.

By my early teens I was already developing a counter-story, an embrace of my African heritage that was profound. My mother's introduction to Africans—firsthand and face-to-face—was catalytic in my developing deep abiding love of Africa.

My mother taught me to always have the highest respect for and valuation of self. That is not to say she taught me to be arrogant or to consider myself superior to anyone. She just wanted my sister and I to understand that we mattered and that we had an obligation to be the very best people we could be. Anything less than that would be unacceptable. Then, logically, how could we, African Americans, not love Africa if we loved ourselves? It is our Motherland and we are its children.

Such an embrace opened up so many wondrous possibilities. This was such a pervasive theme in her daily socialization of us. At every opportunity La Savage would say to me, "Frank Jr., you can be anything you want to be. One day you're going to be the president of the United States." And this was in the 1950s, when a black man being president was just as unlikely as the White House being painted black. It was not conceivable in the mind of most people, black or white. But not in the tireless, questing mind of Madame La Savage. She constantly spoke to me in a special sort of way that made me feel, well, special. Unique.

Frances and I were fortunate to be good students. I once received As in all my classes at Banneker Junior High School. I went to mother's shop to show La Savage my report card. She was thrilled and made an announcement to her clients, which I will never forget. She had me show my perfect report card to all of the customers whether they were interested or not. As I did I could hear her say, "Oh, look at these grades that my son Frank brought in. Frank is a borderline genius."

Although she probably used the term in jest, I never forgot it. A generation later, I loosely adapted it to inspire my own children. I could never get enough of my mother's compliments. Already highly motivated, I found that her spoken approval pushed me even harder to excel in school. And I did.

Even at Dunbar High School, where I took an adolescent detour into fast cars and even faster girls, La Savage constantly reminded me that I was—despite my falling grades—still a "borderline genius." She didn't lose faith.

La Savage also inculcated in me a sense of responsibility that I think was very important as the oldest of my cousins in Washington. As the oldest boy, La Savage gave me a tremendous amount of responsibilities. She said that these were things that I should do because my aunts and my sister had taken over all of the cooking, washing, and ironing. Consequently, it was my job to keep the house clean and to run errands for them.

"When you grow up to be a man, you will have to take care of your family. So right now, we're your family and you have to take care of us," she would tell me. "And we will take care of you." I still, more than half a century later, live by those sentiments.

I will never forget the brutal winters in DC during my teenage years when we still lived in the house on Center Street. I would get up around 6 A.M. to make the fire in the coal-burning furnace in the basement. When my Uncle Thomas helped, we would first shovel the previous night's ashes from the furnace, take them up a steep set of steps to leave for pick up. Then we'd make the fire. All of this had to be done before I went out to deliver newspapers on my paper route. Once my papers were delivered, I returned home to have breakfast with my sister and cousins, and then left for school. That was my routine Monday through Friday.

Although my mother never ceased to find occasions to compliment me, she also made it very clear that she had always had high standards for me. One thing that she insisted on was that I respect women and quickly come to understand—prefeminist—that they were equal to men. My sister and her friends had many sleepovers at the house on Center Street. By the time I was in junior high school, some of those girls started to look pretty good to me. And I, of course, began to want to get closer to some of them.

I will never forget how La Savage dealt with this situation. She knew that we were all growing up and having been a teenage mother herself, she didn't want any of us to follow in those particular footprints of hers. One day, just out of the blue, she called me. "Frank Jr., I want to talk to you."

"Yes La Savage."

"Frances is bringing a lot of her friends over here and these are her good friends," she said, her tone firm but patient. "They come over here because they want to be with Frances, and I can see that you are looking at some of these girls and that's okay too. But Frank, I want you to remember just one thing: You must treat those girls with respect.

"I want you to know," she continued, her words picking up weight as she slowed some to make a point, "that you must not do anything to those girls that you wouldn't want some boy to do to your sister."

The statement hung in the air before dropping on my head like the apple that awoke Newton to gravity. My twin sister is someone I love and always felt the need to protect even though she's technically my older sister—by 15 minutes. When I was a teenager, the thought of any boy touching her was unthinkable to me. From that day on, I never pursued any of my sister's friends. I used to tell my buddies, "You know something, any girl that is in my sister's inner circle, I don't touch them. I don't mess with any of them.

"But if they are outside that circle, they are fair game."

They would laugh so hard at that because it meant more "fair game" for them. But I looked on my mother's pronouncement as a serious bit of business.

As a matter of fact, Frances later told me that La Savage told her the same thing as it related to her and my friends. "You know," Frances said half joking," I think I missed out on so many potential boyfriends because of La Savage preaching to us."

Again, by example, my mother taught me of the importance of family in sustaining and supporting life. I could not have survived the Enron crisis without my family's love and support. And in designing the interpersonal architecture for my life, my mother made sure that Frances and I were always surrounded by loving family. La Savage was a hard worker so we did not have her physical presence around us as much as Frances and I would have liked. But in the most important aspects, La Savage was always there in her teachings, in her spirit. That remained true when we lost La Savage in 1981 after she suffered a stroke, a complication from her battle with diabetes. She was shopping for presents in downtown Washington for my one-year-old son when she collapsed. I thank God that she didn't suffer.

■ ■ ■

On the weekends, while Frances and I were out of school, La Savage worked away in her shop. During the week she was in the shop, too. When she came home she was usually exhausted. So our aunts and cousins and Uncle Thomas became, again, like a cooperative, vital to our household, and to our lives. And there was my maternal grand-mother, Hattie Pitt.

Grandma, as we called her, had a tremendous influence on my life through my college years. She grew up in Rocky Mount, still a small town that today nestles I-95 as it winds through rural North Carolina. She came from a family that had just recently been released from slavery. They were industrious, but there were few opportunities for recently freed blacks in a land that still largely regarded them as slaves—just without specific masters.

Like most blacks in Rocky Mount, my grandparents made a living by picking cotton and tobacco. It was grueling work that paid very little.

I am told that when my grandmother was young, she was absolutely gorgeous. I remember her being tall with black, velvety skin and keen features. Hattie Pitt was soft-spoken, unlike my mother who "owned" any room she walked into. My mother was gregarious and confident. I do think that my mother inherited her beauty from my grandmother, just like her sisters did. They shared a luminous brown skin and a kind of pleasing symmetry of mouth, nose, and twinkling eyes that turned heads. I'm certain that my mother inherited her nature, her charm, from my grandfather. It was quite a combination.

My grandmother loved me and I loved her. We spent a considerable amount of time together during those early years in Washington as La Savage built her career. Grandma was the one who took care of me and my sister while my mother took care of us all. It is not an unfamiliar story, especially in so many families in the black community.

The difference between the modified nuclear family—minus my father, of course—that I grew up in and the single-parent families of today is that I had an extended family of aunts and my uncle and my grandmother in the household. They all had full authority over me. We all lived in the house and everybody there knew that if La Savage was not there they could do whatever they had to do to make sure Frances and I stayed on the right track. But my grandmother was a typical grandparent. You know what I mean. I could do no wrong in her eyes. I knew I was clearly her favorite.

Secretly, all of her grandchildren probably felt the same way. But I had evidence. Whenever my grandmother went to the shop or to the grocery store, she would always take just me. My mother never had to worry about my well-being because I had my grandmother with me. And Grandma's sweet, warm voice had been so important to me throughout my life, even long after she passed away in 1967. I would hear that voice when I most needed to, particularly during some of the most challenging and grueling times in my life. Ancestral voices, like in many African cultures, are often the most resistant to trifles of life and death.

My grandmother was passionate about our education and wanted to make sure that we received the best schooling. Our family knew that without education, we had no chance in life, and so like many black and first-generation immigrant families at the time, my family encouraged academics. We were very lucky because our family gave considerable thought to what path Frances and I should take to help ensure that we got into a good college, and one that would accept black students. The family looked at all the black schools in Washington—this was years before Brown versus the Board of Education Supreme Court decision in 1954, so public schools were segregated by law at the time. In the end, the family decided on three.

These were Morgan Elementary, which was in downtown Washington, off U Street NW. It was actually on Champagne Street, just to the west of 16th Street near Meridian Hill Park, which locals later christened Malcolm X Park. It was known to have the best black elementary school teachers in the town. Aspiring black, college-bound students went on to another top black public school, Banneker Junior High School, which was right next to Howard University on Georgia Avenue and the DC Teachers' College.

The best college preparatory high school was Dunbar, revered for its track record of having graduates matriculate. And at that time, there was only one college that we were all thinking about: Howard University. It was then, and still is after more than 150 years since its founding, the leading black university in America. Howard was our target.

Each of these schools had the top black teachers in the country, since this was before integration opened broader opportunities for them to work in white colleges and universities.

■ ■ ■

In 1943, I started at Morgan Elementary School. I soon discovered that our teachers there took a special interest in my sister and me and supported students who came from families that valued education. Throughout my school years, I studied with fantastic teachers at exceptional schools. A case in point is that Dunbar High School is where I first got my exposure to foreign languages. The first foreign language I studied was German with Mrs. Saunders, my homeroom teacher. In the course of studying German, I, of course, was able to learn something about Germany and Europe. This was an incredible experience for me, although speaking German was very tough. It was at Morgan, Banneker, and Dunbar—what I call the Magnificent Three—where I made friends for a lifetime. Some were classmates from elementary school and many of them followed me all the way through Howard.

I am certain that I got a first-rate education, one comparable to any offered by the best private schools in the country. When I arrived at Howard University in 1956, I was prepared for college and life.

When my classmates and I graduated from Dunbar most of us went to Howard University. The tuition was affordable because the federal government partially subsidized the university, a practice that goes back to the school's founding in 1867 as a federally chartered, nonprofit private institution. It is named for General Oliver Otis Howard, a white, Civil War hero and a founder of the historically black university.

Ultimately, our parents and our grandmother were able to see Frances and me and my cousin, Janice, graduate from Howard University, the same school that graduated Thurgood Marshall, who would become the first black juror on the U.S. Supreme Court. It was a historic day for our family, especially for Grandma Pitt who had long dreamed of such a day for us.

As we were growing up, my grandmother made sure we went to Sunday school and church every single Sunday and the belief in God and Christianity were 100 percent ingrained in me. So, when, as a young man, I said something to her that seemed to call into question the existence of God, my grandmother was absolutely taken aback. I had attended a philosophy course at Howard that day and had a stimulating discussion on Friedrich Neitzsche's views on whether God was dead or had ever existed at all. Brimming with youthful hubris, I told my grandmother about the classroom discussion and the German philosopher and she became very upset, saying, "Boy, is that what they are teaching you at Howard, to question the existence of God?"

What ensued was an animated discussion about God and religion, from a religious standpoint, and maybe even a personal one. This had to be a difficult subject for her. But she was able to engage me in an intelligent conversation on the topic, honoring her college education at Shaw. That is what was so fantastic about her. She, also a college graduate, had an expansive mind and open heart. I could sit down and talk to my grandmother like I was talking to a college professor.

When I learned years later, thousands of miles away from Washington, that Grandma Hattie had passed away, I would be inconsolable. I loved her so, so much. She was 75 years old and a beacon of warmth, and love, and caring.

I was in Liberia at the time, working for Citibank when I was told of her death. I raced home to attend the funeral. I cried during the entire service. I had so many wonderful memories of the support and love that she poured into me. Thinking of that beckoned the tears to pour.

My family has been such a treasure. I often think of my mother's sisters, Naomi and Hazel, and her brother, Uncle Thomas. And there is my Aunt Louise and her husband, Willie, who was probably the closest thing I had to a father. And my cousins, Janice and Teddy. Amazing people.

Although all of my aunts were born in September under the Virgo sign (like my wife, Lolita), they all had very different personalities. All of my aunts eventually divorced the men they had married in Rocky Mount.

My Aunt Hazel, who is just the greatest, and is still alive today and in her nineties, was a firebrand. She had a temper. She was hot! She was the disciplinarian and nobody wanted to run afoul of her. Yet, she was also full of love and affection for us. My Aunt Hazel would call herself "Pretty Hazel." Even when I see her today, the first thing I say to her is, "Hello Pretty Hazel." And she laughs now, just like she laughed back then. She took on the role of family enforcer with gusto. When any of the children stepped out of line, she was there to put us back in place.

I will never forget coming back from a party in the neighborhood. I must have been 14 years old and was starting to feel more man than boy. My cousin Janice, Aunt Naomi's daughter, was going with this guy Robert Lee. She was crazy about him and ended up marrying him; they have four kids and a few grandchildren now. After the house party, some of my friends and I walked around the corner, back home to Center Street. As I strolled up, talking with my friend Sonny Johnson about the night's cutest girls, I noticed my Aunt Hazel standing close to the front door waiting for us to get into range. Sonny and I just kept talking. I walked up to her all breezy and teenage cool and said, "Hi, Aunt Hazel."

"Where's Janice?" she snapped. With my mind still more on my conversation with Sonny than her question, I blurted out, "I don't know Aunt Hazel, she's back at—"

POW!

She stepped hard on my foot and popped me upside my head and said, "Boy, you go back there and find Janice and bring her—."

"Okay, okay, okay . . . Aunt Hazel," I said, still a little dazed. It was that kind of looking out for each other and love that my mother knew would be fostered by raising Frances and me in an extended family. Without that arrangement, La Savage could never have worked hard and long enough to build and sustain a good life for us.

But, as the saying goes, the only constant in the world is change.

My Aunt Louise was the first of the sisters to move into her own house. She and her husband, Willie, had stable government jobs and were big savers. So without children to take care of, they were able to buy their own home on 13th Street in Northwest Washington. Although they were apart from us we would visit their house often.

They adored us without reservation. I think they loved the fact that although they didn't have children, they had us. We returned their love like we did with all our other aunts and uncles. Later on, Aunt Louise and Uncle Willie did very well, so they ended up moving into a nice, big house in northeast Washington. My sister and I would often take all of our Howard friends to their house to party.

Unfortunately, a jealousy developed between my mother and Aunt Lou over Frances and me. I could sense that La Savage needed reassurance that she occupied a special place in my heart. I reminded her that "when we were growing up, you always told Frances and me that I should look upon all of my aunts and uncles as mothers and fathers and that's what I did. I see them all that way.

"Of course," I told her, "no one can take your place. You're my mother, but I do love them."

Yet she still just could not get over the fact that I was very close to my Aunt Louise. That caused Frances and me a lot of pain. I guess that's life.

The youngest daughter was my Aunt Naomi. We all call her the "angel" of the family because Aunt Naomi is the kind of person who doesn't have a bad bone in her body. She's simply a wonderful person. Now 90 years old, she took Hazel into her home after Hazel's husband died and she had to leave her own home. I cannot think of one bad thing she's ever done to us or to anybody else—not a curse word or impure gesture or action. It's hard to describe it, but if you look in her eyes all you can see is bottomless humanity and compassion. She is a rare human being.

Uncle Thomas was the youngest and although he was the man of the 3522 Center Street house, he had been spoiled by the women in my family. His mother and his sisters did everything for him—cooked for him, did his laundry, always gave him whatever he wanted. He got married but the relationship did not last. He never had kids. He never really had to take care of any of us either because our aunts and grandmother took care of us, and of him, too.

Nevertheless, Uncle Thomas was a wonderful man, sharp and always put together from hat to freshly shined shoes. He dressed impeccably, as a matter of fact. If anybody ever thinks I dress well, the credit goes to my uncle's example and encouragement. With probably the exception of going off to World War II, which, I think, gave him a sense of responsibility, he mostly lived a charmed life.

Like many Southern-bred families, especially black, Southern families, my family's diet—heavy with fried, fatty foods and meals high in salt—was a prime contributor to the onset of diabetes.

Both my mother and Thomas died way, too, early from complications of diabetes. Both died at age 62. Fortunately, my aunts Hazel and Naomi have managed not to succumb to the disease that strikes so many black people, especially those of us who are Southern-bred and prone to consume too many fatty foods. I've worked hard to break the cycle. So far, none of my generation has the disease because we have purposely followed a careful, preventative diet.

■ ■ ■

It is an interesting aspect of our family that even though we were raised in a segregated Washington, there wasn't a lot of talk about race or segregation in the house. I don't know whether that was by design or whether it was something our elders didn't want to talk about around us. Maybe they wanted us to grow up not thinking about segregation, but thinking about success. It's also possible that they thought it best not to talk about race because we kids were in effect living "double lives"— partly with whites and partly with blacks. Up until our second year in junior high school, our daily lives were divided into an all-black day at school and an all-white afternoon, evening, and weekend in our integrated neighborhood. We were only the second black family to move onto Center Street besides a very elderly black couple with no children. As a result, up until the time I was 13 or 14 years old, all of my friends, whose houses I went to, and whose games I played in my neighbor-hood, were white. Teddy Crystal, and several other white children who were raised in my neighborhood, were my best friends. We did everything together. We went together to nearby Rock Creek Park to play games, hike its paths and wooded hills, and ride our bicycles. I went to Teddy Crystal's house to eat. He and his family came to mine to eat. Race never came up between us. All we wanted to do was have fun, and so we did. Ah, the wonders of youth.

But when we went to school, I had to get on a bus to the all-black Morgan Elementary School in the predominately black community. This was effectively "busing" in reverse, black kids being gathered and shipped past white-only schools to maintain racial segregation. In the 1970s, notably in Boston, busing to desegregate public schools was met with white violence and protests.

At the time, I could not imagine such a consequence of racial exclusion. Frances and I just continued to live a double life as if that was the way everyone lived. I know it might be hard to believe, but we didn't talk about race because we were too busy having fun, playing baseball, basketball, and riding our bikes.

And when I went to college, I still lived in a kind of racial twilight as my undergraduate years at Howard were almost all black, and my graduate studies at Johns Hopkins was mostly white.

So did any of this have an impact on me as I moved through what was essentially an all-white financial industry? I've thought about this a great deal.

When I first moved into international banking in 1963, I was the only black officer I was aware of at the time at Citibank. Yet, I felt like I belonged there because I had the required training and education. I had no sense of inferiority. All my life, La Savage had drilled into my head how great I was and how I could be anything. I had played with white kids for most of my life so working with them was not anything new to me. Nothing in my life has changed in that regard.

Alan Dynner, one of my two best friends in the world, is a white, Jewish man. We're friends because we have so much in common professionally and personally. Of course, we talk about race, but it does not impact our relationship. Our race talks are never personal. If either of us had a chip on our shoulders over racial or religious issues it would undermine the foundations of our friendship. We'll never let that happen.

Obviously, as the civil rights movement picked up steam in the early 1960s, race became an explosive issue. Either way, I've always been aware and proud of my blackness. And that characteristic was even further enhanced by my early exposure and subsequent work and charitable activities in Africa, my motherland. My race has been a source of pride to me, not anger or angst. That's somebody else's problem.

I truly believe that my childhood experience of living in racially bifurcated world enabled me, at least, to successfully navigate both the predominantly white financial world as well as the diverse cultural and religious world I encountered while working in such places as the Middle East and Asia. I never felt inferior or intimidated while working in such diverse cultures because I had the good fortune of representing some of the most powerful financial institutions in the world such as Citibank, Alliance Capital, and Equitable Life. I represented billions of dollars and access to its power and potential profits.

That's all that counts. All of my clients and associates around the world respected the authority, power, and influence of my corporate positions and uniformly treated me with respect. Thankfully, La Savage laid the framework for me to be just as comfortable in my black skin as I was working in these diverse environments.

Of all of the lessons La Savage taught me about life's success, it was her way with people that instructed me on how to live a life of not only self-respect but respect for others. She had tremendous interpersonal skills. People loved her. For as long as I can remember, she met people with her enthusiastic, *"Hello, darling!"* She even underscored her trademark greeting with a hint of a French accent. She was very charismatic and knew it, turning up and down its volume when and as she needed. She was always in control in every social encounter. She was a marvel to watch in action.

I vividly remember when La Savage came to visit me in New York. I was rapidly making my way up my career ladder and was working for the chairman and the president of Equitable Life on Sixth Avenue. She was decked out in one of her favorite outfits, a stunning gray number draped with a sort of fox cape, when she stepped out of the elevator on the 38th floor, looking out on the forest of gleaming corporate high-rises. My mother had this beautiful hairdo with the white streak and a black mole on her face, just above her mouth like Marilyn Monroe's. When she entered the office, it was as if she owned the building, she would make every inch of the impression she had intended. Equitable's chairman and president were bowled over.

Before the visit I tried to prepare her for it. "Now La Savage, I want you to come and meet the chairman and the president of this Fortune 500 company." She was unfazed. When she walked into our offices, she greeted every person I introduced her to, including the chairman and president, by first extending her hand, followed by a fabulous, "Well, *hello* darling! Madame La Savage. Nice to meet you."

Even today many people remember my mother for her dramatic flair and warm, outgoing character. She had this absolutely phenomenal way in which she would captivate you. My daughters, Brett and Grace, are exactly like her, each outgoing, entrepreneurial, family-oriented, with well-honed interpersonal skills. A former TV anchor, Brett is raising a family of four while working in a major position with a large communications company. Gracie is an aspiring actress who recently wrote, financed, and shot her first film, a short entitled *Saving Grace*. La Savage would be proud of them, but no more than I am.

La Savage was simply an incredible woman. She exemplified good character rather than lecturing me about it. I saw the high quality of her character through her ceaseless work and through her extraordinary gift of interacting with other people and making them feel as good about her as they felt about themselves.

■ ■ ■

La Savage had a plan for my life. As a result, she wanted me to befriend other kids who shared my aspirations. She softly steered me toward others with big dreams and big plans to make them come true. One of those new friends I met when my mother moved us to 1129 Columbia Road. His name was Edward "Sonny" Johnson, one of my best friends to this day. Sonny introduced me to many new friends, some of whom were not in school. My mother loved Sonny, but she didn't like a lot of the other friends that she saw me hanging out with. But, as with most kids, the more that La Savage would warn me about them, the more I was drawn to them.

She knew that they weren't aspiring to go to college. She just didn't want anything that would deter me our shared mission. I still insisted on their friendship. Sometimes I would even cut high school and hang out with them.

I had an impeccable academic record at Morgan Elementary School and Banneker Junior High School. I was considered to be a top-flight student. But by the time I went to Dunbar High School, I was barreling down the wrong track. My grades slipped, then suffered. The teachers were disappointed because they knew I was capable of so much more. They eventually did what good teachers do, they brought my poor performance to my mother's attention.

La Savage was livid but more important, she was disappointed in me. Were her dreams for me about to die? Unfortunately, she couldn't immediately get me back on the right path. But she didn't give up. She kept hounding me to do better. I barely squeaked by and graduated from Dunbar, but was admitted to Howard on academic probation. I had to stand by and watch my sister and my other friends get admitted to Howard without any embarrassing conditions.

This was hard to bear, and it should have been enough to wake me up. But it didn't. I continued to hang out with my DC buddies. I had grown into a tall, sturdy young man with my own charms. I was captivated with chasing the absolutely beautiful girls of Howard University (as much as some who were captivated with chasing me). In this race, studying came in a distant second.

So the inevitable happened. I was kicked out of school.

Fortunately, this shame lasted for only a semester. But its effects on me were profound. I was no longer in school with my classmates. I had nothing to do all day except hang around Columbia Road. My mother and grandmother were angry at me and didn't mind showing it. For the first time in my life I was frightened. I didn't know what was going to happen to me. I was in shock, and that moved me to act.

I vowed to get serious when if I was readmitted to Howard. I knew La Savage was disappointed in me, but I also knew that deep down she never lost her faith in me. She encouraged me to use the time off to study and get ready for my return to Howard. She reminded me that I was still a "borderline genius." I appreciated that, but knew I had to prove it all over again.

Luckily, after that one winter semester, and the summer, I was permitted to return. I had learned a hard lesson at the hands of Professor Life.

I'll never forget that one of the first lucky things that happened to me when I returned was that I ran into a former girlfriend from both Banneker and Dunbar. Her name was Eunice Henderson. She was always a smart honor student and a beautiful girl. She reminded me of my mother and my aunts. We renewed our friendship. One day, she asked me to meet her at the Founder's Library on Howard's campus. This is a hallowed place, like a cathedral of scholarship where great works by prominent African-American authors are kept. And guess what? I started reading again. I sometimes wonder if Eunice really knew how much she helped me by nudging me on to a high-speed rail to my dreams.

Of course, talking was prohibited in the library, so no flirting, no playing around. I had no choice but to read. That was the beginning of my academic rebirth. I did well at Howard University and graduated in very good standing. And whenever I think of that great institution I can only smile and feel great warmth of gratitude spread over me.

I was fortunate that my mother, grandmother, aunts, uncles, and all my instructors at Dunbar and Howard never gave up on me, even when I was really screwing up. I found my way back. I don't think that I'm the only teenage guy who has been through this phase in growing up. Parents—and teachers—should never give up on the kids, even when they go temporarily astray. Today, so many are so quick to discard children if their climb to academic excellence isn't a straight line. This is especially true for boys.

Girls still seem to mature faster than guys. They seem to know how to balance fun with studies. My daughters are very good examples of this. They have helped to convince me that women are perhaps a little more disciplined and better able to multitask than men. My mother could wear many hats at the same time, spin many plates and juggle many responsibilities.

But she had her faults. La Savage put her trust in many people, some of whom did not deserve it. I didn't discover this until much later in life, while I was in college, that misplaced trust took a costly toll on La

Savage's Beauty Clinic. Because it was always extremely busy, she hired several new beauticians to work with her. These positions also afforded them an opportunity to be trained by Madame La Savage. She took a liking to one beautician, in particular. She was tall, beautiful, and young with a distinctive beauty mark just above her lip—not unlike the mole on my mother's face.

This woman was always very polite, as most people were back in those days. Her language was stuffed with lots of "yes ma'ams," "pleases," and "thank yous." She learned quickly from La Savage and she gained La Savage's trust. My mother decided to give her more responsibility, making her the cashier to take payments for services and to account to La Savage for those payments.

One week, the beauty shop's door saw an almost constant stream of paying customers. After the shop closed at the end of this remarkable week, La Savage decided to take a look at some of the books and the records of funds received. The two did not seem to jibe with the number of customers served. This disturbing discrepancy raised some serious suspicions. My mother did not actually accuse this young cashier of any wrongdoing, but she began to watch her more carefully. After a while it became obvious that the cashier was, in fact, skimming money off La Savage's accounts. After taking this young woman under her wing, La Savage was very upset and hurt by the obvious betrayal.

She fired the young protege.

La Savage learned that in business trust in people is as necessary as a good bottom line, but blind trust is dangerous. My mother learned that she would have to check and verify trustworthiness.

In the fullness of my life I find myself reflecting on my youth. I've come to realize the fuller meanings of La Savage's success, how she scaled the tremendous odds against her in her era of blatant racism and sharp segregation in the United States. And sexism. She slayed those dragons that block the gates of success for millions of black women. Yet, during those decades of struggle and triumph, I never saw her portray herself as a victim. She only stood taller than her physical height as a successful businesswoman. She refused to be put into a racial box, although she was infinitely proud of her race. She wanted to be a person of the world, and was, and if some people didn't get the memo they were informed in her name: Madame La Savage International. *Madame* from her role model Madame C.J. Walker, *La Savage* from the French language and *International* from the International Beauty Show.

There will never be another quite like my mother.

I felt a deep sense of pride well up in me every time I accompanied her on business-related outings, such as the many different parades in which she participated. These parades were organized by the Washington area business associations and started at 16th and U streets, running east on U Street to Georgia Avenue then north to Park Avenue. She was her biggest promoter and she really knew how to advertise herself. For these parades she would get a convertible and have the name of her shop on the car's sides. Beautiful girls, modeling her hairstyles, rode in the car, too.

I would drive the convertible with La Savage seated next to me. You can't imagine how that felt. It made me feel incredibly good as a person, as her only son. I always liked being swept up in enterprise of my mother, her business, and the shop and the reoccurring magic of *something* made from *nothing*.

When Frances and I attended Howard University, several of our Howard friends went to the shop to get their hair fixed. I used to have a British sports car, an MGA, black with pink stripes down the middle (which I might add I paid for myself from my college job). I used to park that car right in front of my mother's shop because she would tell me "girls will think you are in the shop and come." Always the consummate saleswoman.

La Savage defined success for me. For her, success was not only about one's material possessions. It was also about how one succeeded against all odds by believing in self, exhibiting integrity, and working hard and working smart. La Savage gave me the benefits of these lessons as surely as she gave me life back in 1938.

God gave me La Savage. Her impact is indelible. Her life and love light the fixed star on which I navigate the waves of life itself.

Chapter 4

The Journey to True Origins

The world is a book and those who do not travel read only one page.
—*St. Augustine*

T here are times in your life when you are given glimpses into the life that will one day be yours. These moments can come at any time, without warning, and usually, on their face, they seem quite insignificant when they occur. Their power often only coalesces into brilliant clarity years later when you are standing safely on the shore of your future looking back from where you sailed. Then it dawns on you: Destiny was whispering on the wind.

In the early 1950s, when Frances and I were attending Banneker Junior High School and living with La Savage in our home on Columbia Road, such a destiny not only whispered, but stood right in front of me. At the time, I had no way of recognizing the true meaning of what was unfolding before me. My mother, now comfortably settled into her global identity as Madame La Savage International, had turned our home into a sort of hub of hospitality. She always loved people. But since she had attended her first International Beauty Show in New York, she was especially drawn to people from distant lands.

She was frequently entertaining foreign dignitaries and their families at the house. And our home reflected her tightening embrace of the greater world in evenings filled with the music of exotic accents, of warmly told stories of cultures and lifestyles that held little direct relationship to the working-class, Washington streets that made up so much of my world back then.

In the midst of all of these cozy communions with the larger world, La Savage loved to show off me and Frances to the diverse guests she often hosted. On one of these occasions, I was introduced to a young Liberian girl named Clavender Bright, the daughter of the Liberian ambassador to the United States. She was lovely and poised and self-possessed in all the best of ways. On the streets of Washington, dressed as any preteen girl in the United States might, she could have been easily mistaken for a "cute colored girl." But no, she was more than an undiscerning eye could see.

She was authentically African, and I was taken with her.

This was nearly 20 years before James Brown would defiantly sing, "Say it loud, I'm black and I'm proud." In those days, most black people were offended if you called them "African," even if you called them "black," for that matter. But here was this girl—Clavender Bright—who didn't need Soul Brother Number One to tell her in a hit song what she was born and bred in her native Liberia to proudly be.

I quickly learned all I could about Liberia, that it was a coastal West African nation bordered by Guinea on the north, Sierra Leone on the west, and the Ivory Coast on the east. More important, at least to me, is that in the early 1800s the area was colonized by freed American slaves aided by a private group of mostly whites called the American Colonization Society.

By 1847, these black colonists established the Republic of Liberia, naming its capital, Monrovia, after the fifth president of the United States, James Monroe.

The black-American colonists, who modeled the country after the United States, would come to be called Americo-Liberians. They would dominate affairs in the nation for generations, often at the expense of the indigenous Liberian majority who had been there all along. Clavender Bright was an Americo-Liberian. She was beautiful, and we became very close. As it turned out that she also attended Banneker Junior High School, too. I developed a case of puppy love for Clavender.

I would one day refer to her as my girlfriend, but nothing ever went any further than a game or two of spin the bottle. We were children, really. Little did I know that many years later, Clavender and I would meet again in Liberia where I would be assigned as a First National City Bank officer. And little could I have known that her husband at that time would be P. Clarence Parker, a figure who would become a major client of my bank, an influential official in the Liberian political system, and a close friend who would meet a tragic end.

Destiny was hard on the wind.

■ ■ ■

During much of my high school years, my inclinations toward all things international went in gradual abeyance, replaced by my growing fixation with girls and sports. And that didn't change much until my sophomore year at Howard University when I happened into a class taught by a relatively young professor. His name was Bernard Fall, a Frenchman in a predominantly black university, who crackled with his love and knowledge of the world, its many peoples and interlocking relations.

The course was International Relations, and again destiny was at my ear. Not quite sure of what I wanted to do with my life, I chose political science as a major and economics for my minor. International relations was, of course, mandatory for political science majors.

It turned out that I found Dr. Fall captivating, electrifying. And I found myself very excited by the vistas he opened for me as he lectured on international politics, economics, and international organizations like the still quite young United Nations. I became very attracted to this arena. He was nourishing the seed of the international that La Savage had planted deep within me when I was a boy. I could feel it beginning to sprout and blossom as I sprouted and blossomed into a grown man. I had found my calling.

I looked forward to Fall's class and developed a personal relationship with him. It wasn't just the plain facts with him. He explained and illustrated the dynamics of relationships between nations. While Dr. Fall lectured us about practically every corner of the world, it was his talks regarding Africa that really motivated me.

Consider this. The year was 1958 and Ghana had recently become independent, freeing itself from years of British colonialism. It was the first African nation to do this. Dr. Fall predicted that all African countries would escape the yoke of colonialism and imperialism. He believed that Africa, with its vast riches, could become a leading continent in the world. He saw Africa as not the "dark continent" much as the West had marginalized it, but as an emerging continent bright with promise and would soon flex with the might of its own power.

That's it! I thought. *Africa is where I am going to focus. I'm a black man in America. Africa is black. I should have a comparative advantage working in Africa.*

Right there in Bernard Fall's deep well of a classroom, I discovered my life's destiny, my life's career path, my fate. With my career direction in place, I then concentrated on increasing my knowledge of the world, and Africa in particular. I took courses with eminent Howard professors like Rayford Logan, a renowned historian and Pan Africanist activist educated at Williams College and Harvard. Like me, he grew up in Washington. Unlike me, he, in high school, was taught by the pioneering black historian Carter G. Woodson, the founder of Black History Month and later worked with one of our first public intellectuals, W.E.B. Du Bois.

Dr. Logan was already in his sixties when I came along, and would be associated with Howard until his death at 85 in 1982. He helped me further understand the influence of African culture on the world and how I and every other person of African descent not living in Africa were part of the African Diaspora. Dr. Logan was an expert on African culture, particularly the movement of Africans to different parts of the world. He helped me see the commonalities of this migration and its impact not only on Europe, but also on Latin America, the Caribbean, and then onto the United States—even on music, food, and other key aspects of culture; it was enlightening.

And there was William Leo Hansberry, another galvanizing Howard professor who taught Swahili, the predominant language in East Africa. These professors helped me become deeply involved in international and African student affairs, serving both as president of the university's International Affairs Club and the African-American Student Association.

In 1960, I met another man who would have a major impact on my life, the Reverend James H. Robinson. He was a black, Harlem-based Presbyterian minister who founded Operation Crossroads Africa in 1958. From its inception, he envisioned his program as a cross-cultural exchange, bringing young North Americans of all kinds in direct contact with Africans living and working in their cities, villages, and farms. Over time, he extended the program's reach to the African Diaspora, including the Caribbean and Brazil, for example. Dr. Robinson's goal, he often said, was to build a bridge of understanding between peoples based on his conviction that people can only truly appreciate another culture by directly engaging it, living and working in it.

So far, more than 11,000 young Americans and Canadians have visited and worked in more than 40 African countries, 12 Caribbean countries, and Brazil as a result of Operation Crossroads Africa.

On a rather innocuous day in the fall of 1960, Dr. Robinson came to Howard to recruit students to participate in Crossroads. He described the many worthwhile community projects that Crossroads students had done in poor, African villages during their summer weeks there. I saw a fantastic opportunity to get to know Africa more intimately. I could, I reasoned, get to actually see Africa on the ground, so to speak. And along the way, I could do my best to concretely help some corner of this vast continent I had come to love and respect from afar.

I had to go.

So, I eagerly applied to Crossroads Africa and was accepted some time that winter. La Savage was thrilled with my accomplishment until I told her that the program wasn't free. To make the trip I would have to come up with about $2,500 to help pay my way. The trip itself—all the air fares and hotels and food—would cost much more, but each student was required to pay his or her contribution. Accounting for inflation over the years, that would be more than $18,000 in today's dollars.

This was serious money, and my mother made this clear to me. And I made it clear to her that I never expected her to pay a penny for my trip. I knew she was putting my sister Frances through Howard; and, besides, I had always paid my way and didn't see why this would be any different.

■ ■ ■

That didn't stop La Savage from helping in other ways. First, she expressed a great confidence that I could raise the money. Next, she started to work on a plan. One day, La Savage bolted into our house, approached me with a great urgency drawn all over her sweet face. "Frank," she almost gasped, "I've solved your problem."

She found me in my usual spot, sitting on the living room couch, engrossed in a typically wide ranging conversation with Grandma. And as usual, I was on the receiving end of her seemingly endless grandmother wisdom. Without the slightest idea of what my mother was trying to say, I turned toward her and waited for her words to start making sense. The glow on my mother's face should have made it obvious to me that whatever she was hurriedly saying had to be good news. But at that moment, I wasn't sure what "problem" I had that needed to be solved.

Then La Savage began to tell a story.

"I just attended a diplomatic reception and I met Angier Biddle Duke, the Chief of Protocol at the State Department, and his deputy, Pedro Galban."

Wow, I thought. I was very impressed that my mother had been invited to a State Department reception. In those days, it was highly unusual for African Americans to be invited to such fancy events—unless they were invited to wait tables or open doors for others to attend. She went on to tell me how nice Duke and Galban had been and that she mentioned my opportunity to visit Africa. Sensing their interest, she moved in for the gentle kill by describing the Crossroads program in as much detail as she could muster, including to the requisite $2,500 contribution. She didn't fail to mention that it was a sum I did not yet have. Much to her surprise and happiness, Duke offered to help. To underscore his best intentions, he gave La Savage his card with instructions for me to contact him and Galban.

As my mother's words floated around the living room, I sat there, incredulous at her account. *Could this be possible?* I thought.

"You should call them Frank Jr.," La Savage urged.

"Are you serious?" I asked. "You want me to call the chief of protocol at the State Department? He is a very high official!"

She gave me that piercing La Savage look, pointed her finger at me like a weathervane and doubled the strength of her voice. "Boy, do not ask any more questions. Just call them. Just do it!"

With my mother's command still ringing in my ears, I agreed, thinking that I would humor La Savage by calling the State Department. I had very little expectation of any help.

When I called Duke's office the next day, a kind voice answered, "Chief of Protocol Duke's office."

I identified myself.

"Yes, Frank," she replied. "Mr. Duke said you would call. When can you come in to see him?"

I was nearly speechless, but I managed to make an appointment. I was stunned that the meeting was actually going to happen in a couple of weeks, that it was going to happen at all. I immediately told La Savage of my progress, thanking her profusely as I did. She was, as she said, "tickled pink." She then instructed me to get prepared to make the best presentation of my life. She had faith that Duke and Galban would find a way to help me. But I still had to personally convince them of the merit of my case.

When the day of my meeting arrived early in 1961, I had not completely gotten over my jitters. So much was at stake. But when I walked through the big iron gates of the State Department's entry, I felt my confidence rising. Once I cleared all of the security checks, I was directed toward Angier Biddle Duke's impressive first-floor office. And I found my calm along the way.

Duke's assistant welcomed me, warmly ushering me into the waiting room. I was in awe of its beauty and officialdom. Pictures of President Kennedy, Secretary of State Dean Rusk, and other dignitaries adorned walls that soared to high, ornately trimmed ceilings. *I am actually in the State Department!* I squealed into the silent pandemonium in the privacy of my own head. It was like a dream. Then, Deputy Galban came out to greet me and we entered Mr. Duke's office together.

It was fantastic, a place teeming with the machinery oiled to create history. Duke was a tall, regally handsome man with an unforced charisma. He greeted me with compliments regarding my mother, especially the hopeful way that she spoke about me and my bright future.

"So Frank, tell us about this Crossroads Africa program and why you are so eager to go."

I explained the program and how it would help me to further explore my considerable interest in international relations and Africa. This was a rare thing. There weren't many young African Americans talking about going to Africa and committing themselves to a career overseas that didn't involve the armed services. They were impressed with me. I could feel it. And for good measure, I also told them that about my recent acceptance into the Johns Hopkins Master of Arts graduate program at SAIS to bolster my credibility. It was encouraging to see that Duke appeared genuinely moved by what I had said. At the end of the all-too-brief meeting, he suggested that I meet with his contacts at the Kaplan Foundation, a major education philanthropy. Duke said he would be sure to make certain the foundation's officials knew that he believed Crossroads Africa was a worthwhile project.

Duke was such an extraordinary man who lived a most extraordinary life of service to his country, tirelessly working with local and international charities; he supervised the protocol for the state funeral of John F. Kennedy in the shock-warped wake of the young president's assassination in 1963. Duke went on to serve as the U.S. ambassador to Spain, Denmark, and Morocco. He died in the spring of 1995 at the age of 79. He was killed after being struck by a car near his Long Island, New York, home, while Rollerblading.

But before that, I met him by chance in 1971. Without saying it in words, I could tell that he was pleased that he had helped me, that I was living up to the promise he saw in me a decade earlier.

When I left the State Department meeting with Duke I was dumbfounded. I finally permitted myself to exhale and embrace the belief that my trip to Africa was actually going to happen. La Savage had done it again. I learned time and time again to never question her. And when I told her about the outcome she accepted the news with a kind of inevitability, but I knew she was just as thrilled as I was.

I soon found myself making a full presentation to the Washington offices of the Kaplan Foundation. Again, I detailed what the Crossroads opportunity was and what it meant to me, especially how it would help me advance my burning interest to pursue a career in international relations. I emphasized that this trip would likely be a life-altering crossroads in my desire to make the most of my education and ambition.

I found surprisingly little resistance or push back from the Kaplan officials. It was clear to me that they had spoken to Duke and were relying heavily on his judgment. The foundation agreed to loan me the $2,500 I needed. I accepted right away, but at the time I was so excited that I had no idea how I was going to repay all this money. Much to my surprise, the Kaplan people told me that the foundation would work out a repayment plan when I returned from Africa. They basically told me to relax and enjoy the experiences that awaited me overseas.

On the eve of Frank's first trip to Africa in 1962, Vice-President Hubert Humphrey is flanked by President John F. Kennedy and the Reverend James H. Robinson, founder of Operations Crossroads Africa, at the Rose Garden reception in its honor.

All of this had been such a long shot, and now I could imagine myself actually standing on the continent. I immediately had two reoccurring thoughts as I walked out of the foundation building and into the cold, afternoon air that wintry day: My Africa dream was coming true. All thanks to Madame La Savage—the dream maker.

■ ■ ■

In the late summer 1960, I married my first wife, Beryl Bowser. She was a smart, pretty Howard classmate who found promise in my determination and security in my dreams that had a way of coming true. She found my love of all things international *intriguing*.

We had dated for two years and got along well. She was from New Orleans but was living with her mother's sister and her husband, Leroy J. H. Brown, a professor of architecture at Howard. I will never forget their house on 22 Bryant Street NW.

The Browns were good people, generous and hard working. But they were also strict guardians. Once I wanted to take Beryl somewhere on a date and Professor Brown said no. I was not pleased with that decision, but for Beryl it became the no that broke the back of her relationship with her aunt and uncle. She moved out and in with a girlfriend.

I knew Beryl did this for me, and I came to feel responsible for this split. I also knew she wanted to get married. In the early 1960s everybody seemed to be getting married, especially when they were in their twenties like we were. I was finishing up my degree at Howard and feeling the pressure to get married.

I popped the question and Beryl accepted without hesitation.

By the time the 1961 Crossroads students were scheduled to depart, Beryl and I were expecting our first child. It was a difficult decision, but I decided to defer my Crossroads dream for a year. I would only be a first-time father once, and Africa was not going anywhere. But these major events, combined with my acceptance into Johns Hopkins's international relations program, SAIS, which was in Washington, made for a crucial period in my life.

I stayed close to Washington; in fact, Beryl and I were living with her aunt and uncle in their three-bedroom townhouse on Bryant Street. We were given the third floor. I had not received any word on scholarship dollars to pay for my Johns Hopkins education, so I had enrolled in Howard's graduate African studies program. I also had a chance to work for Washington's health department. Ninety-nine percent of my DC friends took public sector jobs like that after they finished college. And there was nothing wrong with that. It was stable work, providing them a good life with the opportunity to buy a house, raise a family, and put their kids through college.

But I wanted something else. I was told that if I attended the graduate program at Johns Hopkins it would be much too demanding for me to have an outside job the way I did when I attended Howard undergraduate school. To help out, Beryl did secretarial work at an advertising agency in the city.

This was a critical juncture in my life. Was I going to stay true to my dream or choose a safer course? In sailing when you go offshore, you're going from one land mass to the other and you have to cross the ocean. You don't take that lightly because you could die out there, and people do die out there. But you've got to do it. So you're nervous before you set off. You're foolish if you're not prepared. You have to stay focused. In much the same way, I felt prepared and was certainly focused to take on my dream, to make this crossing into my destiny.

I felt much like what Steve Jobs expressed decades later in his commencement address at Stanford University.

"Your time is limited, so don't waste it living someone else's life. Don't be trapped by dogma—which is living with the results of other people's thinking. Don't let the noise of other's opinions drown out your own inner voice. And most important, have the courage to follow your heart and intuition. They somehow already know what you truly want to become. Everything else is secondary."

I had little choice, really. At the time so much of my head and heart was in Africa. It didn't help that although my hometown friends respected my interest in Africa, they did not share my interest in the great continent. I didn't blame them that much. African Americans back then had such a complicated relationship with Africa, if they had one at all. It was a natural result of American blacks being essentially breached from their mother continent after being stolen from the land and enslaved in the Americas.

Along the way, blacks had been "miseducated," as Carter G. Woodson would write, and as a result sensitized to look down on Africa. To disconnect. In the late 1950s and early 1960s, it seemed that only a handful of African Americans felt any kindred spirit or connection with Africa. When I was a boy I actually heard black boys rooting for Tarzan to vanquish the Africans in the movies. Not me. I knew from a very early age that I was an African, too. In that regard, I suppose I was sort of an oddity.

I especially came to understand Malcolm X's response to a black American's claim that as an American born thousands of miles away from Africa he had left nothing there. Malcolm's retort?

"You," he said, "you left your soul in Africa."

Despite a new wife, a baby on the way, and the demands of graduate school looming, when the summer approached, all I could really think about was reclaiming my full soul. I wanted to go back to my true origins. I knew I was ready to join the hundreds of other students who had been accepted by Crossroads Africa. I was ready to make the big trip.

The following year, in May 1962, I did.

■ ■ ■

There were 250 other students, known as *Crossroaders*, heading for Africa that year. We assembled at the Washington National Cathedral for our orientation and training before embarking to the various African nations each group of us had been assigned. I never knew why, but Dr. Robinson selected me to be the spokesperson for all of the students. One of my first tasks was to deliver a speech to express our thrill and appreciation for being selected to visit Africa and have the opportunity to help the African people once we arrived.

I knew it was an honor to give this speech, but I was scared to death the whole time I spoke. I had never been asked to be the voice of so many people, and to speak in such an imposing and majestic landmark like the Cathedral. My family came, and despite my nerves, I managed to muddle through my talk and somehow make my family proud.

Crossroads Africa also caught the attention of the new man in the White House. Within days, President Kennedy invited all of the students who were at the Cathedral to visit him for a ceremony he was holding in our honor in the Rose Garden. I will never forget that day. I wished my wife, Beryl, could have seen this.

First of all, President Kennedy was incredible. He said some extremely complimentary things about Dr. Robinson, the job that he had done of bringing all this together, and the hope that we all represented for the future of the world and for relationships between Canada, the United States, and Africa. This was quite a heady moment for me and for all of the kids at this special ceremony. Crossroads turned out to be a precursor to the Peace Corps, which Kennedy established in 1961, hence playing a significant role in the genesis of American service organizations operating abroad.

My group had been assigned to build tennis courts at an all-boys school in Northern Rhodesia, still a British colony. We were a diverse mix of students, including white Americans and Canadians, two African Americans, including myself, and an Asian American. We were also scheduled to make stopovers in Paris, Kenya, Southern Rhodesia, (Zimbabwe), and to visit the famous Copperbelt of Northern Rhodesia, now Zambia.

We had great chemistry right from the start; everyone got along and there were no superstars who tried to hog the spotlight. And even though I had some notoriety because of the speech at the National Cathedral, I handled that brush of celebrity with great care so I wouldn't alienate or intimidate others on my team. Our shared excitement about the prospect of bringing help to Africa transcended all else, and it didn't take us long to blend ourselves into a cohesive unit. Brought together by our common desire to experience Africa, we worked hard together, took care of each other, and got the chance to really get to know each other.

This was summer camp on steroids.

The travel began at 9 P.M. May 25 as our Boeing 707 took off for Europe. Our first overseas stop was Paris. The City of Lights exceeded my wildest dreams. Yes, I grew up in America's capital city, but this was an Old World capital, and you could feel this fact with every step you took on its quaint, winding streets, along its roads laid out by the ancient Romans, and in the way you were engulfed by the shadows of great churches, monuments, and museums that awed the likes of Thomas Jefferson and John Adams when our own nation was in its infancy. And in more recent centuries there was the Eiffel Tower, Arc de Triomphe, the Champs-Elysées, and the studied ease of café life.

I wrote as many of my impressions into a journal I carried with me on the trip. I decided to use it to help me write detailed, weekly dispatches back to the Kaplan Foundation. I wanted its officials to know that, yes, Operation Crossroads Africa and my experience because of it, was worthwhile, indeed. I managed to do this and have that journal to this day.

This was my first trip to Europe. I was overwhelmed even though we were there less than eight hours. Paris was an incredibly beautiful city and very active like New York, yet always buzzing with a distinct flair. I felt like a million dollars. Yet, I was, like my fellow Crossroaders, anxious to get to Africa.

We boarded a British-made jet airliner and took off for Eastern African nation of Kenya. It was a brief layover in Nairobi, but not so brief that I didn't have a chance to drop to my knees and kiss the ground. I was that overjoyed. I knew how my ancestors had suffered in the dark, dank holds of slave ships in their coming to the Americas. I made the return trip as a young, college student reclining in the ultramodern, air-conditioned splendor of a sleek jet while sipping Coca-Cola and munching salted peanuts high above the clouds.

I had returned to my native land. Africa. In 1962, Nairobi was a modern, bustling city with wide boulevards and skyscrapers, like any other major city in the world. We were totally caught by surprise by the cool, dry weather and the fact that Kenyans wore winter clothes and heated their homes. This was far from the popular image of Africa as a continent of steamy jungles and shirtless villagers who never built much of anything larger than a thatched mud hut.

This revelation gave me my first appreciation for the diversity of Africa, in this climatic instance. Kenya felt like September back in Washington.

The highlight of our time there would come at the end of our time in Africa. On the way back to the United States we made another stop in Kenya and were given the chance of a lifetime. We were granted a meeting with Jomo Kenyatta, the former head of the Mau Mau Society, a group of freedom fighters that fought the British for Kenya's independence that would come the following year. He would be independent Kenya's first president. When my group of Crossroaders visited with him, Kenyatta was under house arrest. But as a gesture of good will, the British administration permitted us to visit him.

This was one of the most incredible experiences of my life.

Kenyatta was a giant of a man with striking, high cheek bones and a smile that was like a slice of high noon. His gaze was penetrating and his color not much unlike the deep, rich brown of my own. I immediately felt a sense of kinship with this leader who, while a prisoner in his own home, exuded the aura of a leader-in-waiting. It was as if he had heard his own destiny on the wind and it informed him that he would one day lead Kenya to freedom, that he would one day assume his rightful place as its head of state.

Kenyatta spoke to us with a great ease that only magnified our awe of the man. I kept thinking, *what a way to end our trip to Africa.* Jomo Kenyatta made a lasting impression on me because he was suffering his incarceration with such dignity, just like Nelson Mandela faced down his 27 years of incarceration that began in the winter of 1964. It was quite humbling to witness such a rare quality in a man.

Crossroads brought me to Kenya amid a historic time when, as my professor Dr. Fall had predicted, Africa was slowly but steadily liberating itself from the shackles of colonialism and imperialism. In effect, the continent was looking the prospect of independence straight in the eye.

But the entrenched colonizers, especially those who had made their homes in the colonized regions, resisted this drive for independence. By and large, these whites lived a very fine life—big houses, servants, high-paying jobs, and dominance over the local black populations. In Kenya, colonists came to fear the Mau Mau, as an infamous group of bloody rebels determined to drive whites from Kenya.

In a rare moment in African history, traditionally tribal enemies, the Kikuyu and the Luo tribes, put their long rivalry aside and came together to fight the British. The colonizers had every reason to want to remain in Kenya. It is among the most beautiful countries in the world where tea and coffee can be grown in abundance. With this, it took a lot to force the colonists to leave. The Mau Mau fought very hard and many people on both sides died, suffered, and lost their homes during this period of the Mau Mau Uprising from 1952 to 1960. Although their leader, Jomo Kenyatta, was under house arrest, the period of British colonialism in Kenya was rapidly coming to an end.

As we sat with Kenyatta in the summer of 1962, it was clear we were talking to a man who knew that he had made history and was looking forward to building a multiracial Kenya where, he said, all people could be free and benefit from the riches of the country.

■ ■ ■

Our first prolonged time in Africa was in Southern Rhodesia, 1,200 miles from Kenya. We went to its former colonial capital of Salisbury (now Harare) to visit a native school called University College. It had only recently been integrated, in a government effort to placate the nation's black majority that was severely segregated from its privileged white minority. Our appearance and the fact that we were a thoroughly integrated group seemed to baffle the native students. It seemed as if they didn't know how to interact with us because we were all so close—black and white, white and black, Asian and black and white.

Rather than break up into racial subgroups, as black and white students at the school did, the Crossroaders did everything together. Albeit slowly, the black Rhodesians students became comfortable with us and we were thrilled about that. They were curious about our backgrounds, family, school—anything to give an insight into how we lived back home. Sadly, the white Rhodesians never got to that point. We learned that they perceived our ease with racial integration as a threat to their way of life. But to their credit, some of the white Rhodesian students eventually warmed to us. I remember we once all played a game of basketball and we had an integrated party where some whites and blacks danced together. So, I think we Crossroaders had a positive impact on some of the white students there.

Yet most of them at the school made little or no effort to befriend us, to get to know us, or to even welcome us into their country. To say that most of them were standoffish would be an understatement. Their general lack of communication only further increased our alignment and identification with the black Rhodesian students.

The African students seemed especially intrigued with me because they perceived that I was respected by the rest of the white kids in the group. Some said they had never seen whites hold a black person in such high regard. They would find moments to talk to me privately. One black Rhodesian student wanted to discuss racism in America. Even 8,000 miles away, this student knew that we in the United States were experiencing a tumultuous trial in confronting race relations at that time. He was interested in knowing how I felt about that situation. I tried to be honest about my concerns, but gave him an overall perception that America was moving in the right direction. That, more than anything else, reflected my own hopefulness.

I had seen so much to test that hopefulness for black Rhodesians. As Crossroaders, we had toured deeply impoverished townships where blacks lived terribly, several families crammed into stacks 10 feet by 10 feet, not big enough to garage my mother's car back home.

All the while, white Rhodesian government officials came around to promote their propaganda that conditions were improving for blacks there, that the minority government were the good guys. In almost every country we visited we were a center of attention. Local newspapers would show up to cover us; government officials would buzz around us.

When I and my fellow Crossroaders finally left Southern Rhodesia, I realized that the brothers and sisters there were in for a rough time in their struggle for independence. If the hardnosed attitude I saw among those white students was the norm, I was thinking, *God help them.* I also realized that country's white-minority government was getting the active support of the white-minority government of apartheid South Africa, a government that ruled a country with a white population that was less than 10 percent and its black population almost 80 percent.

When we left Southern Rhodesia in early June, I was convinced that an armed conflict by black Rhodesians was likely. And that is precisely what happened during the Rhodesian Bush War that waged from 1964 to 1979. The bloody struggle eventually brought Robert Mugabe to power in 1980, where he remains today as the president of the nation that was renamed Zimbabwe.

Our next stop was to Southern Rhodesia's neighbor on its northern border, Northern Rhodesia. We boarded a public bus for the eight-hour trip that turned out to be a hot, bumpy ride. Everybody was packed like too many pickles in a jar too small. An odd thing happened when the Crossroaders started to board the bus. Its driver knew right away that we were all Americans, even the black students among them like me.

The driver, who was black, asked us all to sit in the front seats. We noticed right away that the black Rhodesians all had to sit in the back of the bus. I'm sure this request surprised the segregated Africans crammed into the rear seats. They could see that I was as black as they were.

We all decided on the spot that we wanted no part in Southern Rhodesia's racist system. But contrary to our wishes to do otherwise, we had no choice but to sit in the front of the bus as we were told. Mind you, as a black American, I grew up under the sting of segregation, so it was not strange to me to see blacks in the back of the bus. But I had also grown up aware of the early civil rights movement's success in the American South beating back such humiliations. I knew how Rosa Parks had refused to give up her seat and move to the back of the bus in Montgomery, Alabama in 1955.

In Africa that day, I could see how her act of defiance and bravery was not just for me and my people in the United States, but it was for all segregated people everywhere—even in Africa.

Almost without my noticing it, I fell in deeper and deeper solidarity with black Africans and the degradation they were being forced to suffer. Until I opened my mouth, it was increasingly not unusual for me during my Crossroads trips to be mistaken as African by Africans. That happened on the bus as some of the black Africans stared at me and wondered, some out loud, how it was that this African can sit up front with those white and Asian people.

When we arrived in the capital city of Lusaka, the first person we met was Shaughan Kelly, a member of the United States International Services (USIS) and Mr. Burgess who represented the Northern Rhodesian government. They escorted us to a school called Chalimbana, which had a huge campus, with both new and old buildings where we would construct three tennis courts. We were welcomed by the principal, Mr. Robertson, a former missionary who had been in Africa for more than 17 years.

Mr. Robertson, who was white, said he was aware of the success of another Crossroads project in Northern Rhodesia, so he safely assumed that we were motivated and would actually finish the project. Given the school's reasonably well-kept facilities, it was immediately obvious to us that the school had been built for white African students. However, when we arrived whites and blacks were attending the school.

In those days, when a group like Crossroads showed up in a country, the first thing people suspected was that this is some kind of

CIA front. So we were initially suspected to not be what we said we were. But when the Chalimbana students discovered that we were a church-sponsored organization, and when we buckled down to work, the suspicions slowly faded away.

We were a group of idealistic American do-gooders and were in Africa solely to help the local population. So, we were shocked to learn that both the entrenched power centers, the white government and the black political groups vying for national control, such as the National Freedom Party (NFP) and United National Independence Party (UNIP), viewed us as a platform to present their cases. Consequently, we received an enormous amount of attention from all of the political groups in Northern Rhodesia; from the Governor-General, representing the white leadership, to Kenneth Kaunda, leader of the UNIP, who eventually became the head of state when Northern Rhodesia became independent and renamed Zambia.

We even went to a UNIP rally and spent time with party's leadership, which may have been unbeknownst to the white politicians. It didn't matter how much we assured these political groups that we had no political influence in the United States, they weren't convinced and so they kept approaching us. In addition to accomplishing our mission of constructing the tennis courts at Chalimbana, we also got to know almost every single leader of any significant capacity in Northern Rhodesia. We had the chance to meet with some leaders from the African National Congress (ANC) from South Africa, as well as men like Harry Nkumbala.

The ANC took refuge in South Africa's neighboring countries of Southern and Northern Rhodesia to escape the brutal apartheid army and police. The rebel ANC also launched attacks against South Africa from those countries.

The three to four weeks that we spent in Northern Rhodesia were extremely eventful. We gained a tremendous insight into the dynamics of what was happening in this British colony, a unique and rewarding experience. Yet, we never lost sight of our main goal of building those three tennis courts, which was serious work. This was the first time any of us had ever done work like that. Luckily, we had the help and guidance of a local contractor. Several African students also formed a "counterpart group" to help in the task.

Until then, I never realized how complicated it was to build a tennis court. We had to clear brush, level the site and lay down a suitable foundation—all before even laying the final surface. We formed a brick detail to go to the kiln early every morning to pick up bricks and we helped to make the cement, too. The Chalimbana students would come by every day to watch us slowly build the courts. They were especially fascinated to watch the white Crossroaders do physical work, apparently a novel sight in Northern Rhodesia.

The weather made our job even more difficult. It was winter there, so the air was very dry and the mornings were windy and cold. The winter breezes blow up calamite, an indigenous red clay dust, which got into our noses, our hair, and turned our clothes red. At one point I contracted a very bad chest cold from working in the elements.

As we American and Canadian students worked together with our new African counterparts, a meaningful bond was formed. This project demanded teamwork to finish on time.

Getting to know fellow Crossroaders Pete, Clara, and Marilyn was the best part of the Northern Rhodesian project for me. All of us spent many hours working on that tennis court. It is an interesting phenomenon— how you really get a feel for people and they begin to open up to you when you are together in a situation like that. It was the same with our African friends. They started opening up to us about the grim situation in Zambia. We often spent all day discussing politics; the African students would share their assessments of African politicians such as Kenneth Kaunda, Arthur Weena, Sakota Weena, and other leaders. They also sang throughout the day. We loved their African songs, especially the UNIP independence song, which I found myself humming as I wrote this part of the chapter. Singing made the days go faster.

Outside of Chalimbana, although we maintained contact with Mr. Rushing, the U.S. Counsel General, our closest relationship was, without question, with USIS's Shaughan Kelly. He became like a father to us. If we had problems, we knew we could call Shaughan and he would always be there for us. We also loved to go by his comfortable government house. His wife was a great cook and he let us swim in his pool. We loved that pool.

On the other hand, we had Burgess who seemed determined to brainwash us with the white Northern Rhodesian perspective on

African politics and culture. Often, at the end of our work day, he would take us to various government buildings such as the Legislative Council. He would have various officials make presentations on government policies to improve the condition of the local population. Sometimes we were bored, but we would politely listen to them anyway. Reverend Robinson would expect no less.

While working at Chalimbana alongside our African peers, we were insulated from the stark apartheid-like system, which most Northern Rhodesian lived under every day. However, when we decided to venture into the capital, we confronted the stark reality of Rhodesian racism face-to-face.

Pete Schmidt (his full name) and I hitched a ride into Lusaka for provisions. I was also anxious to get a call through to my wife. I hadn't spoken to her since our layover in Paris. We had no mail service from May to July. Pete and I arrived at the post office to find that it was closed, so I decided that I was going to have to make a collect, international telephone call.

Pete, who's white, and I started going around the city's local shops searching for any phone capable of making an international call. We ended up in some modest watering hole called the Lounge Bar. We walked in to find only whites drinking around the bar and tables. I asked the bartender if he had a phone I could use. He looked at me blankly and with a guttural tear of a voice he mumbled something unintelligible. His outstretched arm, however, couldn't have been more clear. He was pointing me to the door.

"I'm American, so I don't know what you're saying," I said half knowing what was going on.

He unfolded his next words very carefully.

"I don't give a damn what you are," he said, his statement so clear I could almost read it floating in the warm, moist air between us. "Get out!"

I was at once surprised and unnerved by his tone. And while I was sorting this all out in my head, everyone in the bar—a very tough group by their beefy, rugged look—turned to cast a cold stare at the commotion.

"Get out!" the bartender repeated.

I turned to Pete, and spoke softly but insistently, "Hey, let's just get out of here."

As we turned around to go, somebody shouted something incoherent at us. Pete, now quite upset and red-faced, turned around and asked no patron in particular, "What did you say?"

Suddenly, all the men in this place jumped out of their chairs and bar stools and rattled beer mugs to answered Pete with a mounting menace in their bearing. I knew we had stepped into trouble, so I grabbed Pete by his upper arm and dragged him out of the Lounge Bar much faster than we had entered it.

In fact, as we walked briskly down street we looked over our shoulders to make sure we weren't being pursued. When it seemed that we were safely away, I turned to Pete and told him, "Well, now we know how racist some African whites are. They didn't want me in the bar because I'm black. And they especially didn't like that I was with you, a white person ready to defend me."

The irony hit me hard. Here I was in Africa, in a black country, and racial segregation had followed me like a bad smell. I knew places like the Lounge Bar back home, knew whites like these Rhodesians who could only see the color of my skin, and only see me as being less than they were.

So, this was Northern Rhodesia's "color bar," I thought. These men were obviously of Afrikaner stock, that Southern African ethnic group of Dutch, French, and German origin with a long history of oppressing black Africans. These men in the bar simply detested black skin. It didn't matter what country I was from. The rest of our Crossroads team was shaken when we told them what happened. We realized more than ever that Northern Rhodesia could be a very dangerous country for blacks and their sympathizers, no matter what color they were.

This incident was one of the factors that solidified my desire to do everything I could to help overturn the racist regime in South Africa, which had exported apartheid, the strict control and separation of black from whites, to Northern and Southern Rhodesia.

During our weeks in Northern Rhodesia, I had the opportunity to discuss apartheid with native South Africans. One of the best forums for these open and honest talks occurred when the ANC gave a reception in our honor shortly after our celebration of July 4. There, Crossroaders learned that when the ANC referred to South African apartheid it included, by extension and explicitly, the white regimes in Southern and

Northern Rhodesia where we were. He heard ANC spokesmen and policy makers, in the strongest of language, say that the group was committed to freeing all of these regional countries from the effects of the highly regimented system of racial oppression.

I met a "coloured" South African (a person of mixed race), Mr. Jee. He was from the South Africa's eastern coast and was living in exile in Northern Rhodesia. In South Africa, the racial categories, based purely on skin color, were black, coloured, and white. Of course, under apartheid, whites had superior standing overall, but coloureds, due to their lighter skin tone, had a slightly higher standing than native blacks. This was in sharp contrast to the United States, where a person was either black or white, and only one drop of black blood was enough to have someone considered black. Period.

Mr. Jee was a member of the ANC and fighting against apartheid along with black South Africans. He talked to us at length about the political and social situation in South Africa. I could easily relate to his experience and his sense of partnership with blacks of all colors. After all, I, a dark-skinned man, was working alongside my fellow African-American Crossroads teammate Linda, who was light-skinned but was as much African American as I was.

Despite the overwhelming wealth and power of their foes, the ANC member, even those living in exile or in jail as political prisoners, continued to prepare for the day when they would take control of South Africa. They were encouraged by one of their imprisoned leaders, Nelson Mandela, to study economics, law, development, and finance through extension programs. This preparation proved extremely valuable when the ANC assumed leadership of South Africa in 1994.

The ANC representatives were friendly to me, perhaps because, as a "black" African American, they identified with me. My Crossroads colleagues observed this, but did not take offense as I always made it a point to later tell them about the conversations I was privy to. The ANC members encouraged me to return to Southern Africa as soon as I could to help rid the region of apartheid, and one day help provide leadership once the land was free. It was yet another peek at destiny. I would, decades later, return to the region as a businessman in an attempt to help Northern Rhodesia evade a South African economic blockade, and as an investor of foreign capital into the new, postapartheid South Africa.

By the middle of July 1962, we had nearly completed our first tennis court. Progress was not as we wished, mainly because the delivery of bricks, cement, and other supplies were painfully slow. We began to fear that we would not finish on time, so we significantly increased our work schedule and pushed harder to speed up the delivery of building materials.

One day, an African student on our team told us that there was going to be a UNIP rally about a half mile from us. Shaughan Kelly was going, so we decided to attend as well. On the way there, we saw many people headed in the same direction and we knew this was going to be something big. It turned out to be a major event with about 300 people gathered at the rally.

We learned that this was the first step in the UNIP's effort to build a base of support in the area. Kenneth Kaunda and his fellow UNIP leaders showed up. Kaunda was the main speaker and after some opening speeches and songs to excite the crowd, he took the stage. He was striking, with bold eyes and a shock of white hair, like Don King's yet much less theatric.

Kaunda was highly articulate, delivering a rousing speech that raced chills up my sweaty back. The energy in the crowd was electric, too. He condemned the Northern Rhodesia's white leadership for its apartheid-like policies, and to my surprise, focused on the multiracial character of UNIP. Kaunda welcomed Northern Rhodesians of all colors into the UNIP. He envisioned a multiracial new nation, where, he said, every person would be treated equally; this was the sweetest music to my ears.

I thought, *Here is a man who has been persecuted and denied his demo-cratic rights. And yet, he is still willing to work with people of different colors, some of whom may have treated him very badly.* He understood that the UNIP needed to work with all Northern Rhodesians if they were going to advance the nation. Kaunda gave our entire Crossroads group a good feeling.

Without warning or fanfare, Kaunda came to visit us at Chalimbana the same day. We were amazed. We were a group of young students, visiting the nation to simply build three tennis courts. Yet, there he was. The presidential aspirant of the country made time to talk to us and answer our questions. Kaunda was accompanied by Arthur Weena and Sakota Weena, two of his lieutenants. We had so many questions because we had been told many different things about Kaunda and his party. But we wanted to hear all of this directly from the man himself.

He gave us one and a half hours of his time to learn about his vision for the country. It was a bold and imaginative one. Above all, it was a vision that was inclusive rather than exclusive. It was designed to increase the living standards and the working conditions of blacks in Zambia without calling for whites to be thrown out of the country or for their property to be confiscated. He used none of that vengeful rhetoric. We thought ourselves extremely privileged to have this private moment with Kaunda and left the session feeling optimistic about the prospects of the country under his leadership. As the group talked later, we observed how fortunate we were to have been in the region during this exciting period of transition. Before our time in Africa was over, we had met with two prospective black leaders of imminently independent countries—Jomo Kenyatta of Kenya and Kenneth Kaunda of Zambia. How lucky could we get?

As we got closer and closer to the end of July, we increased the pace of our work. Rather than working only from 8 A.M. until 1 P.M., we took an hour-long break and then kept working until dusk.

As a matter of fact, we decided to start working even earlier, starting at 7 A.M. When the African laborers showed up at eight o'clock, they were awestruck to see us, the full team of Crossroaders already working like heck to finish those tennis courts—which we completed on time.

Everyone at Chalimbana was ecstatic that the tennis courts were finally done. And, of course, Shaughan Kelly and the U.S. Counsel General were proud of us as well. We had a big going-away party the night before leaving. It was great fun and we were pleased with ourselves for accomplishing our ambitious goal.

■ ■ ■

Next stop: the Copperbelt, the economic heart of Northern Rhodesia. Our hosts, the management of the Copperbelt, were ready for us when we arrived. It was evident that the companies and the government had spent considerable time compiling an impressive program for us. The Copperbelt was a major industrial complex and we got a chance not only to see things above ground, but also below ground, about 1,500 feet, at the actual copper veins. We saw every aspect of the copper extraction, packaging and transportation system, a remarkably big operation.

All the underground mine workers were black and all the supervisors were white. Mine workers were paid relatively good salaries compared to other laborers on farms or in stores, but the work was hard and dangerous, typical of mine work worldwide. Moreover, the black miners lived in atrocious housing conditions. Several workers were packed into single hostels made of wood, which reminded me of the slave quarters I read about in history books back home. There were no indoor toilets, only a latrine running outside, rife with disease.

The black miners were fed fairly well, with basic foods to keep them physically able to perform the grueling work. Although living conditions were poor, these men were desperate to make money to send back to their families, so they did not protest. This was a deplorable situation to witness. It was the first, but not the last time, that I saw people living under such conditions.

As a result of what we saw, the Crossroaders decided to try to get closer to some of the deprived miners of Northern Rhodesia. We had the opportunity to talk to some of them; we learned that many were migrant workers from what is now Malawi, the poorest of the eastern regional countries. In some cases, they had not seen their families or returned home for many years; it was terrible to hear.

I carried these images of Africans, most treated like chattel in countries governed by white majorities, back with me to the United States. I also came back with a new appreciation for black African's perseverance, patience, and their steady move toward their own empowerment. I returned to the States and entered Johns Hopkins SAIS a much-enriched person. My commitment to Africa and my respect for its people were further reinforced. I had added another edifying chapter to my life. And last, I gained a rewarding feeling of satisfaction from performing a good deed that helped people in need of aid.

I could not have asked for more. I became 24 years old while in Africa and I felt transformed.

■ ■ ■

While I was in Africa, almost every week I wrote a letter to the Kaplan Foundation describing the week's activities. When I returned to the United States, I attended a final debriefing session at the foundation. I shared my enjoyment of my African experience with its officials and thanked them for their help. I also raised the issue of how I could repay my loan.

Right away, the leading staffer nonchalantly asked me to wait outside while staff talked among themselves. I walked outside, with no idea what was happening, but figured they had to negotiate different loan repayment options among themselves, before presenting the final one to me.

After only a few minutes, they called me back into the room. The lead staffer began.

"Frank, we have thoroughly enjoyed your weekly letters telling us about your experiences in Kenya, Northern and Southern Rhodesia. We have gained so much from them, and we feel you have already paid us back by sharing your journey.

"What we're saying is that we are going to forgive your loan."

Once again, I was speechless. This was the last thing that I expected. It undoubtedly was good news, considering I had no idea how I was going to come up with all of that money, especially when I was about to start graduate school. I am forever grateful to the Kaplan Foundation for its generosity.

La Savage was thrilled about its decision and knowingly added, "Frank, I told you everything would work out."

Disappointment did find me, however, when I returned from Africa. I learned of the death of the Howard professor, Bernard Fall, who had ignited my interest in the international arena. He was killed in Vietnam on a fact-finding mission there, where he had apparently stepped on a land mine. I never had the chance to share with him the tremendous international experience I had on my first trip to Africa.

But, somehow I felt he knew.

Chapter 5

My Journey Deepens

One of the signs of passing youth is the birth of a sense of fellow-
ship with other human beings as we take our place among them.
—Virginia Woolf

My Crossroads experience made me more fully appreciate how
much Howard had opened my intellectual curiosity about
the world beyond America's shores. I could trace my
development to a collection of my undergraduate courses and the gifted
and dedicated professors, like Rayford Logan and William Leon
Hansberry, who taught them. But once back from Africa, I had little
more than a week before starting another journey that would bring me
closer to my destiny of international finance and being a man comfortable practically anywhere in the world.

My first year at the Paul H. Nitze School of Advanced International
Studies of Johns Hopkins University was about to begin. It was September 1962. I was living with my wife, Beryl, and our infant son, Eric,
in the 22 Bryant Street house with her aunt and uncle. I was ready to
focus on my studies and take my understanding of international issues
to an even higher level.

I quickly realized that I could not have made a better decision than to attend graduate school at Johns Hopkins; SAIS, as most people referred to it, gave me an in-depth understanding of the forces that drive international relations, namely international politics, economics, culture and language, and its requirements were rigorous.

The school's location—on Massachusetts Avenue near DuPont Circle in the heart of Washington—provided a fine opportunity to meet with government and business leaders who were actually developing, influencing and executing foreign policy.

SAIS opened up a whole new world to me. My professors and fellow students hailed from all over the world and were extremely smart and able. Admittedly, SAIS was an academic challenge for me. I quickly came to realize what the "advanced" meant. But I faced that challenge, took even on the most demanding courses, and eventually succeeded.

When I arrived at SAIS, I learned that I was the only African-American student in the program. That didn't faze me. I had a wonderful reception from the school. No one there made me feel as if I didn't belong among them. But before my first year was finished, an old buddy from Howard, Acklyn Lynch, transferred to SAIS from Harvard. Acklyn, a black native of Trinidad, was an interesting guy; among his many loves was classical music. He would attend chamber music concerts at the Library of Congress, and I would join him sometimes.

As a result, I became very fond of classical music. Looking back, it's funny how life plays out sometimes. My appreciation for classical music would serve me years later when I was asked to join the board of directors of the New York Philharmonic, a position I would hold for more than 20 years. Thank you Acklyn.

At SAIS I had to choose a career path. It wasn't enough to know that I only wanted to work abroad. I was surrounded by students who were committed to the international arena and were fairly sure about what they wanted to do. I was at a loss at first, and then I decided on the United States Foreign Service; quite frankly working overseas for the U.S. State Department was the only option that I could see for myself at that point. After all, it was a government job. Solid. Respectable. Steady.

So, I hunkered down and began to work toward that career path. Almost right away I came to a detour. The program, quite reasonably, required that all students speak a foreign language. I was told that Swahili, which I had studied at Howard, would not qualify as my mandatory language. It wasn't even taught at SAIS. Furthermore, the language department would not recognize it as a major "world language," like English, French, or German. Naturally, this upset me. I thought this diminished the importance of Africa and the language spoken by millions of East African people.

I soberly voiced my concerns, but lost that battle. I was told to choose another language. I settled for French. I had never studied a day of French in my life but in time I had to become proficient enough to pass a written and oral exam. But more on that later. I was determined to succeed and I knew that I could not get what Madame La Savage, who didn't speak French, called "my piece of paper," unless I mastered the French tongue.

Another challenge came by way of the school's head of the African studies program. It was an issue of ideology. I cannot say that this professor was necessarily pro-apartheid when it came to the struggles of the black majority of South Africa to smash that racist system. I can say that he certainly didn't support the liberation movement there. I may be wrong, but I believe he even worked as a consultant to some of the South African apartheid leaders. This troubled me, especially in the wake of my Crossroads Africa trip. I had seen with my own eyes, up close, the terrible costs apartheid was exacting on millions of "non-whites" living there.

Yet, I found myself putting his politics aside because he was teaching me ever more than he knew he was about Africa and the challenges the continent faced abroad. I realized that I had to at least tolerate his views, whether I agreed or not. That was the American way. Right?

■ ■ ■

In the fall semester of 1963, I decided to take the Foreign Service exam. I failed miserably. But the Foreign Service exam was a great deal different than the exam is today. It was blatantly culturally biased, designed in such a way that unless the test taker had grown in the United States upper classes he or she stood little chance of passing. Not surprising, most people who were in the Foreign Service had attended some of the best preparatory schools in the country, had gone to Ivy League colleges. And many had come from money, like Angier Biddle Duke who attended Yale University and was born an heir to a vast tobacco fortune (Duke University is named for his family).

At first, I didn't let this "failure" bother me too much. I knew that I had received a very good education at Howard. It was that I just didn't have any of that background, that sense of the world you can hardly learn in school. Still, here I was seemingly at the end of the path staring at a white, brick wall. I didn't really know what I was going to do next.

The Foreign Service had so much cachet, which I associated with its important work in international relations. I wanted to be a part of that elite group, and it was frustratingly just behind this wall that I couldn't scale because someone had deemed me too heavy with the wrong race and class. Somehow it didn't matter that I was psychologically ready for an international career. It didn't seem to matter to anyone who counted that I was qualified, that I was getting an excellent education, that I was extremely motivated, that I had, against all odds, traveled to Africa—not as a tourist, but as a shining representative of my country, building relations and a few tennis courts along the way.

I became depressed.

What am I going to do now? I applied for a couple of government jobs, just like my mother had done when she first moved us from North Carolina to Washington more than 20 years before. Fortunately, a number of major companies were coming to SAIS to interview graduating students for jobs. An international position with a private company had never occurred to me. I didn't realize the extent to which U.S. companies were doing business outside of the United States. These companies needed to hire trained Americans to staff their overseas operations because there were, at that time, few foreign nationals with proper training and education. Consequently, these companies hired Americans, sending them abroad, and having them run their various operations in these faraway places.

Acklyn and I saw all of our white classmates scheduling interviews with these companies and we were inspired to take a chance.

"Frank, look, let's apply for some of these jobs," Acklyn said.

We had no real expectation of being hired, but we consulted with Aldus Chapin, a SAIS career counselor, anyway. He encouraged us to schedule the interviews, so we did. In retrospect, I think Aldus knew something that we didn't know. He must have sensed that these U.S. companies saw change coming around the world, just like there had been great change in the United States in the early 1960s. Racial segregation was beginning to dissolve across the United States; Africa was shaking its colonial masters. The need for U.S. companies to hire people of color for their overseas operations was slowly becoming apparent.

On Counselor Chapin's advice, Acklyn and I scheduled interviews with a number of banks, oil companies, and the like.

I was more excited than I had anticipated when the recruiters arrived at SAIS in the spring 1964. Despite the great wealth and power these companies represented, when I sat for interviews with their officials I immediately found comfort in a certain familiarity. I was transported back to the business environment that I was raised in at La Savage's shop. Although the elements were different—beauty shop versus international bank—the formula was the same. The more I participated in the interviews, the more my deep-seated interest in business came rushing to the forefront. The interviewers could sense this, too. I found myself standing out, standing out positively.

I was enthusiastic about some of the opportunities, especially those at international banks. Chase and First National City Bank Citibank, the two largest, were headquartered in New York City, which I had loved since La Savage took me for the International Beauty Show when I was a kid. Gradually, I came to think that an international business career may be a viable option.

This was also a critical juncture.

With surprising ease, I talked to these bank recruiters and easily related to everything they were talking about. They were, after all, speaking a language I heard from La Savage almost all my life.

After the first round of interviews, much to our shock, Acklyn and I were invited by almost every single company we had spoken with to travel to their headquarters for a second interview. I had set my bearings on companies based in New York, like Mobil, Exxon, Chase Manhattan Bank, and Citibank.

One of my first interviews happened to be with Chase Manhattan, a Rockefeller-controlled bank. This was big time. I boarded an Eastern airlines shuttle to New York for an 11 A.M. meeting. When I arrived, it was still early in the morning. Although the city famously never slept, it appeared a little groggy as I walked its canyons of skyscrapers. I marveled at how some of the tallest buildings that seemed to go on forever disappeared in the low, morning clouds and mist.

My heart began to beat rapidly as I walked down Wall Street. Oh, my God, I am walking on Wall Street in New York City about to interview for a job at one of the biggest banks in the world. I felt like I was on top of one of those highest towers of glass and steel. Thoughtlessly, I went into a cigar shop and bought a celebratory cigar. It was about 9 A.M. and I was prancing down the street in my discount-store blue suit, smoking a cigar of all things.

By the time I met with the Chase personnel officer, I noticed him quizzically looking me over. Perhaps I imagined it, but he seemed to sniff the air around me a few times. Suddenly, I realized what was going on. I probably reeked of cigar smoke. How foolish of me to have smoked a cigar first thing in the morning before such important interviews. I had started off on the wrong foot and the interview went downhill from that point. I was young and had gotten caught up in the emotion and excitement of the moment. Lesson learned.

■ ■ ■

In a series of different trips to New York I interviewed at Mobil Oil, Exxon, and finally Citibank. I had a good feeling about the Citibank International Division talks. I liked the atmosphere at Citibank and I felt that I had good chemistry with all the young officers I met at the bank. They were dedicated to international business; that was their most important characteristic. They had all traveled and lived abroad, and they could talk to me in great depth about their experiences. It was fascinating to hear them describe what they had seen and done during their time overseas. This got my juices flowing. I could visualize me being such an experienced young banker.

Then there was the pièce de résistance. My looming meeting with Walter Wriston, then the head of the bank's international division.

Years later, he would become the CEO of Citibank and make it the major international bank that it still is today with operations in more than 100 countries and territories.

Wriston was a warmly charming man who looked like a million—No!—a billion dollars. I have to admit that I was bowled over. I enjoyed every minute of our interview, and I knew right then and there that Citibank was the organization I wanted to join. I just knew it. I could feel it in my bones.

During the interview, Wriston's phone rang. He picked it up then leaned over to me. "Frank, I'm sorry but I've got to interrupt this meeting. It's been great talking to you. I hope we can talk again, but I have to take this call from Aristotle Onassis."

Man, I thought, *he's got Onassis on the phone and the great, Greek shipping magnate was calling him.*

Without hesitation, I shot to my feet. "Mr. Wriston, I totally understand, and I look forward to talking to you again."

Well, I knew enough about international business to know that Aristotle Onassis was one of the biggest businessmen in the world, who had a tremendous fleet of ships. I knew that he was big, big time and I was hit with a rush of excitement thinking about how awesome it would be to land a job at Citibank.

A few days later, Citibank, as well as some other corporations, offered me a job. Needless to say, I was thrilled. Without question, I knew right away that I wanted to be a part of the international division of Citibank. I accepted the offer, a salary of $7,500 (about $53,000 in 2011 dollars), and a promise to be assigned overseas within a year. What could be better?

I was the first African-American officer of Citibank and member of their international division. This was an incredible turning point in my life, considering that only a few months before, my only solid job prospect was working as a civil servant in the DC Health Department.

Times had changed.

However, I had a problem. I had not officially graduated from SAIS because I had not officially completed the last requirement—passing my French language exam. I would not receive my master's of arts in international relations until I did. Fear overtook my joy for landing my fantastic new job. Frankly, I was scared to death when I called the

Citibank personnel officer to tell him the news. I assured him that I would take and pass the exam later. I held my breath on the phone. I could feel the personnel officer sensing my chagrin. A couple of very long moments later he assured me that the job offer still stood.

What a relief.

I had another scare when I took a required physical. The doctor discovered a lump on my right upper chest. He said they would have to perform a biopsy to determine if it was malignant. If it was malignant the lump would have to be removed. I could not believe it! I had never even noticed it. Did I have cancer? I had come this far and. . . . At that moment I saw my whole new and promising world fading like dreams you can't recall by noon.

My wife and family were very frightened. Grandma Hattie and La Savage were beside themselves. When I awoke from the operation, the doctor told me that he found that the lump was an adhesion, probably something that resulted from a blow that I may have received while playing football. It was not cancerous and I was fine. I breathed a sigh of relief and my dream came back to me.

In June 1964 I walked into the bank and took my seat on the platform of the Middle East and Africa Desk in the international division of the First National City Bank. Up until that point, it was the best day of my life. I had arrived!

This happened to be among the earliest years that big New York companies started in earnest to hire African Americans. A path of opportunities had opened before us, one that some of us had been walking toward even if we could only see our way there in our dreams. There were many African-American men and women who were much smarter than I was, but were born at a time when these opportunities, for them, were largely limited. A business career in the private sector was just not much of an option. I was lucky to be in the right place at the right time. I was even luckier to have had a mother who made sure I received a good education and empowered me with the confidence to take advantage of an opportunity once presented. Even with these advantages, I really could not have imagined that I would get a job in the private sector.

The first African American to graduate from SAIS was Cliff Wharton Jr., who was some years my senior. One of his first jobs was in the field of education, though later he became the CEO of TIAA-CREF, one of the largest retirement funds in the world, and still later, deputy secretary of the U.S. State Department in the Bill Clinton administration.

La Savage was over the moon with my appointment to Citibank. She would proudly tell everyone, "My son Frank is with the World Bank."

I would always have to remind her that I worked for First National City Bank, not the World Bank, and she would always respond, "Never mind, it's the same thing."

Being the only African-American officer at the bank was lonely at times. Looking back on it, my situation reminds me of Ralph Ellison's 1952 classic novel, *Invisible Man*, about a black man seen but yet unobserved by his white counterparts. In Ellison's words, "I am invisible, understand, simply because people refuse to see me."

The only other blacks I saw at Citibank in those early days were the maintenance staff. Those working-class guys were always really happy to see me on the platform and took every chance to walk by and greet me. Luckily, Acklyn, who also landed a job by way of his brainstorm, was also in New York. He had joined Chase and befriended a black credit officer there named Hughlyn Fierce.

Acklyn introduced us and we immediately hit it off. Hughlyn, a Brooklyn resident, was a Morgan State University graduate with a master's degree in business administration from New York University. He was the consummate banker who adored credit analysis. Hugh was a fun guy, too. We formed a tight-knit group—Hugh, Acklyn, and later Ernie Khalibala of Manufacturers Hanover Trust Bank. Every Thursday evening we would get together at Cellar Restaurant on 95th Street and Columbus Avenue on Manhattan's Upper West Side near Central Park. We'd swap stories about our black experiences at our respective banks. Remarkably, given that we were the only ones, our tales all had a similar ring.

The "Cellar Group" became an important support base for us. God knows we needed it.

I was looking forward to going on my first assignment at the Citibank affiliate, Banque International pour L'Afrique Occidental (BIAO) in Abidjan, a progressive, French-dominated West African nation of the Ivory Coast. Great, I thought. This would help me perfect my French so I can easily pass my French language test and get my SAIS diploma like I promised.

But, much to my disappointment, in the spring 1965, Warren Wheeler, my division's vice-president, summoned me to his office. What followed was a life-changing conversation. I eagerly took my seat in his office, ready to start our meeting.

"Frank, I'm sorry to tell you that the BIAO just contacted us and said that due to the wide disparity between our compensation systems, they think it would be unwise and disruptive to send any New York Citibank officers to West Africa."

He cleared his throat and pressed on. "We are only minority shareholders of BIAO so we must accept its decision. Unfortunately, we can't send you to West Africa and we don't have any openings right now in Liberia, so we want you to go to the Middle East."

All of my excitement about returning to Africa drained from me like the color from a dying violet.

Stunned, I responded the best way I could. "The Middle East, Mr. Wheeler? I don't know anything about that region. Where would I go?"

"Jeddah, Saudi Arabia to join our bank there. Jeddah is one of our most profitable bank branches and the city is growing rapidly. We could use you out there."

Still taken aback, I asked for time to think about it and we decided to discuss it later. Like I told Wheeler, I knew nothing about the Kingdom of Saudi Arabia or the Middle East in general except that the region was mainly Muslim and characterized by continuous fighting with Israel, as well as among the Arab countries themselves. And yes, that Saudi oil there put the king in kingdom. I had to learn more about this chunk of the world before making a decision. Fortunately, one of my good friends at SAIS, Bob Terkhorn, had also joined the Citibank International Division and was a Middle East expert. I called him to get his insights.

After a long discussion in which Bob explained the politics, economies, and religions of the Middle East, I became somewhat interested. I came to see that this assignment could promise new and different experiences. Again, my risk taking and curiosity kicked in.

Finally, in a steady voice Bob said, "Frank, you know, it's a different world, but you should seriously consider it. I am going to Beirut on assignment so we can see each other in the region."

I discussed it with Beryl, who left the decision up to me. After much consideration, I decided that it was the only way, at the time, that I could go overseas and begin to have some real experiences. I definitely did not want to stay in New York and process loan applications for the overseas branches. I longed to go overseas. I took the risk and went to a completely unfamiliar destination.

■ ■ ■

The trip to Saudi Arabia was, shall I say, interesting. Beryl and our son Eric had never flown before, much less across the Atlantic Ocean to Europe and then on to the Middle East. Our first stop was London. It was a thick stack of picture post cards, illustrations from history books, come to life. Next we landed in Paris. It was thrilling to show my family this beautiful city and reminisce about all the sights I had seen when I last visited as a fresh-faced Crossroader en route to Africa. We switched to a passenger ship for a several-days-long voyage from Genoa, an historic seaport in Northern Italy to Beirut, Lebanon.

Long known as "the Paris of the Middle East," Beirut was such a lovely, cosmopolitan city on the sea and clearly much deserved the title. Nestled on the Mediterranean, it was absolutely breathtaking. It was a modern city with an intoxicating blend of Arab and Western cultures. The climate was mild most of the time and the city was flanked by majestic mountains, tall and covered with huge cedar trees. Walking down the Cornich, a waterfront alive with designer shops and shoppers busily eyeing, buying, and chattering away in so many languages, you could easily think you were strolling along the Champs Élysées.

Lebanon felt like the whole world. Its history is peppered with conquest, by the Romans, then Greeks, and last, the Arabs. Almost everyone in Lebanon spoke—sometimes in a single sentence—Arabic, French, and English. What a great way to be introduced to the Middle East. We were convinced that Beryl and I could easily find comfort in a city like Beirut. We could live there, but we had to remind ourselves that this was not our final destination.

Frank Savage as a corporate executive at Equitable Life

Amidst all this elegance and beauty there was one significant blight. The city housed the teeming Palestinian refugee camps, which housed Palestinians who had been pushed out of their neighboring homeland to make room for European Jews emigrating from war-torn Europe. They were coming to settle the still new nation of Israel. Of course, I knew about the creation of the modern state of Israel by the United Nations in 1948. I sympathized with the European Jews and their desire to leave Europe after the Nazi Holocaust. I also had read numerous newspaper articles on the ferocious Arab resistance to the arrival of the Jews and the creation of Israel, a fact that many Arab states refused to acknowledge.

What I had not read about was the inevitable horrendous impact of this forced migration on the uprooted Palestinian natives of Jerusalem, for example. It simply was not adequately reported in U.S. newspapers. When I visited the refugee camps in Beirut, I could not believe my eyes. The living conditions were absolutely appalling, almost inhumane. The refugees lived mainly in tents, exposed to the elements at times when the weather ranged from extreme heat to heavy rains to temperatures at night cold enough for snow. There were no proper bathing or lavatory facilities and mothers were cooking outside on portable stoves.

I was sickened by the sight. How could such degradation and poverty coexist with the wealth and modern comforts of Beirut? To me, this was clearly an untenable, potentially explosive situation—a breeding ground for an uprising. Who could blame the fathers and sons who felt obliged to fight their way out of these camps, especially when this beautiful city full of ordinary families living ordinary lives was in plain sight? I knew this could not last.

I also saw the potential for the Palestinian unrest to destabilize all of the Middle East. Virtually all the regional Arab states deplored the establishment of Israel and cited the mass displacement of the Palestinians as evidence of the injustice visited on them. For the first time, I saw their side of the story. Unfortunately, as I feared, the Palestinians in the refugee camp subsequently revolted and over time, other Arab countries came to support different Palestinian factions. Lebanon was destroyed in the aftermath and many of its most valued citizens fled the country. Even today, more than 40 years after my time there, Lebanon has not fully recovered from such a great loss.

Although the refugee camps were disheartening, I had redeeming experiences in Beirut. I met Peter Wodtke, the senior Citibank officer in the Middle East, who became a mentor and life-long friend. Peter is a sweet-natured man, extremely well-educated and sophisticated, in the true sense of the word. I was impressed to learn that he spoke numerous languages, even Swiss-German, having lived in Europe for many years. I found great comfort in his especially warm hospitality during my time in Beirut.

Arriving in Jeddah, my family and I entered a radically new environment, vastly different from Beirut. Even before the plane landed, my wife had to put on an abaya, a long, black dress that covers a woman from head to toe. In Saudi Arabian culture, women are prohibited to be uncovered in public. Although Jeddah is on the Red Sea, the desert temperatures were 90 degrees or more all the time. And the city was nothing like Beirut, with very few tall buildings, only one respectable hotel, the Kandara Palace, and few supermarkets. Many of the streets were not even paved. Beryl and I were disappointed, but this was it. This would have to be our home for a while.

Because my assignment to the Middle East was not expected, there was no available space for us in the compound that housed bank officers and their families. We had to move into a house in a Jeddah neighborhood. It was okay, but nothing to write home about (and I didn't for a while). We had a Jordanian driver, Omar, and an Eritrean maid, Heddeghah, who were both lovely. The Citibank branch, known as "BankalAmerica" was in the center of town near the souk, or marketplace.

BankalAmerica (pronounced Ban-ka-LA–Ma-reck-kay) was the biggest bank in the city at that time, followed by the British Bank of the Middle East. The bank opened at 8 in the morning and closed at 1 P.M. for lunch (and a nap) to reopen at 4 P.M. and then close at 7 P.M. It was entirely too hot to work during midday. I had the exalted bank title of "accountant," which meant that I had to do anything and everything required (read: gofer). In this role, I learned all the nuts and bolts of banking. In Jeddah I learned how to run a bank, an experience that has been invaluable to me throughout my professional life. Remember, my education was not in finance, but in international relations.

It was also during my Jeddah tour of duty, from 1965 to 1967, when I came to realize that I possessed certain credit analyst skills, which would hold me in good stead in my future financial services career. Actually, I didn't so much come to realize this as much as I was told this. Peter Wodtke made regular due diligence visits to Jeddah. During one of those visits he told me that he had read some of my basic credit reports on bank customers. In a private conversation, he shared an insight.

"I detect an intuitive understanding of credit," he said of my work. Looking up from his notes, he went on. "I think you have a future in banking and I hope you stick with it, the bank needs officers like you."

I could feel La Savage smiling over my shoulder. For a moment I felt like the "borderline genius" she always told me I was. This assessment from Wodtke was very encouraging. I had not yet fully considered myself a banker. I was still growing into my expertise. But here was my big boss and he was validating my selection of international banking as a career. I felt reenergized and more motivated than ever to become as competent as possible in banking.

But there were two sides to this Saudi Arabian halala (a copper coin inscribed in Arabic with numerals marking the coin's denomination)

Working in Saudi Arabia was rewarding professionally but difficult personally, especially for my young wife. Beryl had totally lost her independence; as a woman, she was not allowed to drive or go shopping without a male chaperone. She always had to wear the abaya when outside, which was difficult for her as a Western woman who might be wearing miniskirts and sleeveless tops back in Washington. But she did her best to adjust. Thankfully, Beryl developed a close relationship with Barbara Brody, the wife of Jim Brody, a black Lieutenant Colonel who was the military attaché at the U.S. embassy. Their bond made up for some of the isolation Saudi custom and culture placed on her.

And there were other supportive people in our lives in Jeddah, like Bill Roberts, a colleague at the bank, and his wife, Gail and family that supported us through some tough times we had there.

Beryl and I decided to have our second child while I was assigned to the Middle East. Instead of delivering the baby in Jeddah, we decided on the American University Hospital in Beirut because it had superior facilities. That was a very fortuitous decision. Expecting to return within a week or so, we left our baby son, Eric, with the Roberts, who had a son about Eric's age.

Once our daughter Brett was born, we learned that she had a congenital malfunction in her digestive tract. This required urgent surgery and a period of recuperation. Henry Mishalani, the doctor who performed surgery, literally saved our newborn daughter's life. He said operating on Brett, who was three days old at the time, was like operating on a Swiss watch. She survived the operation and we all returned to Saudi Arabia. But less than a year later, Brett was stricken with a related problem. Adhesions had formed around her earlier surgery, again preventing her from fully digesting her food. Baby Brett had to be rushed back to Beirut for another operation. Dr. Mishalani saved her life, again. After her relapse, we decided it was too dangerous to take Brett back to Jeddah. The level of care that she apparently needed just wasn't there.

This was 1967 and my tour in Saudi Arabia was coming to a timely close. We soon started packing our bags to return to the United States, but I couldn't quite fold away my profound experiences. The 1967 Arab-Israeli war broke out while we lived in Jeddah. The bank's head office instructed Bill and me to evacuate our families to Greece. But we concluded that the war breaking out was far north from us and so we didn't feel at all threatened in Saudi Arabia. Life was going on as usual, so we unilaterally decided to stay put.

I never will forget that after we made that decision, the head office in New York told us we could stay in Jeddah. The war ended quickly, but the office insisted that we must never override its orders again.

I still remember our rebuke: "We know things you may not know about dangers you may face. And when we order you to evacuate, you evacuate."

"You know, Frank," Bill said after we were lightly dressed down by our superiors, "I know we thought we made the right decision. But we shouldn't have stayed because we could have been putting our families at risk."

I agreed. We should not have taken that kind of risk when living in a war zone, even if we were south of the war zone. But we were young and made an irresponsible decision. Thank God, it worked out in our favor. But I will never do that again.

Looking back on my two years in Jeddah, I saw an oil-soaked country begin its transition. I saw Jeddah itself grow from a sparse, desert city into a world-class modern city with excellent infrastructure. And why not? Saudi Arabia has the second largest oil reserves on the planet and today is the second largest exporter of oil in the world. Culturally though, Saudi Arabia did not change. It continues to adhere to strict Muslim teachings. I interacted with Saudis, Yemenis, Jordanians, Africans, Lebanese, and other Arabs on a personal and business basis there. I twice witnessed the Hajj, the annual Muslim pilgrimage to their holiest of cities, Mecca and Medina, both adjacent to Jeddah. What a sight to behold—thousands of pilgrims of all races and colors, from all parts of the world, coming together for this holiest of Muslim pilgrimages. Many pilgrims would bring their worldly belongings with them, like amazingly beautiful Iranian carpets, which they would often display in our bank's lobby. It was in that lobby when I first fell in love with Iranian carpets. My stocking feet rest on one as I write these lines.

Although I arrived in Saudi Arabia as a fish in unfamiliar cultural waters, I gained an appreciation for Islamic customs, religion, and people. I also gained a more balanced view on the Arab-Israeli conflict. Of course, I understood the determination of Jews to establish a new homeland after suffering such profound loss at the lands of Nazi Germany. I also understood the desperation of the Palestinians, who had been removed from their homeland so Israel could be born.

The world must find a way to enable both sides to live peaceably side by side or the consequences can be more terrible than we can ever imagine.

My time in Saudi Arabia also taught me the essence and rationale of certain Islamic practices, which may seem cruel to Westerners. Only by living in the area, immersed in the culture, can you appreciate some of the Koran's major tenets in practice. While working at the bank, I realized the impact of having strict Islamic laws, under which, for example, stealing is punishable by amputation of a hand. The deterrent power of such an unequivocal law was demonstrated on a daily basis in the bank's activities. One of our major customers was a trading company, Al Raji Trading, named for its owner. He was headquartered in the souk and although I was an officer of the bank, I had to go to the marketplace often to collect deposits from Al Raji.

Al Raji would give us bags heavy with money, which we took back to the bank and hauled into the vault. We never had a problem. No armored cars with armed guards were ever necessary. Sometimes, Al Raji's people would bring large cash deposits directly to the bank. Again, they had no problems. They could walk through the streets with millions of riyals without fear of being robbed. People hardly worried about theft in Saudi Arabia because of its dire consequences. Who wants to gain a dollar, so to speak, and lose a hand?

There is very little vagueness in Islam when it comes to sentences for deeds prohibited by the Koran. Perhaps this came about after centuries of living in unforgiving deserts. Jeddah borders the desert and Riyadh sits in the middle of one of the harshest deserts in the world, Rub Al Khalib. The early Bedouin people who formed the foundation for modern Saudi Arabia lived in this brutal place. Food and water were nearly impossible to come by, so if people stole these items, families died. It was that simple.

Although I am not a Muslim and don't condone all Islamic practices, I came to respect Islamic culture and religion, just as I respect my own, while I lived in a Muslim state. As I went on in life, this Middle Eastern experience would come back to me, help me to be successful in the region as an American businessman, one equipped with a unique perspective.

It had been a good decision to accept this post. My success there reconfirmed my philosophy that it is far better to try and fail rather than to not try at all and wonder what if. I hadn't failed, and now I was returning home in a stronger position in the bank than the one I held two years earlier.

■ ■ ■

Once back in the United States with my wife and children, I had only one thing on my mind: pass my requisite French examination so I could finally fulfill my last requirement to Johns Hopkins and receive my master's degree from SAIS. I had made a promise to myself, to La Savage and, of course, to Citibank that hired me on the condition that I pass that test and get my degree.

I figured that I would be in the United States for at least six months; Citibank was putting me through some credit courses to prepare me to be a credit officer, a step up the career ladder. Also, we all needed some time to recover from the trauma of Brett's last health crisis.

I wasn't going to let anything stand in the way of my passing that exam. Using my own money, I enrolled in an intensive French course at Berlitz on 54th Street and Sixth Avenue, not far from the Citibank headquarters. For the next four months I did only three things: I worked at the bank, took the credit courses, and studied French, lots of French. For the past couple of years I had been speaking Arabic. Suddenly my tongue was struggling to curl around French words and phrases.

It became clear to me that total immersion in French was the only way I was going to ace the exam. I could hear La Savage in my ear. Failure was not an option. The bank had believed in my promise enough to hire me and then give me an invaluable international experience in the Middle East. There was no way I was going to let the bank down.

Then, before I could completely accept the fact, I passed the SAIS French exam. It was a great day. The bank seemed surprised, yet happy with the news. I'm not so sure at that point it was important to Citibank that I learned to speak French and got my graduate diploma. It was May 1968. The bank's officials who dealt with me seemed to have already decided that I had a great career ahead of me.

But for my family, and for me, acing the exam was a tremendous accomplishment. Sometimes you just have to do a thing not for the promise of rewards at the end, but you do the thing because it is simply the right thing to do. I made a promise and I was going to keep it. I had become, up until that time, the only man in my family to earn a graduate degree. I emphasize "man" because my twin sister, Frances, had already earned her master's degree in social work. Furthermore, she went on to earn an MBA from Pace University in New York.

La Savage's "two twins" celebrated our success, and our mother's satisfaction could not have played more sweetly on her lips.

"I never doubted you two," she said. "Never doubted. Not once."

Chapter 6

The Longer Road Home

There is a kind of magicness about going far away and then coming back all changed.

—Kate Douglas Wiggin

T hings had changed for the better back at Citibank's New York office. While I was overseas, the bank had hired two African Americans, Edward Lewis in the financial engineering department, and Cleveland Christophe in the corporate office. I was thrilled to meet them. We quickly became close friends. Whenever we were together Ed would talk about his idea of starting a national magazine for black women. There were national black news and lifestyle magazines, *Jet* and *Ebony*, being the most popular. Both of them were produced by the pioneering black publisher John H. Johnson in Chicago. But a magazine focused essentially on and for black women . . . ?

Before I could see exactly what Ed had in mind with his magazine idea, I was given my next assignment. Citibank had a branch in Monrovia, Liberia in West Africa. The bank was called the Bank of Monrovia and was that nation's de facto central bank. I was finally going to be posted in Africa, I thought. But knowing the Americo-Liberian history of the country I also knew this would be a mostly English-speaking country.

I was disappointed that I wasn't going to get a chance to actually use my French, but looked forward to going back to Africa anyway.

One day my vice-president, Warren Wheeler, approached my desk at Citibank with an African man in tow. "I want to introduce you to Clarence Parker, one of our best customers in Liberia." Motioning to me, he went on, "Clarence, this is Frank Savage, one of our newest officers. He just returned from a tour of duty in the Middle East and I'm happy to say that for his second tour of duty, he will be joining you in Liberia."

"Well, Frank, welcome," Clarence said with an easy smile. "We look forward to greeting you in Monrovia."

I told him how much I anticipated my upcoming trip, especially because my first brush with Liberia came by way of a Liberian girl I once dated in junior high school. I don't know why I mentioned her name, but I did.

"Her name was Clavender Bright."

First his eyes laughed at the sound of Clavender's name, then came a lightness in his voice.

"That's my wife," Clarence replied, to my shock.

Mr. Wheeler glared at me as if to ask, "What have you just said, you young, foolish boy?"

I was so embarrassed.

Clarence Parker just laughed harder, "Don't worry about it. I know that was a long time ago when both of you were kids. I just can't wait to tell Clavender that you are coming to Liberia. I know she will be happy to hear the good news. We're looking forward to seeing you and your family."

At that moment Clarence Parker started to become one of my greatest friends.

I arrived in Monrovia with a lot going for me. I was the first African American to come to Liberia in a senior executive position; I would be living on the serenely beautiful bank compound, and I knew Clarence and Clavender Bright. The Bright and Parker families were Americo-Liberians and part of the Liberian elite. They were also close to President William Vacanarat Shadrach Tubman, also an Americo-Liberian.

These distinctions are important. The Americo-Liberians are descendants of the "freedmen" who migrated to Africa in the early 1800s to escape the prejudice and discrimination in the United States. With the support of the American Colonization Society, which advocated that free African Americans should return to Africa, the group settled in Liberia. Over time, the Americo-Liberians amassed all the political and the economic power in Liberia. During my stint in Liberia, Tubman, the President, was a benevolent leader who sought peace between the Americo-Liberians and the indigenous African people who had lived there long before the Americo-Liberians arrived.

Tubman moved to personally blur the differences the best he could. He maintained a very close relationship with a woman from an indigenous tribe, provided the indigenous people with economic benefits, and treated them with respect. Although he maintained tight control, he placed a lot of emphasis on making sure that the indigenous population felt included in the greater Liberian society.

Clavender's family was known for their many palm oil and rubber farms. The Brights were wealthy, well-educated, and highly sophisticated. Clarence Parker owned the biggest paint-producing factory in West Africa. He and Clavender were socially active and, like President Tubman, were members of the True Whig Party, the predominant political party in Liberia.

When I landed in Roberts Field, Monrovia, I kissed the ground just as I had done the first time I arrived in Africa with Crossroads. I'm happy to be back home, I said to myself as I took in this country of mangrove forests, towering palm trees, and ample beaches. And Liberia was hot, equatorial hot.

The feelings, the aromas, the African people . . . it was all there for me. A wonderful group of people lived on the bank compound, where we had all of the facilities and amenities that we could want.

My experiences in Liberia and in Jeddah were as different as the sun from the moon. In Saudi Arabia, although I came to know a number of people, I never developed a close, personal relationship with anyone to the extent that I did in Liberia. On my second tour, it was totally different. I went there as a foreign staff member, but the Liberian people embraced and regarded me and my family as if we were coming home to Africa.

There was an intriguing irony in this. Liberia was deeply Americanized in almost every respect—culture, language, lifestyle—you name it.

Because of our relationship with the Parkers, Beryl and I were immediately launched into the social scene. At one party among the first events Clarence and Clavender took us to, everyone danced a popular Liberian dance called the *quadrille*, a mixture between the waltz and the popular African-American line dance called the *electric slide*. It was an exclusive event attended by the upper crust of Liberia, mainly Americo-Liberians. President Tubman and his wife led the quadrille and Beryl and I joined in after watching the steps.

The Parkers introduced us to their gracious, bespectacled president and to all the other dignitaries at the party—the Minister of Finance, the Minister of Commerce, the head of the Central Bank and the head of the Ministry of Agriculture. We met everybody who was anybody to meet in Liberia. Looking back, my stay in Liberia was like one big, never-ending party.

■ ■ ■

My family was so lucky to have friends like Clavender and Clarence. We had many wonderful times with them and their two boys.

Word soon spread around the bank of my Liberian social connections. This gave me tremendous standing—and advantage. It was a new and exciting feeling. Up to this point in my life I had never been in the empowering environment of an independent African country complete with black leadership and black affluence. To see blacks run a country bolstered my sense of pride, and to be a part of that governing group, to actually know these people, made me feel even better. And I was 30 years old. For my children, Eric and Brett, this exposure was very healthy. They were still young, but old enough to notice that everyone in charge in Liberia looked like them.

In sharp contrast to Saudi Arabia, my wife could now live a normal life and have friends, go to luncheons and dinners, get to know people and go shopping—all by herself. Monrovia was like a little America where she could live happily ever after. We had an incredibly active social life. The Americo-Liberians spent their entire weekends going to brunches, lunches, dinners, or parties. Their lives, and ours by extension, were one great big social event. And I cannot lie. It was fun; there's no question about it.

However, at some point doubt began to creep in. I found myself locked into a heavy conversation with myself. Am I having too much fun here? Is this the way I'm going to build my career?

While I was in Liberia, I noticed that, with few exceptions, most of the businesspeople who ran the hotels, shops, supermarkets, and restaurants were not Liberians. They were either Arabs, primarily from Lebanon and Syria, or Indians. They were excellent businesspeople, and some of the biggest clients of the bank. Most of the Liberians I knew, such as Clarence Parker, worked for the government. They held high and prestigious positions in government but not in business. This public–private break struck and disturbed me because I knew that for Liberia to further develop its economy, it would have to develop a solid African business class.

Knowing human tendencies as I do, I now understand what may have happened. First-generation immigrants work unusually hard, struggling mightily to build wealth and financial independence. In Liberia's case those first waves of African Americans who migrated from the United States would be that generation. Like all immigrant groups, they probably wanted their kids to aspire to greater heights, to move up into the leadership class. And I imagine that this is what, in essence, happened in Liberia.

It was the later generations of Americo-Liberians who were in place when I came to Liberia. They were the intelligentsia, the political leaders and the owners of the economy. But in terms of business they were like the owners of farms but oversaw them like absentee landlords. They hired indigenous people to work their farms and then counted their dividends, so to speak. And newer immigrant groups, like the Arabs and Indians had their shoulders to the wheels of commerce.

This left the indigenous population to perform all of the nation's grunt work. They were the maids. They were the construction workers. They were the bus drivers. They were the cooks. They comprised the greater working class. Rarely did one find an indigenous person who went to work in a suit and held an executive position. A clear demarcation existed between the Americo-Liberians and the indigenous populations. This essentially two-class system concerned me.

This structure was a recipe for a disaster. Eventually that great gap between the haves and have-nones led to a revolution by the indigenous people. The consequences of this still weigh heavily on the country and shadows its future.

Back in the late 1960s, when my family and I lived in Liberia, President Tubman made a valiant effort to make the indigenous people feel that they shared a common destiny and bond with the Americo-Liberians. But in the end his efforts failed. He died in a London clinic in 1971.

From time to time I would voice my concerns to my counterpart officer at Chemical Bank, Hilary Dennis, a Harvard graduate from a leading Liberian family. He and his wife, Liz, a medical doctor, would socialize with us, but they were not social creatures. Hilary had a serious streak and spoke at length about his country's need for economic development. I also befriended Hilary's American colleague at the Bank of Liberia, Tom Duffy. He met his wife, Moya, in Liberia while she was working as a Pan Am stewardess; Moya would come to be a dear friend of my future wife, Lolita.

Tom was an expert banker, someone Chemical Bank could send anywhere in the world. He could fit in and become comfortable in any land—Africa, Europe, or Asia. The economic climate in Liberia was a constant topic of discussion among my new peers.

My Liberian stint was briefly interrupted when my grandmother, Hattie Pitt, died in 1968. Next to La Savage, my grandmother was my rock—my babysitter when I was a child and my intellectual sparring partner during my college years. Her long-time battle with arteriosclerosis finally came to an end when she had a fatal heart attack. When I received word of her death, I started crying and couldn't stop. My wife tried to comfort me, but there was no consolation for losing someone so dear, someone who played such a crucial role in my life.

As the only family member of her generation who had gone to college, she cherished education and did everything she could to support me as I worked my way through school, particularly through Howard and SAIS. I boarded a plane for Washington, DC, leaving my family in Liberia so the kids wouldn't miss any school.

The funeral was very difficult for me. Once again, I started bawling endlessly. I couldn't accept that my grandmother Hattie Pitt, one of the lights of my life was gone. When I returned to Liberia a few days later, I was still mourning my grandmother's death. I threw myself into my work and continued to advance my background in banking operations. Antranig Sarkissian, an experienced bank operations executive, joined Citibank around this time and I began to learn quite a bit from him.

Sarkissian ultimately became an executive assistant to Bill Rhodes, another experienced international hand who rose to become Chairman of Citibank and the principal negotiator for many of the emerging market bailouts in the 1980s. But by the time I left Liberia in the summer of 1970 for home leave, I was ready for a new challenge.

■ ■ ■

The new head of Citibank's International Division, Carleton Stewart, had something else in mind for me. He asked if I would return to Liberia that year for another tour with a promotion to the bank's credit platform. As much as I liked it there, I had mixed emotions about returning because of my concerns about the direction Liberia was moving. It could turn dangerous, which it did. I was also growing more anxious about the fragile health of my daughter Brett. She had developed atopic eczema and the humid, often rainy climate of Liberia exacerbated her condition. I conferred with Hilary Dennis; he shared some of my concerns but was generally optimistic about the overall stability of Liberia. He believed there was a group of people led by President Tubman who were determined to keep Liberia united and to improve the living standards of all Liberians. He encouraged me to return and help to advance the country. I was impressed, as usual, by Hilary's points and I wanted to do anything I could do to help Liberia, a country for which I had come to feel a real kinship.

As a point of reference, I shared my observations of the state of Palestinians in Lebanon. "Hilary," I began, "I've seen this similar type of situation before. If something isn't done to further enfranchise the indigenous people, there is potential for some very bad outcomes."

Hilary understood, but held to his confidence that the divide between indigenous peoples and the Americo-Liberians would be peaceably narrowed. This was a compelling statement coming from Hilary, given that his parents came from both Americo-Liberian and indigenous backgrounds. Still, my most important consideration was for my daughter's health. Her doctors predicted she would grow out of her skin condition, as it was genetic and not in reaction to climate.

After taking both issues into consideration, my family decided to return to Liberia for my second tour of duty. In our hearts, it was really what we wanted to do. I never stopped loving Africa and the promise of a promotion to the credit area didn't hurt. Performing credit decisions could round out my banking knowledge and carried an element of prestige. Going back to Liberia as a credit officer would give me the opportunity to put into practice my training in credit and lending. Given the types of Liberian companies, which the bank served, I was not going to gain highly sophisticated credit experience but I certainly would get some important field experience.

With the understanding that I would get an opportunity to work directly with companies, I moved to "the platform," as we call it. The platform was right at the front of the building where everybody could see you, even local customers who wanted to get credit. So I presumed that the two additional years in Liberia would be a compelling time for me. Unfortunately, things didn't work out too well.

After a month or so, I still had not received official notice of my promotion so I asked Kim Abbot, head of the Monrovia branch, to follow up with Carleton Stewart about when it was coming through. Stewart did not respond favorably, essentially reneging on his promise to promote me. I was stunned, shocked really, that he would send me back to Liberia under false pretenses. This was the early fall of 1970.

Having already assumed a seat on the credit platform, I was also extremely embarrassed. At that moment, I lost all faith in the bank and particularly in Carleton Stewart, whom I subsequently learned had made similarly false promises to international staff; actions that led to the departure of several promising executives. Worse, Liberia's rainy season was upon us and as a result, Brett's eczema became more severe. She was miserable, scratching herself constantly with no relief.

Fortuitously, the summer before I left the States for this nonexistent promotion, my sister married a man named David Cherry. He worked at Equitable Life Assurance Society. At their wedding reception, which I attended, Dave and I started talking about Equitable. I had three or four life insurance policies there, so I knew it only as an insurance company. I, like most people, never thought of Equitable as an investment financial institution.

David explained that Equitable was a giant company that had made considerable investments on a private basis in large U.S. companies and some foreign companies, too. David wondered if I would be interested in talking to Equitable. I could not imagine why I would, given my international career path and how far it had taken me so far.

Then David got right to the point.

"Frank, we're getting ready to set up a small business company that's going to invest in black businesses. We need somebody like you who knows finance, and can create this special company."

I was pleased to hear that at long last there was going to be an opportunity for black businesses to access capital, the kinds of capital that could grow black businesses. That, on this level, had never been done before. I had experienced this problem personally; La Savage had built her business out of her own capital because banks would not give her a business loan. This initiative was coming from a Republican president, Richard M. Nixon.

In 1970, Nixon introduced a program called "Black Capitalism," with the goal of helping black and other minority businesses access capital. He said he believed it was important for the black community to build its own businesses because it would help blacks be independent and build stable families. His program would encourage the creation of Minority Enterprise Small Business Investment Companies (MESBIC). The federal government would match, three to one, any capital that a big company put up to invest in black businesses. For instance, if a company provided a black business with $1 million, that black business could get another $3 million from the federal government at extremely low interest rates through a special loan program.

This gave some socially conscious major businesses the incentive to provide capital to some small black businesses. The Equitable Life Assurance Society was one of them. At that time, the president of Equitable was Henry Smith, who supported Nixon's Black Capitalism program. Coy Eklund, executive vice president in charge of the Equitable Agency group, had encouraged Smith to embrace this program.

Frank returns home from Africa to create an investment company to provide needed capital to black businesses.

Coy had started to hire an impressive cadre of black professionals, like Leroy Beavers, Al Carleton, and Darwin Davis, to market Equitable insurance policies to an increasingly affluent black market. Establishing a MESBIC to help African-American businesses would not only be profitable, but socially correct. In the beginning, only a few companies like Equitable and General Mills were motivated to try to help to build black businesses.

I had heard about this program earlier that summer through my friends Hughlyn Fierce and Ed Lewis, who were still with Citibank. We discussed what it could mean for black businesses if they had access to capital. Along with Jack Woods at Chase Manhattan Bank, Ernie Khalibala at Manufacturers Hanover Trust and one or two others, we were among the few African Americans with the kind of financial experience at that time that could take full advantage of the turn of events.

All of us felt an obligation to try to help our community. Still, I was more committed to returning to Africa to pursue what I hoped would be a lifelong career in the international finance and business arena. Nevertheless, I agreed to meet with Bill Cowey, vice president of private investing at Equitable, to learn more about the company's MESBIC plans. Cowey started the meeting by verifying that I was, in fact, an officer in the international division of Citibank. He thumbed through the directory until he found my name, which, I suppose, made me legitimate in his eyes. I could only smile inside.

Our discussion left me convinced that Equitable was serious about establishing and capitalizing the MESBIC; the idea had the full backing of the CEO and the executive vice president of marketing for the company. Cowey was responsible for setting up and staffing the new company and asked if I would like to be considered for the CEO position. I informed him that I was scheduled to return to Africa, but that I would like to do more research and get back to him.

We ended the meeting on a positive note and my brother-in-law called immediately afterward to relay that Cowey was very interested in me. The good news did not change my plans to go back to Liberia. Yet, I left the possibility open.

I was sorely disappointed, perhaps a little angry, that my Citibank boss had reneged on his promise to give me the promotion I expected when I returned to Liberia for my second tour of duty. And I guess it showed. Kim Abbott, the interim head of the Liberia office, tried to talk me out of leaving with assurances that my promotion would come sooner or later. But that was not good enough. I had witnessed the poor treatment of another Citibank officer living in Liberia who had been with the bank for more than 20 years. I watched Stewart emasculate this man, who had exhausted every other option in his life by working for so long overseas for Citibank. He had lost touch with the United States, and although living and working overseas afforded certain luxuries, he was stuck in this foreign world.

My God, I thought, I could be in that same boat 15 years from now. Carleton Stewart actually decimated a whole layer of very talented and experienced international bankers because he didn't have good people skills. He tacked toward betrayal.

I remembered how La Savage took a career path entirely different from government after having been disrespected by that examiner when she was a young mother simply looking for a way to support her family. Like her, I was not going to accept this insult. Whether I had another job, I was going to quit Citibank and return home. Once the decision was made, I started to brainstorm about job options. I wanted to stay in finance, preferably banking. Of course, the recent conversations with my brother-in-law and Bill Cowey at Equitable immediately came to mind. Should I take the CEO position of the Equitable MESBIC? Is this my destiny? Is this a way to get Brett back home so she can get proper treatment? Quite frankly, my wife was disconcerted by Brett's condition and welcomed the prospect of returning to the United States where she could get proper treatment.

This was the fall of 1970. I called my brother-in-law and explained my situation. I told David that I was ready to consider joining Equitable. He called Bill Cowey right away and told him that I might be available, should Equitable still be interested in me for CEO of their MESBIC. They were, indeed, still interested. Cowey had the head of personnel call me a few days later to make a formal offer. We negotiated all the details of my position—salary, bonus arrangements, benefits, taxes, the cost of returning home—on the telephone. A starting date in late November 1970, was set. The deal was sealed. The risk taker in me was still willing to take risks.

I handed in my resignation to a disappointed Kim Abbott. This was nearing bonus time. By leaving early, I forfeited a bonus, which, quite frankly, I should not have done. I could have asked Equitable to compensate me for the lost bonus, but money was not on my mind at the time. I just wanted out of Citibank. I acted, in part, out of anger, which is not always a good thing, but my overall reasons for leaving were sound.

My only true regret was that I left Liberia before my mother ever had a chance to visit me in Africa. She had been so preoccupied with recovering from the destruction of her beauty shop following the 1968 riots in Washington that began with the April 4 assassination of Martin

Luther King Jr. Sadly, La Savage never got a chance to experience Africa except through me, through all my stories and artifacts of my commune with the Motherland.

■ ■ ■

In November 1970, I left Liberia to join Equitable Life weeks later to become president of the Equitable Life Community Enterprises Corporation, the Equitable-sponsored MESBIC long in the making. It was the beginning of a new stage in my life and I could feel my fortunes rising.

Although I left Citibank on unfavorable terms, Liberia still had a place in my heart and Beryl and I kept in close contact with our Monrovia friends, including Clarence and Clavender, Hilary and Liz. When President Tubman passed away in July 1971, he was succeeded by William Tolbert, his long-term vice president. Contrary to Tubman, Tolbert was more concerned about showing that he was "the boss" rather than continuing to build trust among the indigenous Liberian people. As a result, he slowly broke the fragile bonds between the America-Liberians and the original Liberian people. This led to the 1980 revolt orchestrated by Master Sergeant Samuel K. Doe, an indigenous, noncommissioned officer in the Liberian armed services. Tolbert was killed in his bed. The majority of the America-Liberian leaders who were part of Tolbert's cabinet were also killed.

From what I was told, the Tolbert administration didn't know how to handle the power so suddenly thrust on it. In his attempt to establish dominance, Tolbert was nepotistic and put many of his family members in positions of power. One of his brothers, Steve Tolbert, was already a powerful man in Liberia and one of the nation's few black businessmen. His company, called "Montserrat Fishing Company," ran a fleet of trawlers along the West Africa coast. He was a genuine, independent businessman who was not involved in any way in politics. There was also an internal power struggle among the America-Liberians. It was a mess and I'm glad my family and I weren't there when it all exploded in bloodshed and power grabbing.

Tolbert's most grave mistake was to mistreat the indigenous population. His actions made them feel like second-class citizens in their own land. During their revolt, almost all of the leaders of the True

Whig Party, the party of the ruling class, were killed, including my good friends, Cecil Dennis Jr., Secretary of State, and Clarence Parker, who, at the behest of President Tolbert, assumed the chairmanship of the True Whig Party.

Cecil and Clarence were marched half naked to Monrovia's beach, tied to crudely cut telephone poles and shot in a public execution. Thirteen government officials died that dark, sunny day. Americo-Liberians suffered greatly. Women were raped, homes were confiscated then burned or taken over. Hilary and Liz Dennis were stripped and paraded down the streets of Liberia for their Americo-Liberian origins. The whole country was ravaged and Sgt. Doe appointed himself the new president and promoted himself to general.

I recall sitting in New York during this turning point in Liberian history, thinking of the bad feeling I'd had about the future of Liberia in the pit of my stomach. Now it had happened. All of my friends in the Liberian community were treated horribly, including Clavender Bright and her children, who, thank God, escaped. The country embarked upon a long, starless night of corruption, killings, and the total destruction of Liberia's economic fabric. I wondered: What would have happened had I been there? I had become a fixture in the Americo-Liberian community and I had grown close to the leaders of the True Whig Party. Of course, the U.S. Embassy would have attempted to protect me. Nonetheless, I could have been killed, deemed guilty by association.

I had felt that it was time to move on, but while I was in Liberia I had been reluctant at first to heed my own feelings. This is one of those lessons that you learn in life. If you receive a sign that it's time to make a move, if you feel it in your gut, you should not be afraid to act. In my case, a confluence of events sent me that signal: company problems, my daughter's illness, and ominous concerns about the future of Liberia.

But I guess as the winds of destiny would catch my sails, my decision took me on another course, a voyage I had never expected to take. Thank God it turned out to be one of the smartest moves I ever made.

■ ■ ■

By late 1970, I found myself back in New York City. I had not planned to be there as recent as three months earlier. But as my Grandma Hattie used to say, "God works in mysterious ways." Hughlyn Fierce and Ed Lewis were elated that I had returned home to help the all-important mission of building up the African-American business community. Capital was essential to this task and I was determined to supply it.

I began to develop this new company from the ground up with about a million dollars in capital. It was reminiscent of the way my mother started her business so many years earlier back in Washington on Georgia Avenue. I watched her start it from scratch and learned how to do practically the same thing by osmosis. I felt very comfortable in this small business environment even though I was operating within the power and reach of a major company

My family moved into a nice apartment in Riverdale, an old upper-middle-class enclave in the Bronx. Beryl and I now had three children, Eric, Brett, and our newest son Mark, who was born in 1970. Riverdale was a wonderful neighborhood with excellent schools and my family was in good shape financially. Brett's skin immediately began to react positively to the environment, which was much less humid than the one she endured in Liberia. My wife loved being back in New York with her friends, and she could easily get to Washington to see her relatives and vice versa. Things were going smoothly.

I needed a securities lawyer to work with me at the MESBIC because we planned to make securities investments rather than simple bank loans. I turned to a number of my friends for recommendations. I had been abroad so long that I didn't know any black lawyers in New York. My friend Cleave came back to me one day with a strong suggestion.

"Frank," he said, optimism lightened his words. "I've got just the lawyer for you—Reginald Lewis of Lewis and Clarkson. We call him Reg. He's from Baltimore and graduated from Harvard Law School. He's one of the few black lawyers with corporate finance experience because he worked with a big New York securities law firm for awhile."

I thought that this "Reg," who was not yet 30 years old, sounded great, so Cleave arranged to have him brought to my office. After Reg described his background—raised in a working-class family, won a football scholarship to pay for undergraduate school, worked well in corporate law—I knew that he had all the right kinds of experience to support me legally. I explained my mission and strategy, which was to provide capital, not loans, to emerging black businesses. He was already familiar with President Nixon's Black Capitalism program and the role MESBICs could play. He was very self-confident. I asked him to meet with representatives from the Equitable law department. When he did they were equally impressed with his credentials and experience.

I hired Reginald F. Lewis as outside counsel to the company. As his wife Loida still says, "Frank and Equitable were the first big corporation to hire Reg as a lawyer."

Reg went on to become an extremely successful entrepreneur. In 1983 he purchased a small, dress-pattern maker, McCall Pattern Company, for $23 million. He later sold it for $63 million, making a hefty personal profit. Then in 1987, Reg Lewis put together the financing, with some help, to purchase Beatrice International for $985 million. It soon reported revenues of more than $1 billion, making Reginald Lewis the first African American to build a billion-dollar company.

I wonder what he could have accomplished if he had had more time. He passed away at age 50, a victim of brain cancer.

Word spread quickly throughout the African-American community that Equitable Life had set up this MESBIC. Almost from the start, I began to meet many African Americans in New York who I hadn't met during my early days there at Citibank. Through my friendship with my brother-in-law, Dave Cherry, and with another African-American Equitable manager, Darwin Davis, I continued to meet many impressive people with impressive ideas.

Darwin Davis was one of the most accomplished agency managers at Equitable Life and he sought me out when I joined the company. He introduced me to Coy Eklund, who succeeded Henry Smith to become the new CEO of Equitable, and to all of the black managers in the insurance area. He and his wife, Val, also brought my family together with several other African Americans in the business community. Darwin really made a concerted effort to connect me to the right people. Another good lesson: you can't do it alone. Networking is not additive, but exponential.

I grew increasingly close to the African-American colleagues I met during my days at Citibank in New York. One of them was Ed Lewis, who had worked in the bank's financial engineering division. It focused on the forensic analysis of companies, a kind of financial CSI.

Ed indicated to me that he was still thinking about starting a black women's magazine.

"I may be at Citibank now, but I'm thinking about starting a magazine. I have three partners with magazine experience and we're thinking about launching one that addresses the needs of black women between the ages of 18 and 45 because there is no such magazine now."

I thought his concept was interesting. It made a lot of sense to me because I had been raised by women like La Savage and my aunts, who were so smart but were never acknowledged in society in the way they should have been. Ed's magazine could be the first voice of black women. I knew Ed's ideas held promise. Just then, I had no idea just how much and how far he would eventually go with his magazine.

Cleve Christophe, also a new Citibanker, graduated from the University of Michigan Business School. He worked in the corporate department reporting to the CEO. He had already been a great friend by introducing me to Reg Lewis.

My friendship with Hughlyn Fierce continued to grow as well. He literally preached to me about our obligation to help black businesses grow and prosper. He would take every chance he had to introduce me to emerging black businessmen. As I grew the MESBIC, I counted on his support and good judgment. Again, you can't do it alone.

The support of Equitable's chief executive officer was great. Coy Eklund was fantastic and socially conscious; he was absolutely indispensable to the success of the MESBIC. Coy was one of the first CEOs of a Fortune 500 company to practice affirmative action by promoting blacks like Darwin Davis to positions of power and responsibility at Equitable Life. These were the early days of affirmative action in the United States, so few corporations had people of color in positions of genuine authority. Thanks to Coy, Equitable was an exception. The company recognized that the black community represented a significant opportunity and, therefore, as head of the agency division, Coy Eklund had made it his business to begin to recruit black agents to the Equitable agency force to pursue what he thought was a growing black business community.

Coy recruited Leroy Beavers from Golden State Insurance Company in California, Darwin Davis from his post as a mathematics teacher in Detroit, and many more of the country's most outstanding black businesspersons, none of whom could resist the opportunity to join such a substantial company. As respected figures in their communities, they did well in attracting business. They also became some of the most distinguished performers in Equitable's history.

Although Equitable was the leading insurance company to embrace black capitalism, several others like Prudential and Metropolitan quickly followed suit as they saw the success of these black business agency managers. You could see a smattering of blacks who had begun to populate the major corporations. Slowly, our numbers began to increase.

When I met Coy Eklund, a white man, I was greatly impressed. He had an infectious personality and was a true leader, having built one of the most successful agencies in the history of Equitable. We bonded right away. It was encouraging to know that I had his full support for the MESBIC. I had the benefit to get to know Coy very well on a personal level during this period because he insisted that I attend all the agency manager events at Equitable. He said it would serve me well in better understanding the insurance industry and provide a means to meet with the outstanding black agency managers and insurance agents. He also wanted them to see that he was trying to do everything he could to help black businesses, which in turn, helped their business.

Coy was Midwestern, but he also came from Scandinavian stock that immigrated decades ago to the United States. I have always found these people to be honest, upstanding, and socially conscious. Coy was no exception. He forged an extremely close relationship with all the black professionals at Equitable and ensured that we were respected within the corporation. He was a very special man, truly a pioneer in affirmative action without apology.

The creation of the Equitable MESBIC also caught the attention of Earl Graves, the founder and publisher of a new magazine called *Black Enterprise*, widely considered the bible of black business development. Earl often featured me in his magazine, including more than my fair share of covers.

With all this backing, I felt truly vindicated in my decision to return to the United States. Equitable seemed to be a successful, socially progressive company. More important, the President of the United

States, Richard Nixon, was advocating black capitalism on U.S. soil. It was a wonderful confluence and I stood where all of these currents converged. It was a great feeling.

■ ■ ■

The next phase of my life was under way, but little did I know how much of a turning point this was in my life. For my first two years at Equitable, I worked nonstop to identify black businesses that could qualify for our investment while trying to help those businesses grow and expand. We had no shortage of deal opportunities coming to us. The word was out and MESBICs were becoming very popular. In addition to Earl Graves covering us in *Black Enterprise*, mainstream business journalists were discovering us and writing about our work. I landed on the cover of *Fortune* magazine.

MESBIC formed a very strong association. We started to syndicate deals with each other to aggregate larger sums of capital. The amount of capital available through the MESBICs was not large in view of how expansive our work had become. We were dealing with perhaps a billion dollars. However, the impact of what we were doing was significant. It sent a message that things were changing and that black business could now access the capital that it needed to grow, to flourish.

Then the government launched the 8(a) business development program, operated by the Department of Commerce. This was designed to enable black businesses to access contracts from U.S. government agencies. These contracts, often the kind long out of reach of black entrepreneurs, provided black businesses with a reliable source of high-quality revenue. This was especially true because these very same businesses were having trouble securing business from large, private companies.

The MESBIC and 8(a) programs were a significant boost to black businesses in the 1970s. I was pleased with some of the deals that we had already negotiated. Ed Lewis resigned from Citibank to launch what became the enormously successful *Essence* magazine. Our MESBIC was one of its first investors. Earl Graves decided to diversify his business into broadcasting, and we invested in his new venture. Gene Jackson and Sid Small formed a company to acquire radio stations around the country, in which Equitable also invested.

We were growing fast and I needed to expand my staff. I hired an impressive black MBA, Howard Mackey, to help me handle the portfolio. Reg Lewis was proving extremely valuable in negotiating and structuring deals. We had relationships with a minority accounting firm, Mitchell & Titus, that helped us handle all of the accounting and bookkeeping needs of the portfolio companies. I was ecstatic about our MESBIC team. We had some companies that lost every penny we invested and other companies that were profitable. This was high-risk venture capital investing in the truest sense. I was honored to be back home taking part in this effort, and my family, especially La Savage, was proud of what I was doing with my life. Above all, I was certain that I was making a major contribution to advancing the economic condition of African Americans.

At the same time, that international bug was still gnawing at me. I loved what I was doing, but I knew that at some point I would have to return to my first love—international finance.

Chapter 7

Africa Calls
Once Again . . .

The darkest thing about Africa has always been our ignorance of it.
—*George Kimble*

S
ometimes opportunity knocks when you least expect it and under
the most unlikely circumstances. It's like finding the strangest of
bedfellows in the most surprising of beds.

Such was the case with TAW. It was 1973 and I was sitting behind
my desk in the Equitable building on 1285 Avenue of the Americas. I
pored over financial statements and related reports on my MESBIC
portfolio companies. I tossed my glance out of one of my 10th-floor
windows in my newly adopted home. I loved the hustle, the bustle of
New York, the deep thump of its unceasing pulse beneath the concrete
and earthen tissues of streets, parks, and building foundations. I relished
in it all—the infectious rhythm and roil of its people, all wonderfully
contrasting creeds and colors, with their distinctive shoes, bags, hats, and
individualized styles and natures.

It was so different, so distant, from Washington, DC, from Jeddah,
from Monrovia. This was the city that swallowed and chewed me

lightly when I first visited as a child with my mother to attend the International Beauty Show in a building walking distance from this office. A ringing phone broke my sliver of a reprieve as my secretary announced that Hughlyn Fierce was on the line.

"I know you're probably very busy and I don't want to interrupt anything, but I would like to introduce you to Tom Wood, a brother who is a director here at Chase." It struck me to hear that a "brother" was a board member of Chase Bank.

Hughlyn continued. "Tom runs a company called TAW International Leasing, which leases trucks and buses throughout Africa. TAW stands for his name, Thomas A. Wood. The Zambian government just awarded TAW a $60 million contract to build a truck transportation system."

Listening intently, I sat at my desk wondering if I would wake up soon. Africa? Sixty million dollars? Contract? Am I dreaming?

"Here's the catch though," he said, before taking a deep breath and pressing on. "The transportation system needs to be designed to circumvent the blockade South African has put on Zambia, punishing the Zambian government for harboring the ANC. The blockade has prevented them from getting copper to South African ports to be shipped to the European and Asian markets.

"It's killing the Zambian economy, Frank," Hughlyn said.

He explained that the Zambian government had asked Tom to assemble a fleet of trucks to carry the copper instead over land from the Copperbelt to ports in Tanzania and Kenya in East Africa. TAW needed capital so it could buy all the cabs and flatbed trailers from General Motors and Fruehauf. TAW also needed to hire Ryder to help build the infrastructure and manage the system. "Like most small black companies," he went on, "TAW is short of the required capital to take advantage of this opportunity so they would like to see if your MESBIC can help them.

"In short, they need capital."

It was a refrain I was accustomed to hearing from black entrepreneurs.

Hughlyn said he wanted me to talk to Tom. He hoped I could provide him with enough operating capital to get the Zambian venture to the point where TAW could build out the system, and then successfully operate the fleet.

"The implications for Zambia's future are incredible, to say the least," he said, pushing all the right buttons to unleash my enthusiasm for the project. "Just think about it, a black-owned company defying the South African blockade and building a transportation company that can potentially rival the best in the world!"

Hughlyn knew me too well. Africa? Investment? Zambia, where I had visited as a student? Now the chance to build a black-owned, global transportation company? It all sounded fantastic to me. And who was this guy Tom Wood who was daring to think on such a huge scale? I wanted to meet him right away.

But Hughlyn wasn't done. "Frank, TAW has the chance to be really successful. Chase is committed to helping him, but they need equity capital to bridge themselves until they get this whole program up and running. And by the way, you remember Ernie Khalibala?"

I almost couldn't believe I heard that name sizzling in my ear. Is was the same Ernie Khalibala who used to work at Manufacturers Hanover Trust Bank, one of our *band of brothas*, part of the first wave of black bankers to work for the major banks.

"He's working with Tom Wood," Hughlyn added.

This made the TAW deal all the more appealing to me. Ernie was a smart, soft-spoken guy who had a Kenyan father and an American mother. I had many fond memories of our good times in our early days in banking. He was part of our "Cellar Group" of newly minted black bankers swapping stories about our forays into corporate America.

Trying hard to take all of this in, I responded, "Hey, man, thanks for calling. I really do appreciate it. Let me see what I can do. Please send Tom Wood over right away."

I hung up the phone and let a moment of stillness settle over me. And then a flood of thoughts rushed through my mind. Wow, what an unexpected opportunity. This could be huge. When Hughlyn called me about something, I paid attention because I knew that he wouldn't send any opportunity my way that he hadn't already carefully thought through himself. His mention of Africa sent my blood rushing like the frantic taxis flying through the arteries of the streets below. I felt myself becoming emotional when I thought of how this deal might be good for business, but very possibly good for a whole region struggling to free itself from generations-old racial oppression.

Since my Crossroads days in Zambia, I had wanted to find a way to fight apartheid. I was even more anxious to meet this Tom Wood. I was also left thinking, Why me? Why now?

■ ■ ■

Two days later, Tom Wood walked into my office. He was a tall, light-skinned African American in his mid-forties. He was smoothly articulate and exuded a kind of Obama coolness that inspired confidence. I learned that he was a mathematician and electrical engineer. He spoke to me about TAW, what it was trying to accomplish in Zambia, and then confessed that the main challenge he faced was the absence of equity capital to make the Zambian project more than a mighty notion.

"Can you believe it?" he asked. "We have a contract worth $60 million. And I just don't have the money to execute it."

It was a classic problem for black business at that time—an opportunity seen but just out of reach because of a lack of access to capital.

Tom Wood said he had hoped to secure from me a subordinated, convertible loan with warrants or other equity features, which could support requests for bank loans. He explained that Chase and the First National Bank of Chicago were willing to extend the working capital loans. He noted that the Overseas Private Investment Corporation, an independent U.S. agency that supports U.S. companies' expansion abroad, was ready to assist as well. But he still needed equity capital "to be able to put this all together."

This was exactly the MESBIC mission: provide equity to deserving black companies, thus strengthening their financial ability to access loans from banks. I liked the way Tom was thinking.

As I carefully weighed the information that Tom shared with me, I knew that I wanted to be a part of this project. But I did not know if I could convince Equitable's board of directors to participate because of certain company restrictions. For instance, Equitable was subject to an Insurance Department regulation that severely limited investments in non-U.S. companies or in companies that derived the majority of their revenues from non-U.S. sources. This rule extended to Equitable subsidiaries such as the MESBIC. I had already failed to obtain approval to invest in Reginald Lewis's Beatrice International deal for this same reason.

Reg had gone after the billion-dollar international business of Beatrice, a large global food company with operations in more than 30 countries. Given our relationship, Reg, of course, came to me looking for capital and I was very much inclined to do that deal. Not only did I have the utmost confidence in him, but this was also going to be a lucrative investment. Unfortunately, Equitable told me that the MESBIC couldn't invest in the Beatrice deal because we were a wholly owned subsidiary of Equitable. That meant that we could not make an international investment under the current regulations.

Needless to say, this was a huge disappointment to me, to Reg, and to our mutual friend, Cleve Christophe. So I was a little depressed over not being able to get Equitable to see that these companies offered a tremendous opportunity for us, and to lose out on the TLC Beatrice deal really bothered me. But, there was nothing I could do about it because, in fact, the insurance company did have regulations that they had to live by. The rules were there for a reason and I had to respect that.

But with TAW the stakes were so much higher; this wasn't just business. I decided to make another attempt to get approval, to make a good faith appeal. Even as the failed Reg Lewis deal haunted me, I persisted. I apprised the board of Tom's seat on the board of Chase Manhattan Bank and offered countless details about his strong professional background. I spared no aspect of the deal's attractive potential returns.

Nevertheless, like the Beatrice deal, the board turned TAW down. In the final analysis, the same restrictions that Equitable had on foreign investments were applied. Again I was gravely disappointed. I called Tom to break the bad news.

"I'm very sorry about it," I told him, "and if there's anything else that I can do to help you, please let me know."

At that moment, I was ready to end the conversation, trying to prepare myself for the shockwaves of a tsunami of regrets and my own second-guessing regarding this tremendous opportunity thwarted by the rigid policies of Equitable. But before I could hang up, Tom interjected, "Obviously, I'm disappointed. But let me get back to you."

His words hung in my ear longer than they should have had as I wrestled frustration I was having making international deals that I was naturally inclined to make. Although I was exultant about the contributions the MESBIC was making to the growth of black-owned businesses domestically, I felt stymied in making great deals with a foreign flavor. For the first time, I began to wonder if this was the right place for me in the long term.

I gladly invited Tom into my office when he called the next day and asked to meet. As he arrived, I was riddled with guilt over my inability to finance his deal, but he, on the other hand, wore a smile bright with Tom Wood confidence.

"Frank, how would you like to join TAW?" he said in words so bold that they felt like they were conveyed in all CAPITAL letters as they crashed into my forehead. "We could really use someone with your banking, financial, and organizational skills. I know how much you love Africa and Hugh and Ernie feel you could add enormously to TAW."

He caught me completely off guard.

Before I could gather my thoughts, Tom went on. "Before you make a decision I want you to talk to Ernie. Why don't you go out to Nairobi to see him?"

I was stunned at his suggestion. Tom had obviously sensed that I had high hopes to finance his deal. My disappointment provided him an open window to offer me a major role in TAW. What I never came to know, or will likely never know, is whether this offer was some part of a deftly maneuvered Machiavellian plan. Had Tom genuinely hoped the MESBIC would invest in his deal, or was he recruiting me to TAW all along, or both?

I told him that I was honored by his proposition. Joining TAW had not been something I had contemplated. "I just wanted to help you pull off the Zambia project," I told him. "That said, I'm willing to go to Kenya to meet with Ernie to see how I can be of help, but I can't make any promises."

"Of course," Tom replied, smiling.

That evening, I told Beryl what happened and that I was going to Kenya to evaluate this opportunity. She was surprised that the TAW situation had developed so quickly. But I knew her as well as she knew me. I could tell that she was not surprised that I may be considering returning to Africa.

■ ■ ■

In the fall 1973, I flew off to Nairobi, which I had not visited since 1962 with Operation Crossroads Africa. Ernie and his wife, Evelyn, welcomed me at the airport with great enthusiasm. It was super to see Ernie again after so many years. He settled me in at the Nairobi Hilton then took me to the TAW office for a briefing on his East African operations and on the Zambian project.

Although I did my best not to reveal my hand during the trip, I knew I could not resist the chance to work with Ernie and Tom Wood, and to help Zambia overcome the South African blockade. The prospect of working with them was exciting. TAW had a truck and equipment leasing business in Abidjan and Nairobi, but what Zambia required dwarfed both of them.

Ernie and I flew to Zambia to meet with their major supporter in Zambia, Rupiah Banda, head of the government's agricultural production organization. Rupiah was a powerful man with a powerfully booming voice. He was a stern advocate of TAW and offered to do whatever was necessary to help the company succeed. He said the project was critical to Zambia's survival.

It was good to return to Zambia, which had not changed much since my Crossroads days.

As I flew back to the States, I knew Africa was part of my destiny and was already eager to go back. I could feel the winds building to drive me hard along this course. When I got back to New York, Tom told me that the trip had gone very well. Ernie and Rupiah were very enthusiastic about the prospect of my coming on board. Tom offered me the position of chief operating officer of TAW and head of the Zambian project. My initial focus would be setting up the Zambian operation and supporting Tom in the capital and bank financing efforts. I let Tom know I was very interested, but was nonetheless concerned about my lack of leasing experience. He assured me that I would have full access to all of TAWs experience and personnel.

Africa was my calling and now it was calling me. Had it not been for my bad experience with Carleton Stewart at Citibank and my urgent need to support black businesses in the United States, I may never have left the continent. But I felt that with Howard Mackey at the helm, the MESBIC was in good shape and it had skilled management to lead it forward without me.

I accepted Tom's offer.

Once I made this decision, I had the task of talking to my wife and to the CEO of Equitable. Beryl was very supportive. I took her on a trip to Zambia because I knew we may have to move there to run the project. I could see that she did not relish the prospect of living in a developing country once again. After the travails of living in Saudi Arabia and Liberia, I did not have the heart to ask her to go back overseas, especially to a place she might find a little sleepy, maybe even a little sleazy.

Beryl and I agreed that we would keep our base in New York and that I would commute back and forth to Africa.

Breaking the news to Equitable was much harder. I met privately with Coy Eklund and told him about how the TAW opportunity fell lightly into my lap. Coy was on the Chase board, so he knew Tom and was familiar with his Zambia project.

"Why don't you take a leave of absence, and then you can come back whenever you finish with the Zambian project?" he asked me. "We really think you have a bright future here at Equitable in the investment operations."

I was overwhelmed. To hear the CEO tell you that you have a "bright future" at a company the size of Equitable was too powerful to ignore. But I was compelled to be totally honest with him.

"I really appreciate that, Coy, but the fact of the matter is I don't intend to come back. It would be disingenuous and unethical of me to tell you that I'm planning on coming back when I'm not. I just don't think that's the right thing to do.

"I feel really blessed to have had the opportunity to work with Equitable and build the MESBIC. But at the same time, I want to go back to Africa and try to build TAW into a successful global transportation company. I know it's a risk, but it's one I'm willing to take."

Coy was visibly disappointed, but I think he respected my decision. He said he understood and said we should stay in touch. "We are always here for you," were his parting words.

This was the sign of a true leader and an ethical man. I knew that Equitable was the kind of company where I could potentially build a career because its leadership respected and cared for me. But I left the comfort and security of Equitable and set off for ever-seductive yet alluring Africa.

Frank in the African market in Abidjan, Ivory Coast, while chief operating officer with TAW International Leasing, 1973.

Three outstanding people ran TAW: In New York, Tom Wood, the founder, chairman and CEO; in Nairobi, Ernie Khalibala, the executive vice president responsible for the East African operation; in Abidjan, Mahmadou Mba, head of the West African operation. I was joining the company to head up the Zambian program.

The first thing that Tom did was to introduce me to the company's lawyer, a young, Jewish man named Alan Dynner with the law firm of Kirkpatrick & Lockhart in Washington, DC. He was a young partner in the firm and although not the principal partner on the TAW deal, he was assigned to do a lot of the grunt work. As Tom worked with Alan more and more, I think he came to realize that Alan had not only a brilliant legal mind but that he also had keen business judgment. The two of them worked extremely well together and by the time I joined TAW, Tom had substantial confidence in Alan.

While I met with some other partners at Kirkpatrick & Lockhart, the person I really collaborated with was Alan. He is my best friend today. We've known each other for more than 30 years; we know each other's families; we've supported each other though many life changes, including divorces, births, and deaths. I introduced him to sailing and he introduced me to scuba diving.

■ ■ ■

When I first joined TAW, I was intent on getting off to a solid start. I wanted to understand and know everything about TAW's current leasing operations so I could assess how I can use those operations to support the Zambia project. In retrospect, I should have had a total grasp of the scope and details of the other TAW businesses before I accepted Tom's offer.

Tom, Ernie, Mahmadou, and I met in New York to review the business segments. The more I learned about the East and West African leasing businesses, the more I became concerned; both had a high default rate, their customers were fairly new and they lacked sufficient accounting and managerial experience. This resembled the same problem that I had seen with African-American businesses in the United States. The weakness of the East and West African operations was a result of the poor quality of the leases. It dawned on me why Tom had pursued this business in Zambia. If he could successfully execute the Zambia project, it would become, by far, the major source of revenue for TAW, giving Tom and his company an entirely different financial footing.

During our New York meeting, I began to seriously question whether I had made the right decision in leaving Equitable. But the die was cast. There was no going back, only moving forward with TAW.

To understand TAW it is important to know a bit more about Tom Wood. He was not your average entrepreneur. The son of a Pullman train porter, Tom Wood was an honor student and basketball star at

Columbia University. Prior to founding TAW, he started another company, a data processing and systems analyst firm called Decision Systems Incorporated, or DSI, in 1960. He was 39. Tom went on to become the first black member of the board of directors of Chase Manhattan Bank. He was a rare and brilliant human being with an incredible personality and tremendous interpersonal skills. If he were a businessman today, he would definitely be the kind of person who could be the CEO of General Electric or any other major company. During his time, he did not have that opportunity. But these were the 1970s. Tom was ahead of his time. He had a broad vision of the world and like me, he loved Africa.

We all had a lot of confidence in Tom, but I could see that the leasing business he had built up in Africa was small and problematic. In the Zambian project, Tom was going for the gold. And so after we reviewed the leasing business, we talked about the Zambian project, which Tom and Ernie had overseen until I came on board. The project was in trouble. It was running behind on the deadlines they had given to the Zambian government and, as a result, they were at risk of losing the contract all together. In addition, many people wanted to see TAW fail.

But in Tom's estimation, we were well on our way to prosperity and he turned to me to clearly signal that he had faith that I could help pull it all together. I had mixed emotions about his outlook. I appreciated his confidence in me, yet I was not so sure that I had all the skills necessary that we needed to succeed. Tom had a special skill of inspiring people to believe in themselves and be loyal to him. Above all he made people want to succeed and never disappoint him.

I have to be honest. Tom inspired me. I was determined to see the Zambian project make it, regardless of what it might cost me.

We had serious enemies, principally the apartheid South African government. The thought of Zambia being able to avert its blockade by shipping copper to Kenya and Tanzania was unacceptable to South Africa's leaders.

The companies that had been providing trucks and buses to these African nations were mainly European, like British Leyland and Mercedes, which had a lock on the market. As a U.S. company, TAW was going to bring in compatriot companies like General Motors, Ford, Ryder, and Fruehauf. If we successfully provided trucks that were durable enough to overcome the treacherous African roads, we could gain significant advantages within the market, which the Europeans did not want. We also had rivals inside the Zambian government. There were various government officials who had benefited enormously from working with these traditional transportation companies, so they had a vested interest in our failure, too.

It was clear that TAW's Zambian project had political and commercial adversaries. The challenges seemed practically insurmountable, but Tom remained optimistic. He was confident that he had the support of Zambian President Kenneth Kauda and the majority of the Zambian government, who lauded him as the only person with a viable plan to get around this blockade. Yet, there was no escaping the fact that treacherous waters laid ahead.

From a business standpoint, our main challenge was a shortage of funds required to build out the necessary infrastructure. If the trucks were going to travel from the Copperbelt up to Kenya and Tanzania, there would have to be "truck stops" along the way, just like in the United States. We were responsible for building these facilities. Truckers would need a place to rest, refuel, and make repairs. The trips to Tanzania and Kenya were long (more than a 1,000-mile drive from Zambia) and difficult on poorly maintained roads. Moreover, the copper freight was extremely heavy so the trailers we would provide had to be very strong.

Customarily, private companies would only build the truck stops, while the government would build and maintain the roads. But these were urgent circumstances and the Zambian government didn't have the time or funds to maintain the roads. This is why TAW had to make sure the trucks were sturdily built to withstand the difficult road conditions. The truck stops would need to provide full service, with supplies and maintenance facilities in anticipation of breakdowns. This infrastructure had to be built out of our own capital before the contract was complete.

In other words, by the time we delivered those trucks, we had to have the entire physical and human infrastructure in place. Our contract included the estimated cost of building the infrastructure but overruns were common in a contract like this, which was unprecedented.

Because TAW had been unable to raise all of the necessary equity from institutional investors, a minimal amount came from "angel" investors with a promise to pay their investments back from the Zambia revenues or the other TAW leasing revenues. Therefore, we were forced to divert some of the cash flow from the existing leasing business to provide a portion of the working capital we needed for Zambia. Tom would go to Mahmadou in West Africa and Ernie in East Africa to draw down funds to support the Zambian project. Although they both cooperated, this put their businesses under serious financial stress. It was a gamble that Tom obviously thought would pay off.

Tom persuaded the suppliers of the trucks, trailers, and infrastructure to contribute working capital as well. He ensured them that TAW would buy their trucks in the future, thus providing them with a steady stream of new business from Africa. Before this phase of the project I had never actually seen this done, but I have come to learn that if the business prospects are attractive enough, it is very common for major equipment supply companies to provide financing, or even equity as bridge financing. These arrangements provided a much-needed additional source of the working capital

We were pushing hard to deliver the trucks and to have at least the minimum safe infrastructure established. I was constantly traveling from Zambia, Kenya, and New York, meeting with our banks and trying to put the project together. Tom and I stayed in constant contact to keep things moving. It was a taxing process, but we did have one thing going for us. The Zambian government appeared to continue to back us, especially the Permanent Secretary of the Ministry of Transportation, a career civil servant who ran the department and oversaw our project. We kept him fully informed on our progress. Tom had been candid with President Kaunda and the government about the enormous obstacles they faced in trying to get around the blockade. With the knowledge that Tom had their best interest at heart, the government appeared eager to work with us toward our common goal.

Regardless of this support, I became increasingly concerned about our ability to execute the project because we had not yet found a way to overcome TAW's equity shortage. Sensing my doubts, Tom called me one day in Zambia to reassure me. As usual, he was very convincing.

"I know we have challenges, but we can overcome them, Frank. That's why you're here. I want you to help me solve these problems. We have got to convince the banks to help us. They know and respect you, so I want you to attend the bank meetings with me.

"Ernie can support you overseeing the Zambian project while we try to solve this financing problem," he told me. It sounded good.

Tom, Ernie, and I made several trips to Zambia and always met with Rupiah Banda, our guy inside the Zambian government, to get his assessment of the government attitude.

"Well, hello, Frank Savage," Rupiah exclaimed in his thunderous voice. "I'm so glad you have joined TAW and I want you to know that we're going to give you every single bit of help that you need. I will use every influence that I have to help you be a success.

"I know full well that it's going to be a tough and demanding job," he continued, "but it's critical to the survival of Zambia that we make this work. I want to tell you that you have my full and unqualified support."

I was encouraged by his sincerity and intensity of support. He had great respect for Tom Wood, too, believing that Tom would be the savior of Zambia. Rupiah was well positioned within the government and in the business community; I knew he would make sure we obtained as much help as was possible. Rupiah Bwezani Banda was an amazing man who rose through the government ranks until he became president of Zambia in 2008. He was serving as vice-president when Zambia's then president, Levy Mwanawasa, suffered a stroke in June 2008. Rupiah became acting president after Mwanawasa died two months later. Rupiah won election in October 2008 and served until he was defeated by Michael Sata in September 2011.

While in office, Rupiah did an excellent job of shepherding the country through the current worldwide financial crisis. I was very proud of him.

TAW was constantly reevaluating its status on implementing the operational aspects of the Zambia project. We had so many balls in the air. Maintaining the Zambian government approval was top priority and, of course, we were constantly trying to finalize our financing. It was quite a handful, but we were motivated and determined to make this happen. Tom, Ernie, and I spent little time at home and this put additional pressure on our family situations. Tom appreciated our efforts and he was a constant cheerleader. He made sure we all would get together occasionally to have dinner and just blow off some steam. After one of those dinners we would all be flying high and ready to go.

Although I didn't have a background in leasing, I had extensive experience in building a business from anything at all. La Savage had shown me how it was done, starting her business from doing women's hair in my bedroom while I slept on the couch. I had started from the bottom at Citibank. I managed to get hands-on experience in Jeddah and then Liberia, all followed up by start-up experience at the MESBIC. I knew how to get things going. I now had to draw on that background big time.

With persistence and patience we put together our Zambian plans. I knew that I would have to establish relationships at Ryder, which was going to operate the truck fleet. It had the requisite experience in the United States, but this was its first foray into Africa. I needed to build a rapport with the key people I would be working with in Zambia.

I traveled to the Ryder office in Miami to review the Zambian plan and to be briefed on how Ryder intended to manage the fleet. The Ryder team was very impressive. We discussed the system that we had to put in place and even they were daunted by the challenge of creating the network of truck stops necessary to support the copper delivery operation.

We also reviewed the specifications required to build flatbed and covered trucks that were capable of carrying copper. The trucks typically used to transport goods within the United States were not configured to carry freight as cumbersome and heavy as copper. Nor were they configured for travel on dilapidated roads, African dilapidated roads. When we went out on a highway test drive in Zambia, we saw several trucks broken down and abandoned. It was not economically feasible to install a new road system, so we realized that we had to adapt to the given conditions. There were few truck drivers with the experience we needed so we had to train them. The trips were not only long, but dangerous. Copper was a valuable commodity, and there was a genuine possibility that these trucks would be hijacked and that some of these drivers could lose their lives.

Ryder was working with the truck manufacturer to design secure, fast trucks with sufficient weight-bearing capacity and durability. It was a formidable undertaking and I was struck by its perseverance in the face of such an arduous task. But the Ryder team was willing to work with us because they knew how lucrative this contract would be in both the near and distant future. They were among the supply companies that provided financing for the system.

Ryder's primary concern was the status of the contract. They knew that we had already missed deadlines called for in the initial contract, and Ryder's team was anxious about the probability of the Zambian government canceling the contract altogether. Tom assuaged Ryder's concerns, maintaining that we had a great relationship with the government and that we were the only game in town as far as producing a viable plan to overcome the blockade.

When you put Tom Wood in front of a customer or client, he was extremely convincing, even more so if our attorney Alan Dynner accompanied him. The businessman and the lawyer made an impressive team. As much experience as I had, Tom Wood gave the most impressive displays of business leadership under stress that I had ever seen. And still today, I would say that he had one of the strongest impacts on me—to watch him at work, the way he operated, how his mind worked, how he motivated us even in the face of stunning hardships. He's one of the savviest businessmen I've ever seen in my life, and he was not afraid to take risks. He was on par with any of the top executives of the companies we were working with at the time.

I was always amazed at how calm he could remain in negotiations with our bankers and suppliers. I knew that he was concerned about the outlook for the Zambian project, but he never ever showed any doubt that this project was going to work. He was the portrait of serene confidence. That kind of self-assured demeanor is what caused people to continue to support this project against all odds. I came to admire his battlefield calm, his steady hand, his clear eye.

I would go to all the meetings that he had with the banks, the Overseas Private Investment Corporation (OPIC), and the suppliers. Tom would assure them that we were building a strong management team. He often used me as an example in these meetings.

"We have just brought on Frank Savage, who comes to us after building an illustrious career as a young man, 32 years old. He's worked with Citibank in the Middle East, Africa, and New York. He built and ran the biggest minority small business investment company in America. He is part of a first-class management team, which we are putting in place to run projects like the Zambian contract." This inspired confidence among the bankers. It inspired me even further.

Tom also took great strides to empower the members of his TAW team. We were always meticulously prepared for these crucial meetings with the Zambians, banks, and suppliers. We spent countless hours mapping out our meeting strategy. With all the hurdles before us, there was no room for sloppiness. Tom certainly knew how to pump me up before a demanding meeting.

"Now, Frank, I want you to remember one thing: It's a great life if you don't weaken," he would say, invoking one of his inspirational "Tom Wood-isms" as I called them.

I was reminded of La Savage, who said the same things to me when I was growing up. She instructed me to always believe in myself, always have confidence in myself and never ever shirk from responsibility or challenge. In a way, Tom Wood personified La Savage's principles for me as I watched him work with such determination to make the Zambia deal happen no matter how high the waves crashed against it.

Tom assumed tremendous responsibility for his team, knowing that what he did would affect our lives. He fostered an atmosphere of hard work and trust. Along the way, the team became his family.

Tom Wood taught me about leadership and about overcoming odds. Those are the sort of lessons that you learn in life then tuck away, never really giving them a second thought until you run into a situation that demands their intuitive application. The TAW experience provided me, at a formative age in my career development, a framework to achieve some extraordinary successes, as well as cope and overcome the Enron crisis yet to come.

Although Tom had the Zambian government convinced that we were moving forward with all deliberate speed and precision, the process of putting in the project infrastructure was painfully slow because of our relatively meager financial resources. Yet the Zambian government continued to stand with us. Whenever we needed to get an extension on the contract dates, it granted it.

At the same time, Zambia was desperate to find a way, any way, around that South African blockade. The country absolutely had to ship the copper to market or it would have its own revenue problems. During the time of the blockade, world copper prices were high and Zambia had been exporting 700,000 tons of copper before South Africa closed its ports to Zambia.

Politically, the government adamantly opposed kicking the African National Congress (ANC), black South Africa's chief opposition to minority rule, out to appease the South Africa apartheid government. Instead, Zambia's leadership seemed more steadfast in its determination to withstand the pressure from South Africa. But we were working against the clock to put this project in place before the Zambian government sought other options.

We pressed on knowing what set TAW apart; we understood the profound implications of our success, not only for ourselves but also for Zambia and the entire world. This was not just a business venture, not just a way to make money, but a way to change lives. Accomplishing the Zambian project would be a game changer, shattering the popular notion that blacks could not rise to the global level of business. Tom, Ernie, Mahmadou, Alan, and I could demonstrate that an international, multiracial team could build an operation that rivaled any of the major companies in the world.

With our sophisticated financial and legal backgrounds, we all thought and aspired to act on a global scale. We were not thinking small potatoes, half a loaf. We dared to dream much bigger. I think dreams are vital. Without them, nothing happens. Over our many incredible dinners, Tom would carry us away with his dream of TAW, about where we were going to take this company.

"Look, guys," Tom would say. "This is going to be tough. This is not going to be easy, but think about the rewards if we succeed. Think about what we can do. Think about where we can take this company. Think about the history that we'll be making."

More than 20 years later, I would employ the same practice of giving motivational speeches to my team at Equitable Capital and my triumphant racing team aboard my sailboat, Lolita. It's like Mark Twain once said, "Really great people make you feel that you, too, can become great."

Tom had already shared his TAW dream with OPIC, the quasi U.S. government agency that helps U.S. companies gain markets outside of the United States. A Zambian project led by a U.S. company was right up its alley. OPIC assigned Sheldon Gittleman to work with TAW. He earnestly believed in the Zambian project, but characteristic of a government official, he thought and operated conservatively. Still harboring memories of La Savage's early experience with the government, I was highly skeptical of OPIC. Yet, I also had fond memories of the assistance that Angier Biddle Duke and Pedro Galban at the State Department gave me when I needed help to fund my Crossroads Africa trip.

As it turned out, OPIC gave us a wealth of support. Tom escorted Giddleman to Zambia on a field trip to inspect the project. Our objective was to show Sheldon the progress we had made, introduce him to the local government officials and to Rupiah Banda, and to take him to the Copperbelt. Sheldon was a mild-mannered, quiet man who seemed honest and genuine. It was the 1970s when Ernie, Rupiah, and I first met Sheldon and I seriously doubted he had ever done business with either an African-American or African company. But I think he was comforted by the fact that we were all highly educated, experienced, and well trained by New York banks. Ultimately, OPIC agreed to provide TAW with working capital financing.

Everything began to take shape. With the OPIC financing that we had somehow miraculously pulled together, we ordered half of the trucks and trailers that we needed for the Zambia project. We accelerated our plans to construct the truck stops and maintenance centers needed to service the trucks on their long, hard journey. Finally, we breathed a slight sigh of relief. Tom, appreciating that this was a time to quietly celebrate our breakthrough, gathered us for one of our dinners.

In his inimitable way, Tom thanked us, adding his catch phrase, "It's a great life if you don't weaken." But that moment of jubilation was brief.

■ ■ ■

We arranged a meeting with the Permanent Secretary in the Ministry of Transportation to update him on progress. Having put together the OPIC financing and submitted partial orders for the fleet of trucks, we were feeling very good about ourselves as we entered his office. But we were not naive to the Zambian government's desperation to get the copper transportation underway. In an effort to reassure him we were moving forward, we gave him a complete briefing. He listened intently.

At the end of our presentation, he said with solemnity and concern, "Tom, I'm so happy to hear that you're making this progress because, quite frankly, I'm under a lot of pressure."

Fearing the worst, Tom coolly inquired, "What kind of pressure?"

"We can't wait any longer and a lot of people in other government departments don't think that TAW is capable of delivering on the contract. They are arguing that we should begin to pursue other ways to export the copper. Some even suggest we should turn back to our traditional suppliers such as British Leyland."

I thought to myself, Oh my God our competitors are trying to close in for the kill.

But Tom Wood made another one of his tour de force performances and responded confidently, "Look, I know that Zambia has a critical need to get these trucks on the road, and we are committed to accomplishing that goal. We are well on our way to implementing the project, which is a unique one. As I said from the beginning, it would be difficult to raise the financing, design the proper vehicles, and build out the infrastructure.

"But TAW was prepared to take on the challenge because we understand how urgent it is for Zambia to overcome the South African blockade. This is a fight against apartheid, which we both must win. That was our motivation to take this on.

"We are now at a critical juncture! The trucks and the trailers are being manufactured as we speak. As a matter of fact, Frank will take you to the port of Baltimore within the next three months to physically show you the trucks waiting to be shipped to Zambia. We're on the verge of making this thing happen."

Maintaining an amazing cool, Tom continued, "Frank Savage has come here to run this program. He's putting it together. We've got a lot of bankers supporting us. If you want to talk to our bankers, you may do so. If you want to talk to our suppliers, you may do so. But we are on our way. Please don't stop us now."

The Permanent Secretary was visibly moved. "The Zambian people appreciate TAW's commitment and I'm happy to hear about your progress," he told Tom, and added that although the government was anxious to get the copper moving, he would give TAW another three-month extension. He also accepted Tom's offer to have me show him the trucks in Baltimore. "If," the Permanent Secretary said, "I can tell my superiors that the trucks are about to get on the high seas, I believe Zambia will continue to support TAW."

As Tom and I left the Secretary's office I whispered, "My God, we just dodged a bullet!"

He cautioned me not to be overconfident. "You heard what he said. We've got a lot of detractors inside this government who don't want us to succeed. They know we're feeling the financial pressure and this is their opportunity to try to reclaim this business."

Tom told me that the team couldn't relax for a minute, that we had to work more closely with our suppliers. I was told to fly back to the States, sit down with Ryder and GM and push them to deliver these trucks to us as soon as possible.

"Those companies can't just interrupt their production line all of a sudden and put our trucks first," I protested.

"Look, even if these trucks don't meet all of the specifications, we need to get some trucks in the country to demonstrate that we can deliver. Then we can organize a pilot project to show the capability of our trucks. We've got to begin to put this together now! Get to it."

I had my marching orders and knew how vital it was that I fulfill them. I rushed back to the States, sat down with our manufacturers, and impressed on them the urgency to produce some trucks and deploy them to Zambia as soon as possible. I impressed on them that we had no more than three months. Both GM and Fruehauf understood, and because it was in their interest to keep the contract alive, they did, in fact, alter their production schedules to expedite the TAW fleet.

Miraculously, within less than three months, we had shipped a contingent of approximately 30 trucks and trailers to Baltimore Harbor. The Permanent Secretary was pleasantly surprised when I called him from Baltimore to tell him we were ready to receive him on an inspection tour—as promised. He had put his neck on the line by continuing to give us extensions, clearly hoping all along that TAW would succeed. I flew back to Zambia to escort him to the States and when he saw the nearly 30 TAW trucks and cabs ready for shipment, he seemed vindicated in his faith in TAW and I took a moment to exhale.

As we exited the harbor, the Permanent Secretary said, "I am so glad to see this. I'm going to go back to Zambia and give you another extension."

We were given another three to five months to deliver the trucks to Zambia.

I flew back to New York to brief our bankers, suppliers, and OPIC; all were relieved and pledged to continue their support. It was important that I made them aware that we had another contract extension because without their cooperation we never would have been able to get the vehicles to Baltimore. Thankfully, we had put out the fire, so we could get back to building out the infrastructure. But we were not out of the crosscurrents yet.

A month later, Tom received a call from our colleagues in Zambia, reporting that there was a rumor that the TAW contract was going to be canceled. Since the Permanent Secretary had just recently extended the contract, this caught us by complete surprise. How could this be? Tom immediately called Rupiah who confirmed that such rumors were circulating and that they were part of our competitors' ferocious effort to discredit TAW with Zambian government officials.

Tom immediately sought a meeting with President Kenneth Kaunda. Tom had met him on many occasions and he was very supportive, but Tom could not get an appointment. This caused us great anxiety.

Shortly thereafter, we received a fateful, dreaded message in New York: an official Termination of Contract Letter, dated before our extension date and signed by the Minister of Transportation rather than the Permanent Secretary.

This was a tremendous blow, the one we had feared the most. We were obligated to inform the banks, OPIC, and our suppliers. Their reaction was swift. The suppliers ceased the shipment of additional vehicles to Zambia and the production of new vehicles. The banks and OPIC canceled all further discussions about financing the Zambian project pending resolution of the cancellation. The project, which we hoped would catapult TAW into a new business stratosphere, now threatened to destroy the company all together. We immediately requested a meeting with the Zambian government to discuss the cancellation. Once it agreed, we had to develop our strategy. Tom came to me then, in confidence.

"Frank, I think that you and Alan should go to this first meeting. Rupiah is working hard behind the scenes to get the action reversed," he said, his voice low and somber. But if he fails, he cannot go to the meeting on our behalf because he is technically a government employee.

"See if you can get a sense of where they stand and probe them to see if there is a willingness to negotiate," he said, no smiles. "Obviously, we want to do everything we can to get them to rescind this cancellation notice."

He said that after the initial meeting, we could decide our next step.

I agreed with Tom's plan, but I was racked with anxiety. Was everything we had fought for about to crash and crumble?

Tom and I went to Washington to strategize with Alan. If we sensed the government was using the cancellation to improve or change the contract terms then we were willing to make significant changes. That would be a good outcome because the contract would be restored. Alternatively, if they just wanted to terminate once and for all, the implications for TAW were disastrous. The company may even have to file for bankruptcy. As we were dealing with a sovereign government rather than a business entity, we could not be sure of its intentions. This was new territory for us. Although the contract had an arbitration clause, the government could potentially refuse to honor it. All in all, our options were not good, but renegotiating the terms to keep the contract in place was the ideal scenario, even if we did not generate the initially projected profits.

A few days before we were scheduled to leave for Zambia, Alan had a devastating family emergency. He needed to be home. Understandably, Alan's focus switched from TAW's crisis to his family's crisis. Despite his commitment to TAW, he pulled out of the trip. Tom understood.

We were now at a significant disadvantage because our strategy hinged on me and Alan attending the meeting together—the businessman and the lawyer one-two punch. Alan knew the contract backward and forward and he was a good negotiator. More importantly, after working together for more than a year, we had built a great dynamic team.

Tom seriously considered going to the first meeting in Alan's stead, but after much internal discussion we decided against this. Alan strongly recommended that his partner, Joe Brigati, go in his place. Joe had not worked day-to-day on the TAW case, but he was Alan's backup and had kept totally up-to-date on any developments. Alan also believed Joe's facile negotiation tactics would prove valuable under these circumstances.

We also considered asking for a postponement to give Alan's family a chance to recover, but we quickly eliminated that option as well. To say we wanted to reschedule the meeting could be construed as an admission of defeat, and our enemies could take advantage to level a knockout blow. It was settled. Joe and I would represent TAW in the initial meeting—as scheduled.

We were somewhat concerned about Joe's lack of international experience. This was his first trip to Africa and his practice was mostly in domestic corporate matters. Still, Joe was an excellent lawyer and, like Alan, was one of the youngest partners at their firm. We were well represented. Thankfully, he agreed to go, although I'm sure he had some trepidation. Alan thoroughly briefed him, and then we set off to Zambia.

I could tell that our team in Zambia was relieved when we arrived. The rumors had put them under considerable stress. But outwardly they maintained a positive demeanor and tried to encourage us about the possibility of getting the cancellation rescinded. Joe and I immediately met with Ruphia to introduce him to Joe and get his assessment of the situation. Things were not going well. Apparently, once our detractors learned that the Permanent Secretary had seen the completed trucks, they knew that if they didn't make a definitive move to push us out at that moment then they would never be able to stop us. The Permanent Secretary had been overruled and was not permitted to give TAW another extension. We may never know exactly how our enemies pulled that off.

The Zambian representatives at the meeting included legal counsel and Ministry of Transportation officials including the Permanent

Secretary. At the outset of the opening session, I emphasized our surprise at receiving the cancellation notice dated before the official Ministry of Transportation extension date. I spent considerable time advising them of what we had done to meet the contract requirements, referring to the Permanent Secretary's inspection trip to Baltimore where he had seen not only the first contingent of vehicles ready for shipment but also infrastructure assembly and driver training. Under these circumstances we couldn't understand the cancellation of the contract. The room was tense with negative energy. Strangely enough, the Permanent Secretary did not speak a word.

Finally, the government's lawyer spoke.

"Thank you for your presentation, but the fact remains that TAW did not meet the obligations of the contract therefore it was cancelled."

He made no mention of the extension at all. In essence, the Zambian Ministry of Transportation was ignoring its own official extension letter. As far as we were concerned, the session was off to a bad start and growing worse by the minute.

I asked them if there was anything that we could do to renegotiate, as we were on the verge of delivering the first fleet of trucks to Zambia. We knew how instrumental these trucks were to circumventing the South African blockade. I gave what I thought was a compelling argument, but I could tell that my words were falling on deaf ears and minds already made up. So Joe and I decided to take a break. We excused ourselves to speak privately.

"These guys are not going to move," Joe said. "It doesn't seem to me like there's anything that you can do to convince them. They met with us, but only as a formality, not to try to find a way to restore this contract."

He said the government simply wanted out. "The vibes they're giving off, the fact that the lawyer is the only one talking, the fact that your biggest supporter, the Permanent Secretary, is not saying a word," he noted. "These are all bad signs, Frank. I don't think there's any hope of changing their minds."

I agreed with his interpretation, but I suggested we defer to Tom before going further. We were granted an adjournment until the next day. That afternoon, we called Tom. I led the conversation with Joe by my side, relaying the bad news.

Tom was terribly disappointed. It was unbelievable to all of us that an impoverished country like Zambia would willingly assume the damages and fines for illegally terminating a contract, not to mention the harm to its reputation in the capital markets and its relationship with the United States.

Needing time to absorb all of this, and to contemplate the next steps, Tom instructed us, for the meantime, to continue pushing for a renegotiation and to refer to the legal aspects only as a last resort to bring Zambia around. Even though we were confident that the government would renegotiate if we resorted to arbitration, this was not our goal.

Nonetheless, we needed to remind the Zambians of the consequences of arbitration without appearing threatening.

As we prepared the next morning, Joe said, "Frank, as your lawyer, I must remind you of something. We are negotiating here with a sovereign government. They can essentially do whatever they want to do."

In short, he said, the government could declare sovereign immunity and decide not to go forward, even with arbitration.

His advice gave me a nasty dose of reality. The Zambian government would have to agree to renegotiate, regardless of what was in the contract. And so we went back into the meeting. I led the discussion, the big showdown.

"Gentlemen," I began, "TAW is willing and able to execute the contract. We want to reiterate the extensive preparations we have undergone and the significant financial and other obligations we have incurred to carry out the contract. If Zambia does not honor the contract, we will suffer astounding financial risk and losses to the company. Moreover and most important, Zambia will run the risk of being unable to ship the copper out of the country. The contract must be continued to benefit the people of Zambia."

Despite my passionate entreaty, we were met with the same stony expressions as we had faced during the initial meeting. There was an uneasy moment of silence clearly indicating that we were going to accomplish nothing.

Joe interjected, "Before we conclude the meeting, it is my obligation to remind you of the provisions of the contract, which say that in the event of a dispute, if it cannot be resolved amicably between the partners, the issue will be remanded to the International Court of Justice in London whereupon three judges to be selected by the parties will decide the outcome of the contract and whether or not any damages should be awarded.

"Now, we don't want to go to arbitration," he said in a voice ripe with even tones. "We want to continue to execute under the contract. That is our wish."

Joe went on to explain that TAW did not believe that the cancellation was in keeping with the contract. He said that the government's refusal to rescind the cancellation or be willing to renegotiate its terms left us no choice but to reluctantly go to arbitration. Then he pulled out all the stops.

"Let me repeat that TAW is prepared to go to any lengths to avoid legal action," he explained. "It's bad for Zambia, TAW, the U.S./ Zambia relations and the citizens of our respective countries. There must be a way out of this impasse."

Much to our despair, there was no reaction from the Zambian representatives until their lawyer definitively stated, "Mr. Brigati, we fully understand the contract provisions."

That was it.

■ ■ ■

The Zambians were not going to budge from their position. The meeting was disbanded. I walked out of the government building in disbelief. Was this the same Zambia that I had visited in the summer of 1962? The country I so deeply wanted to help to defeat apartheid? I was heartbroken that my African brothers would do this to a sympathetic African-American company. They had crushed us.

Joe tried to console me.

We knew the ramifications for the project and for TAW in general were dire. We immediately called Tom and told him about the outcome. For the first time since I had begun working with Tom, his voice betrayed a deep dismay. I felt I had let him down; I think he was confident that I could turn the Zambians around, and set things up for him to come into a second meeting and renegotiate the terms. But I could not pull that off, and now we were faced with a totally different and perilous predicament.

"Frank, I need you to come back to New York to sit down with me and develop a strategy for next steps," he said. "In the event we end up having to go to arbitration, we must keep TAW alive until that time, which hopefully will be more than a year."

In the meantime, he said, he was going to talk to Rupiah and some of our other advocates in the Zambian government to try to find some last ditch way to turn the situation around.

As I traveled back to New York, I was deep in thought. What is TAW's future? Will Zambia honor the arbitration clause? Will the TAW team stay together until arbitration? Can I trust Africa? Is the continent ready to do business with African Americans? All of these questions swirled round and round in my conscience throughout my fitful sleep as I crossed the Atlantic.

Tom made one last valiant effort to change the minds of the Zambians. He talked to several people, but not even the ever-persuasive Tom Wood could convince them to rescind the cancellation order. When it became clear that the contract wasn't going to be restored, I became very despondent. We were back in New York by this time and I will never forget Tom's reaction to my expressions of disbelief and defeat.

"Let me tell you how the world works," he said wistfully. "Many people in a position of power follow the mantra 'For my friends, accommodation. For my enemies, the law.'" He punctuated his pronouncement with a raised fist.

Perhaps he was suggesting that somebody in a high position in the Zambian government decided that it was in his best interest to cancel the contract. It didn't matter how negative the impact might be on the country. Some person or persons benefited enormously from the cancellation, and that was that.

I was distraught, troubled, and profoundly disappointed. I coughed up a confession.

"Tom, I'm leaving Africa," I said, my voice low but building strength. "But I'm not leaving forever. I'm going to come back and when I do, I'm not going to need anything from anybody.

"I'm going to be able to execute with my own resources," I told Tom, who began to smile. "When that will happen, I don't know. But for now, I have to leave Africa."

The experience obviously left me greatly disenchanted. Though I hate to make generalizations, I'm a human being, and with all the sacrifices that we had made and all the work that we had done, this conclusion devastated me. I had to leave Africa.

Tom asked me to stay on with TAW so we could continue to fight the cancellation and try to win the arbitration. I believe he asked me largely because I was a banker and I had a close friendship with Hughlyn Fierce, who was leading the banking group at Chase. But I didn't have my heart in any of this anymore. But Tom persisted.

I ended up promising him that I would stay with TAW and try to restructure the company and negotiate with the banks to forebear our loans until the arbitration. But at some point I needed to get back to New York and figure out what I was going to do next. He nodded that he understood.

Our new challenge was keeping the company alive until we went to arbitration. We were absolutely confident there was no way we could lose. The facts were on our side. The contract had been terminated while the extension was still in place, with almost two months remaining. With the sizeable losses we had incurred, we needed to win the arbitration to pay off these obligations. We were talking about millions of dollars.

The mainstream press hardly seemed to notice our plight. But the black press did cover our business travails in Zambia. *Jet* magazine, the news weekly published by John H. Johnson's Johnson Publishing ran an article in its May 16, 1974, issue. The cover featured a picture of a contemplative Angela Davis.

The headline read: Black Firm Suffers Loss of $22 Million in Africa.

I started to formulate a survival plan and visited most of the various branches of TAW International Leasing, both in East and West Africa. I had to gather information about the cash flow we could generate to service the outstanding loans we would have with Chase Bank, First National Bank of Chicago, and OPIC as a result of the cancellation.

I presented the plan to Tom, Ernie, and Mamadou. I figured that we could probably survive for about a year. My plan required a major overhaul of the business, including closing offices and layoffs. It would be tough to implement, but it was absolutely necessary for the company to survive until the arbitration. We needed to push for arbitration within that yearlong period. After that, all bets were off.

The team bought into the plan, which entailed some draconian cuts and the assumption, which proved to be accurate, that the arbitration would be ruled in our favor within the year. But then we had to ask ourselves the larger question: Where do we go from here? Assuming we won the arbitration, about $5 to $10 million was all we could reasonably expect the arbitrators to award us. So even if we won, the long-term viability of the company was questionable. And I personally had some concerns about whether TAW could afford me. I was being paid about $200,000 a year.

I confronted Tom on this very issue.

"I think that after the restructuring, you may be better off without me because then you will not have the burden of my salary expense," I told him. "I think it's best that I get back into the finance business in New York. I'll be there for you at the arbitration if you need me but I don't think it makes sense for me to stay on while we wait for the arbitration."

Tom asked me to just focus on the restructuring for now and we would revisit my situation later. I thought that was reasonable.

I hired my New York colleague, Seth Dei, a brilliant Ghanaian MBA from Mass Mutual Life Insurance Company. Together we met with the banks and OPIC at Chase Manhattan Bank to present the restructuring plan for their approval. After my presentation, the bank executives asked for us to reconvene after lunch.

That afternoon, Hughlyn Fierce opened the meeting. "We reviewed your plan, and we would be prepared to change the terms of the servicing of your loans for a period of a year until the arbitration. We would even consider giving you a further extension if your plans don't work."

I was ecstatic.

"But Frank," he went on, "we have one condition. We want you to replace Tom Wood as the CEO of TAW International Leasing and run the company."

"Wait a minute," I said, utterly shocked. "I'm not looking to take over TAW, and I'm certainly not seeking to advance myself at the cost of a remarkable black-American businessman like Tom Wood, who has my utmost respect."

"We hear you and we respect you, but those are our conditions," Hughlyn replied.

Unbeknownst to the bankers, I was preparing to leave TAW after the restructuring; their unexpected request left me in a difficult situation. Undoubtedly, this was an opportunity to take over TAW, refinance it through the banks, and expand it. I had no doubt in my mind that I could do this. At the same time, I was greatly disillusioned about the Zambia situation, concerned about the business opportunities in Africa, and skeptical about TAW's future. Moreover, as much as I loved Africa, I felt the continent was not ready for an African-American businessman to come in and replace the Western Europeans Africans had grown accustomed to and depended on.

Beyond all of that, I was loyal to Tom Wood and the idea of my pushing him out of his own company was totally implacable to me, not to mention that I could not stomach a falling out between us. I didn't want to flat out refuse the bankers for fear that they would pull the plug entirely, so I asked for time to contact Tom in Nairobi. They agreed to speak with us again the following day.

Seth and I were both speechless as we rode in the taxicab from Chase to the TAW office at 866 UN Plaza on Manhattan's East River. The banks had thrown us a knuckle ball. How was I going to handle it? Seth saw this as an opportunity to save TAW. He thought the banks would probably agree to a total recapitalization of TAW if I met their condition of becoming the CEO. He, too, was unaware of my plans to leave the company. And he obviously didn't have the same issue of my respect and closeness to Tom to consider.

I had to make Tom aware of this development and think it over for myself. I went back to the office, took a deep breath, and called Tom. What followed was one of the most difficult calls of my professional life.

"Tom, I have some good news and some bad news."

"Well, tell me what the good news is."

"The bank accepted the plan that we submitted to them."

"And what's the bad news?"

"Their approval is contingent upon my replacing you as CEO."

There was a palpable silence on the other end of the phone, and I knew right away that our conversation was going over a cliff from there.

"What did you tell them, Frank?"

"I told them that this was not what I had in mind, and that I'm not interested in being the CEO of the company, but I would discuss it with you. I didn't want to close the door completely because I didn't know how an outright refusal would affect TAW. Tom, you and I have talked about my future with the company and the future for TAW and, as you know, I am really disappointed by what happened in Zambia. I'm not convinced that I even have it in me to conduct business in Africa because I still haven't gotten over that."

Tom suggested I come to Nairobi to talk with him further. He didn't say anything else one way or another and I agreed to fly over. I notified the bankers that although we were pleased they accepted our plan, their condition that I replace Tom was one that needed to be discussed internally.

■ ■ ■

I immediately flew to Nairobi, Kenya to meet with Tom, Ernie, and Mahmadou. As soon as I walked into Erie's office and looked into Tom's eyes, I knew this was not going to be a happy meeting. Rather than their usual warm and jovial demeanors, Tom and Ernie were dead calm and chilly to me. They just looked at me with businesslike stares that made me wish I were somewhere else. Tom asked me to repeat what happened at the bankers meeting. I did, stressing how shocked I was by the bank's condition.

"Tom, I am not in any way interested in replacing you," I told everyone in the room. "It has never entered my mind, and I would never do anything to undermine you. As you know, I want to help you to get through this transitional phase, as I promised. But I am planning to return to New York. I just want to help you to win the arbitration."

Tom listened but I sensed he was skeptical of my motives. I think he suspected Hughlyn Fierce and I were teaming up against him. Nothing could have been further from the truth. I admired Tom; he was one of my role models. Plus, sabotage is not the way I do business. In addition, I was young compared to him— I was 33, he was fast approaching 50.

Looking back on this now, I honestly think Tom, Ernie, and Mahmadou thought that I had conspired against them, that I saw this crisis as an opportunity to take over TAW then go back to the bank and extract not only enough money to get it through the crisis and a commitment to get more capital available as a condition of my running the company. These thoughts never occurred to me much less came up in discussion with the banks. I can understand how Tom could have felt that way, but it pained me deeply that I had lost his trust. Even though this was a trying moment for me, I remained calm in the storm.

"Here's what I recommend," I offered. "We get back to the banks and tell them we cannot not accept their condition that I replace you because it would imperil the company and weaken our position in the arbitration."

There is a risk they may reject us, I told Tom, but I think we should offer it. "Regardless of what happens, I'll stick to my plan to restructure the company and leave TAW at a suitable time."

"Okay," Tom said. "That's fine." But at that moment I knew that our friendship and professional relationship were forever changed. I held my hurt inside.

I flew back to New York and met with the bankers to relay our decision.

Surprisingly, Hughlyn responded, "We don't like it but we'll work with you guys, and we'll give you as much leeway as we think is prudent."

Frankly, I don't think the banks wanted the bad publicity that may have resulted from firing Tom. Although pleased by this decision, Tom remained distant toward me. Nonetheless, at that point I did what I promised and began restructuring the company, which proved to be an unpleasant job indeed.

■ ■ ■

One of the branches I visited was in Bamako, Mali, a desert city with a distinctive Arab feel to it, which was once part of the African gold and slave trading route. The office really had never made money, and although we speculated that some employees might have been skimming money from the company, we were reluctant to take punitive action because the head of the office was the nephew of a powerful general who supposedly led a successful coup against the former president.

Everybody was fearful about confronting the head of the Bamako office, but a colleague in the Abidjan office was willing to go with me.

He and I agreed that rather than just barging in and firing him, we would first have to meet with his uncle, the General. I was a little reluctant about it, but we went anyway. The General had this huge, incredible office reminiscent of Versailles, which spoke volumes about his power and position in Mali.

"General, I wanted to see you in regards to some upcoming changes at the TAW office," I said, trying not to sound tentative. "Due to business pressures, we're going to have to close the office and terminate the staff, including your nephew."

"I'm very disappointed that TAW will be leaving Mali," the General informed us. "I'm even more disappointed by the fact that this will lead to the termination of my nephew. Mali will continue to support TAW if you decide to stay. We are also prepared to support your business financially, on the condition that my nephew stays on."

"I'm very sorry," I replied, "but while we appreciate your support, we just can't agree to keep him on staff because we have had some issues with him."

"Mr. Savage, I'm going to ask you again. Please try to find a way to keep the office open and salvage my nephew's job," he said sternly.

I paused for a moment and then answered, "As I said, I'm afraid that business will not permit us to comply with you. We've reached agreements with our bankers and lenders, which we are obligated to live up to."

He looked at me dead in the eye.

"Mr. Savage, you do what you have to do, and I will do what I have to do."

As my colleague and I left his office, naive of the nature and implication of the General's comments, I commented, "Well, that wasn't pleasant but I think he accepted our decision."

In a cold sweat my colleague snapped back, "He just threatened us!"

"Is that what you think he was doing?"

"No question about it," he said. "When he said he will 'do what he has to do,' he was making an open threat." Petrified, he explained that for the General this was all a matter of pride for him. He had offered us financial assistance provided that his nephew got to keep his job. "You rejected his offer. He can't allow that to happen."

As his words sank in, I couldn't help but think what an idiot I was not to recognize his ultimatum. I had to think quickly. I didn't want to endanger my life or the life of my colleague so I decided that I could not execute the plan. It just wasn't worth putting ourselves in danger. I met the General again the following day.

"General, we value our relationship with Mali and have decided to accept your gracious offer of financial and business assistance. We will not close the Mali office and your nephew will remain on staff. But we urge you to please speak with him and advise that he refrain from any activities he may be taking part in, which would be injurious to the financial condition of TAW."

"Thank you, Mr. Savage," he said with charm replacing menace in his tone. "I could tell you were a reasonable man. I personally assure that all will go well for TAW in Mali."

That evening, my colleague and I were so relieved when our plane for Abidjan took off. Back on the Ivory Coast, we recounted our close encounter to our co-workers, one telling me, "You were lucky to get out of there alive."

Chapter 8

Walking Over a Bridge Not Burned

Goodness is the only investment that never fails.

—*Henry David Thoreau*

Shortly after implementing the restructuring plan for TAW Leasing International, I decided it was time to leave the company. I called up Coy Eklund, the chief executive officer at Equitable Life and requested a meeting. He welcomed the visit. Coy was already aware of the recent developments.

"It sounds to me like TAW did everything it could to exercise that contract," Coy reassured me. "I knew that you were determined to do this. I really did. That's why I didn't want to stand in your way.

"But, at the same time, you know, I knew the challenges that you were going to face," he said, his voice and manner almost fatherly. "This is why I wanted to give you the option of coming back. You still have that option."

I felt my thanks before I could say it. He went on to ease the sense of failure over the whole TAW affair.

"You should not at all be disappointed in yourself or think that you have failed," Coy told me. "Dealing with countries that are still in an early stage of their economic development, these things are inevitable. I respect you for your effort in Zambia, but we'd love to have you back here at the Equitable. You know that."

"Thank you, Coy," I finally managed. "What role would you have in mind for me?"

Coy suggested we take some time to think about it and talk in a few days. I left the meeting thanking God that I didn't burn the Equitable bridge when I left to join TAW.

In the meantime my Equitable buddy, Darwin Davis, let me know that Coy had an exciting position for me at Equitable's parent company in the works. Coy invited me back to his office after a few days.

He began by telling me that Jack Fey, the chairman of the board, could use someone with my investment and financial skills to act as a liaison between the two of them and the company's investment divisions. "Quite frankly," he said, "we're mainly insurance people. We have a limited understanding of the investment strategies and allocations."

Coy said that I could really help them stay on top of that and ask questions that they might not think to ask. "So," he said, "we'd like to offer you a position on the staff as the investment liaison officer to the chairman of the board and the chief executive officer. We hope that you'll accept."

I listened with great interest as he continued, "You will be seated with us on the 38th floor and will attend all of the investment meetings as our representative."

This was an incredible opportunity. Working for and representing the chairman and the CEO, I would not only have an open door to the investment operations, but I would be interacting with the investment divisions under their imprimatur. I was well aware of how much power that would bring to me at Equitable. This is what had brought me to the company initially—to learn about their investment operations after being introduced to Equitable by my brother-in-law. Accepting Coy's offer was a no-brainer.

"Coy, thank you very much. I really appreciate this," I said. But I accepted with one request. I explained that I am an operations person, someone used to getting his hands dirty and being involved. As generous as the liaison post was, I realized that it was a staff position. I asked if I could work in the post from one to two years and then be permitted to transfer into the private placement or fixed income departments.

This will give me a chance to work on investments at a highly sophisticated level, something I always wanted to do.

"Frank, that is a given," Coy said. "I will talk to the people in the investment department. If they agree to it, then that will be a given."

Needless to say, they agreed to my terms. Coy gave me a royal introduction. He publicly announced my new position in the company newsletter and presented me to the full board and the investment committee.

■ ■ ■

I had now come full circle with Equitable, having joined in 1970 to set up a successful Minority Enterprise Small Business Investment Companies, leaving with TAW in the aborted Zambia project and returning to work for its chairman and CEO. I was also asked to chair the board of the MESBIC, which was being exceptionally led, as I knew it would be, by Howard Mackey and his team.

I had left Equitable on excellent terms and learned a valuable lesson: You never know when your journey may take you back over that bridge you didn't burn. I did what I felt was the right thing—I chose not to play games with Equitable and tell them I was coming back. I left with no intentions of returning and I told them that and I think they appreciated my honesty.

But the negative consequence of this experience was that I became disenchanted with prospects for Swan business in Africa, and it took me a long time to get over that. As for TAW, it did hold itself together even if by the thinnest of lines. It was not until five years later that arbitration took place at the International Chamber of Commerce in London.

TAW International Leasing vs. the Government of Zambia.

Tom Wood, Alan Dynner, and I went to London for the arbitration. I was the last of us to take the stand and by the time I did, it was so clear that Zambia was at fault that the Zambians actually caved in and gave us an offer to settle the arbitration. TAW had won. The company received a substantial financial award but the question still remained: What happens to TAW now? Our victory was bittersweet, a defeat against a black African country was never what we wanted. The apartheid regime of South Africa may have won this battle but they never got Zambia to expel the ANC and we all know ultimately what happened. That evil regime collapsed, replaced by a majority government first led by Nelson Mandela as its president.

I think those five years took their toll on Tom Wood. He too had lost his desire to return to Africa and start TAW all over again. The company never really dissolved, but it went into a dormant stage, a long sleep from which it never fully awakened.

It was not the end that I had hoped for, but I had gained enormous experience in leasing, project management, restructuring a company, and persevering through adversity. I also gained a lifelong friend in Alan Dynner. By far, the greatest single benefit of my TAW years was working alongside Tom Wood.

After some time, my Zambian wounds began to heal and I found myself pursuing business once again in Africa. I could no longer stay away from Africa than I could stay away from my family. Africa is part of my soul. Nothing can change that.

■ ■ ■

During my first year on the Equitable staff I had the unique opportunity to observe all of the investment operations, meet with all of the company's top investment professionals, and accompany the CEO and chairman to all of the key Equitable board, committee, and operational meetings. I also was invited to attend all of the major insurance award events where I got a full understanding of the insurance operations and the interrelationship between the investment and insurance sides of the company.

Most important, I continued to form strong relationships with top Equitable African-American insurance agency managers like Darwin Davis, Al Carleton, Leroy Beavers, and Jim Obi. It was an incredible reintroduction to the Equitable. It convinced me that this was the type of company and people I wanted to work with even though at first the company did not seem to have the international character that I loved so much. But as destiny dedicated, my long career at Equitable opened up international doors that were beyond anything my imagination at this time could fathom.

Installed on the 38th floor, in the executive suite flanked by offices of Coy Eklund and Jack Fey, was very heady for me. All of the top executives visited frequently for meetings with the chairman and CEO, which I would often sit in on. I could have hardly even visualized my literal rise from the dusty streets of Zambia a year ago to the glass-and-steel mountaintop of a Fortune 500 company. The black executives at Equitable were visibly proud that I was in this prestigious position. Darwin, Al, Buddy Anderson, and other black insurance executives would sometimes come to see me, and sometimes even bring their clients along.

These executives and clients had never had the chance to see one of their own at this level. Equitable had taken affirmative action to a new height. Never before in any major insurance company had blacks, well educated and bursting with merit and capacity, become so valued and enjoyed such success. This was all Coy Eklund's doing. Neither me nor Darwin and the other black executives would have been given these chances to excel without his leadership and sense of social responsibility. He deserves the credit. Make no mistake about that.

As planned, after a year on the staff of the CEO and chairman, I moved into the private placement division at Equitable. It was during this period from 1975 to 1985 that I developed my investment, analytical, and portfolio management skills under the incredible tutelage of George Stoddard, head of the investment division, and Bill Cowie, head of the private placement division. These men were two of the smartest investment professionals I had ever met. I worked closely with them along with other colleagues in the investment department, including John Miller, Susan Penny, Jim Wilson, and my CEO, Brian Wruble.

We focused on making the right investments for the Equitable policyholders and annuity holders. It was pure investment analysis, nothing else. I worked in various divisions of the Equitable private placement department, including the energy, transportation, and, most important, the problem loan division. I got some of the best on-the-job training anyone could get in analyzing credits.

Since restrictions on such investments had been relaxed at the time, I also participated in many of the loans that Equitable made to foreign countries. I was able to travel to Spain, Finland, and Japan on due diligence trips. I had the most international investment experience in the division, so it made sense. Now I considered myself a true investment professional.

In 1981, during the final days of the Carter administration, I was appointed to the board of directors of the U.S. Synthetic Fuels Corporation, a government funded corporation devoted to increasing the use of non–fossil fuel energy sources. It was seen then as the cornerstone of President Carter's energy policy, authorized to commit up to $88 billion to, according to one of the corporation's nominating documents, "strengthen the country and to literally change the way we live."

Just like today, the United States needed to lessen its dependence on Middle Eastern oil. But Carter was ahead of his time and he still doesn't get enough credit for his warning regarding the United States' seemingly unquenchable thirst for foreign oil and the dire consequences such dependence has created.

I came to the Carter administration's attention because of my experience with lending to the energy sector. The CEO of the U.S. Synthetic Fuels Corporation was John Sawhill and the board was made up of top executives, including Lane Kirkland, then the president of the AFL-CIO, Frank Cary, the then chairman of IBM, John D. deButts, the former chairman and CEO of AT&T, and Cecil Andrus, then the Secretary of the Interior. Unfortunately, Jimmy Carter lost the election to Ronald Reagan and the board was replaced with Reagan appointees and never lived up to its promise.

In the shadow of Reagan mid-1980s, the private placement division was offered a tremendous opportunity by Equitable, which had a major, positive impact on my life. Equitable offered to spin off a division into a separate, wholly owned subsidiary, Equitable Capital Management Corporation. Equitable Life provided us with start-up capital, retained us as their fixed income asset managers, and agreed to share with us 30 percent of any profits we generated on third party business.

Brian Wruble, John Miller, and I thought this was an incredible shot for us, so we, unlike the majority of our peers, grabbed it. Not everyone was willing to risk losing the coveted security of "mother Equitable." But we were, and I knew exactly what this could mean for us who were willing to put ourselves on the line and work hard and work smart.

It was requested that I work with two other people in the division to develop the business plan for this new subsidiary. It occurred to me that in order to really make money, we had to bring in third party assets under management. And then a lightbulb flipped on in my head. The division did not have any foreign assets under management. Foreign institutions and individuals want to invest in the United States. I thought to myself, I have this incredible global network of former co-workers from the Citibank International Division, some of them in top positions. I bet they could help me identify foreign customers for our investment subsidiary.

The first person I called to test this idea was Peter Wodtke, my former boss in the Middle East. He liked the idea and was happy to help me. After we looked at all my target markets in Europe, Asia, and the Middle East, we started identifying Citibank branches and the heads of those offices that either Peter or I knew. It was an impressive list. Peter agreed to introduce me to his contacts and then made an interesting suggestion.

"Frank, I think you should also go to the annual World Economic Forum meeting in Davos. It's an incredible gathering of global financial institutions and businesses, and that would be a great place for you to meet potential clients."

Although I was not familiar with the World Economic Forum (WEF) held each year in Davos-Klosters, Switzerland, I embraced the idea right away. Another no-brainer, it would give me an efficient way to meet the leaders of target institutions. I was becoming more con-vinced that setting up this subsidiary was a great idea and that I could actually bring in a lot of foreign money.

I decided to shift my focus from investing to raising funds from foreign investors. My partners, Brian and John, had some apprehensions but were willing to give it a etry. We had people who were focusing on attracting money from traditional sources like pension and corporate funds in the United States, but I-wan-ed to focus on foreign investors, a new clientele.

After we completed the business plan, I turned my entire attention to international marketing. The success that I ultimately experienced was mind-boggling. I had steered this fledging company into the trade winds. Simultaneously tapping into the Citibank overseas network and attending Davos was a winning combination.

My affinity for the international was not limited to my professional life.

■ ■ ■

In 1980, after my marriage to my first wife ended, I married Lolita Valderrama. Not only was she foreign born, but she had already seen much of the world, having lived in Italy and Sweden, and was fluent in more than half a dozen languages. She was poised, lovely, a world-class fine art painter and great partner as I set out to be the international finance maven I had long dreamed I would be some day.

On a softly snowy January day in 1986, Lolita and I went to our first World Economic Forum in the magnificent mountain town of Davos, which is just outside of Zurich, Switzerland. It is nestled between impressive mountain peaks that peel back—blue with reflected sky and green with cedar and pine—like the parting Red Sea. I had never seen mountains so high and broad and a town so sweetly quaint with a uniquely Swiss mix of Old World village and tasteful modernity.

My first sense is that Davos was an unlikely place for a conference of global leaders. Yet its gentle charm proved conducive to personal interaction. It won me and Lolita over. But not right away. We arrived at our hotel to find that it was very small, on the outskirts of town and was obviously the only option left for newcomers like us. We knew that we wouldn't see the people we wanted to see there, so we decided to try to get into another hotel in the town's center.

We bundled up and walked down the main street of Davos. As we approached the town center, we noticed the Steinberger Belvedere Hotel, the main conference headquarters. It was the best hotel in Davos so there was little chance that we could get a room there. But Lolita insisted that we try. As expected, the concierge insisted that the hotel was totally full. We gave him our hotel particulars and asked for a call if anything became available. We told the concierge that we were new to the WEF and wanted to be at its epicenter.

We had almost reached the door when we were called back, "Mr. and Mrs. Savage, wait a minute. We just got a cancellation and there is a wait list, but since you're here, let me take you up to it to see if you like it."

Lolita and I were taken to a terrific room with a balcony over-looking the main street.

"I'll take it," was all I could say.

What luck! Here we were, the only African-American businessman at the Forum and his Asian wife, staying at the premiere hotel filled with many of the top business leaders on the planet. I felt like a kid in a Swiss chocolate factory. For years to come, the Belvedere Hotel would be home base when we attended the World Economic Forums. We would come to host an annual invitation-only dinner at the hotel for our dearest friends and associates meeting there.

Our stroke of luck (or was it destiny blowing my way again?) opened up incredible doors for us. We were directly in the center of all the key activity and being the outgoing people that we are, we didn't hesitate to introduce ourselves to the other hotel guests. In those early Forum days, as a rule, you could meet with anybody you wanted to. Nobody said no to a meeting. Obviously, I took advantage of this and met all of the top businesspeople and bankers from all over Europe and Asia who were in attendance. There were also numerous social events in the evenings and Lolita's command of European languages helped us to converse with almost everyone.

We forged relationships, which led to international opportunities that I could never have made if I had only cold-called people from the New York office. Over the 15 years that I have attended the WEF, I have continually established strong and lasting relationships with world financial leaders. I even reconnected there with former Citibank colleagues like Wahib Binzager, whom I met in Jeddah, and Myrna Bustany, from Beirut. Renewing these old Citibank links made a channel of faded Middle East relationships available to me once again.

Through the help of my Davos and Citibank networks, I attracted billions of dollars of assets under management from foreign sources for Equitable Capital Management. That made me a big hero at Equitable Capital, and also it resulted in tremendous financial reward for me personally. Equitable had become a launching pad for me to reintegrate myself into the international arena. I was now operating from a base of our parent company, Equitable Life, a well-respected Fortune 500 company.

To increase Equitable Capital's ability to attract money from foreign investors and service our international clients, we opened two international offices, one in London and another in Japan. It was during our search for someone to run the London office when I met Axel Hansing, one of the most accomplished international financial executives I would ever meet. We became fast friends and remain so today.

My partner at Equitable Capital, John Miller, had met Axel, a native German, while Axel was stationed in New York working for Hypo Bank of Germany. He had worked all over the world—Hong Kong, South Africa, New York, London—everywhere. John and Axel once worked on opposing sides regarding a troubled investment. John had become so impressed with Axel and found him such a formidable opponent that when I was preparing to open the London office, John suggested that I consider hiring him. I invited Axel to come by the office and within an hour, I knew he was the guy. We hit it off personally and I could see that he was the kind of man who could travel and be comfortable in any part of the world. He was also well connected with the European and Asian banks. I hired Axel immediately.

We then started planning to open our Tokyo office. We registered as an investment manager in Tokyo, one of the first foreign advisors to do this. Coincidentally, Alliance Capital, the DLJ asset management subsidiary, obtained an investment management license in Tokyo as well. I had been introduced to an impressive Japanese international banker, Takahiro Fujino, who was stationed in New York with the Bank of Tokyo. He had spent his entire career overseas with the Bank of Tokyo and was fluent in English. I sought him out to see if he would be interesWd in returning to Japan.

Strangely enough, while Tak had built a great career internationally—Latin America, Europe, and the United States—he had been considering going back home. What better opportunity for him than to join a major company like Equitable and return as the head of one of the first foreign investment management companies in Tokyo?

I was very enthusiastic about these two professionals. I had great working chemistry with both of them, and I considered them key. They were global people just like me and had both worked all around the world. But to me, the most profound element was our respect for one another. I now had the leadership in London and Tokyo to begin creating a full-blown international presence.

During a business meeting in Japan, Frank meets with Japanese Prime Minister Kiichi Miyazawa

■ ■ ■

My renewed relationships with my Saudi friends proved very productive, too. At their invitation, Axel and I visited Jeddah. That trip back to Saudi Arabia was quite cathartic for me; the city had changed enormously—new roads, hotels, and shops. I was able to shed some of the old, negative impressions that I harbored after my daughter Brett's health crises there so many years ago. It was good for me to see the new Saudi Arabia, the petro-dollar rich Saudi Arabia, and interact with enormously successful people there.

An unexpected reward for my return to Saudi Arabia came during the first Gulf War in 1989. I received a cable from the Central Bank of Saudi Arabia (SAMA) inviting Equitable Capital to submit a bid to manage a fixed income portfolio. Though it was a dangerous period to go to the Middle East, I saw yet another opportunity that had fallen into our laps. We were certainly qualified to manage such a portfolio.

"I think we should prepare a bid and go to Riyadh to present it face-to-face," I told my partners. "If the Central Bank is asking us to come over there, we should do it. I'm willing to bet that most companies will not respond in person because of the war."

No one in the fixed income department was willing to go. I couldn't argue with them because Iraqi Scud missiles were landing on the Saudi kingdom like falling stars. But Al Stewart, our chief equity officer, agreed to go so we would have a senior investment person with us. I also asked Axel to accompany us, and as usual, he was game and didn't hesitate.

Before we left for Riyadh, I reached out to my old friend from Jeddah, Jim Brody, the former military attaché there. Jim had since retired from the military and become the head of security for Mobil Oil and was stationed in Riyadh. I was somewhat concerned about the war situation there and wanted to know his opinion. He assured me things were not as bad as they were portrayed in the newspapers and on television news. I asked if his company had a way to evacuate if the situation worsened. It did and Jim kindly promised to take me and my two partners out with them if things got that hot there. That was all I needed to hear.

Al, Axel, and I flew to Riyadh with greater peace of mind. Jim was at the airport to greet us. What a welcome face.

Admittedly, Riyadh was very scary. The military was everywhere and aircraft were constantly roaring and whistling overhead, but luckily none of them was Scuds. The 36 or so hours we spent in the city were nerve-wracking. I hardly slept a wink that night. We woke up the next day and visited the Central Bank to make our proposal, then joined its officers for lunch. After that, we wasted no time getting back on a plane and jetting to London.

We felt confident that we had represented our company and capabilities well. We became even more confident when we found out that very few U.S. asset managers had responded to the request for a proposal. Almost as soon as I got back to New York I got a telephone call from the principal officer in Saudi Arabia.

"We really appreciate the fact that you came to Saudi Arabia," the officer said. "We thoroughly enjoyed your presentation, and we are awarding you a portfolio of $500 million."

My heart thumped like an exploding Scud. Five. Hundred. Million. Dollars!

Struggling to keep my composure, I strained to calmly say, "Thank you very much, sir. We are honored to have been selected."

Overjoyed, I rushed to my boss, Brian Wruble, and informed him, calmly, of the huge win we had just racked up. He was just as elated as I was. Word spread throughout the company and I was pegged as one of the company's rising stars because I went into a war zone to get that $500 million.

This deal brought Axel and I to Saudi Arabia frequently. The portfolio managers would join us, but we knew we had to personally maintain those relationships. The Saudi deal was one of our greatest successes at Equitable Capital Management Corporation.

But there was more to come. Three months after we got that portfolio, Lolita and I were on a business trip in Hong Kong when I got a call to our hotel room from my assistant, Eva, instructing me to call the principal officer in Saudi Arabia as per his request. I contacted him right away.

"I understand that you called me. Is there something I can do for you?" I asked.

"Frank, we are very pleased with how you've put together and managed this account and we have voted to award you an additional $500 million."

Lolita looked on as I started jumping up in the air like I had hit the lottery (but no lottery in the world pays out $1 billion). After thanking the Saudi officer for his confidence in us, I clutched Lolita in joy and exhilaration. What a celebration we were going to have.

"My God," I nearly shouted. "I have raised a billion dollars from a single client!" I was beside myself.

I gathered my colleagues, who were with me in Hong Kong.

"Hey guys, guess what happened . . . ? We just got another $500 million from Saudi Arabia."

They went crazy. We were all going crazy.

This additional mandate significantly enhanced my standing in the company and once again, the company rewarded my efforts with a significant bonus. A bonus the likes of which I had never dreamed, and remember, I dream big. I was handed a check six $1seven million. It was

my first million dollars and I will never forget that. It wasn't just a pile
of money, but recognition, acknowledgment of what I had been able
to accomplish.

As a result of this success I was able to significantly improve the life of
my family and increase my financial support to my alma maters, Howard
and Johns Hopkins. It was an incredible feeling. And it was at this point
that I became known as "Mr. International." On many occasions, I
would touch down in Asia, the Middle East, and Europe on a single
trip. This was especially dreamy stuff for a boy from DC who delivered
newspapers and washed office windoews for extra money.

It was playing out just what Madame La Savage International would
have wanted for me.

Largely because of Takahiro Fujino's excellent leadership and his
fine reputation in Japan, we had equally tremendous success in raising
funds from Japanese institutions. Whenever I went to Tokyo, Tak
arranged meetings with virtually all of the major financial institutions
throughout the country. He had a gold-plated list of clients. He could
open the door to any bank in Tokyo and we raised more than a billion
dollars there, too.

After several trips to Japan, I decided that I needed to develop some
proficiency in Japanese to help me do business. So I enrolled in another
intensive language course at Berlitz in New York just the way I did
when preparing years ago for my SAIS French exam. I thought my
Japanese friends would be impressed, but they told me not to bother
studying Japanese because they all wanted to speak English.

This was one of the first indications I had that English would
become the lingua franca in the global political and business worlds. So,
I stuck to English.

I was living the life I had only envisioned when all I had was a vision
and a mother who could see great things ahead for her only son. I would
jump on international flights like most people jump on buses and
subways. I had seamlessly become interracial, intercultural by simply
being myself, respecting and appreciating everyone I met and worked
with. I have long tried to convince young African Americans to pursue

careers in international finance and international business, not only because it is a great career path but also because it can be an uplifting personal experience. Stepping from jets to limos, from the finest hotels in the world to the world's corridors of power and wealth won't permit anyone who does this to worry about self-esteem. You won't need anyone to tell you that you matter, that you have worth. It becomes self-evident.

I am disappointed that even now as I finish this book that few other African Americans have pursued this route. Throughout my decades in the financial world, I rarely encounter another African American. And although it was at the World Economic Forum that I met Vernon Jordan in the mid-1990s, for the majority of the years I attended, I was the sole African American there. I mentioned this to the WEF founder, Klaus Schwab. I was pleased to see that the following year, black South Africans began attending the Forum, including Thabo Mbeki, then the deputy president of South Africa and Patrice Motsepe, a budding South African entrepreneur.

I have tried to serve as an example to fellow African Americans of what can be achieved in my field—or any field for that matter—with enough self-confidence and proper preparation. Yet, at the same time, I had the added benefit of entering this highly sophisticated global market with the full faith and support of Equitable Life and Equitable Capital. I credit much of my success to Coy Eklund and my partners, Brian and John. But even that assistance did not come by accident. I had to be prepared; I had to be up to the challenge.

My 12 years at Equitable Capital Management were some of the most significant years of my professional life in so many respects.

And I know that Equitable Capital's shimmering successful was, to some extent, a result of my ability to attract foreign assets for the company to manage. Yet, as life would have it, not everything went well. In one personally upsetting incident in the 1980s, a rogue trader at Equitable Capital tarnished our reputation with Japanese investors.

Working with the Long-Term Credit Bank of Japan in Tokyo, Equitable Capital had raised almost a billion dollars in assets under management from Japanese institutions looking to invest in U.S. fixed income securities. I would take teams of my investment professionals to Japan to make presentations to prospective clients. Although Brian

Ruble was CEO of Equitable Capital, the foreign clients knew me as the person who drove that company and their relationship with it. They trusted me and I took that trust seriously. Even though they looked to the portfolio managers to actually manage their funds, they always held me ultimately responsible for their fiscal well-being. After all, I had convinced them to invest in these assets with us in the first place.

John approached me one day with Kathleen Corbet, who oversaw fixed income portfolios, to break some bad news.

"The portfolio manager on the Japanese fixed income portfolio has deviated from his mandate. He has been colluding with a friend in a small investment banking firm's trading operation to buy derivative securities in the Japanese bank's portfolio. He was chasing returns and when the government rates dropped the derivatives totally collapsed as there were no bids. So we had to write down the value of the securities to the current market value, resulting in a substantial loss to our Japanese clients."

"How could this have happened?" I said incredulously. "He was under written instructions from the client to invest in highly rated U.S. government securities. Not derivatives! Didn't you check on him? What kind of monitoring did we have?"

"Yes, we have been monitoring his portfolio as usual, but he had two sets of books. He was showing us one set, which showed us investing in securities that were authorized, and then he had another set on the side where he was trading in these derivatives, and both he and his friend were covering this up."

This was a disaster. *What am I going to tell Long-Term Credit Bank and Mr. Hanakawa?* I thought. Hanakawa was my principal Japanese partner at the Long-Term Credit Bank in Japan. And what are they going to tell their institutional clients?

Well, in Japan when corporate CEOs and other top executives make mistakes, it is sort of expected that they commit hara-kiri. Obviously, I was not going to ceremonially jam a sharp knife in my belly. Nonetheless, I did not welcome the prospect of telling my Japanese partners what had happened. The news would reflect badly upon us, but I had no choice.

I called Hanakawa from New York and disclosed what had occurred. He was speechless. At his behest, Kathleen Corbet and I went to Japan to personally explain the incident to Hanakawa and our friends at Long-Term Credit Bank. This was one of the most humiliating moments of my career. Kathleen was extremely embarrassed as well because this reflected poorly on our system of checks and balances and of monitoring portfolio managers. I felt that we had somehow violated the bank's trust in us.

Yet when Kathleen detailed the actual conspiracy that had been implemented by the rogue manager and his outside cohort, it became clear to Hanakawa and his associates at the bank how such activities went undetected. And yet, the incident significantly affected our business reputation in Japan, and our relationship with Long Term Credit Bank and worst of all, our relationship with Hanakawa and his colleagues.

I learned some painful lessons from that Japanese experience. Trust is everything! I was totally blindsided by this situation, but I was helpless to have prevented it. It shows how dependent we are on the trustworthiness of people we count on. How does one defend against a rogue trader? A criminal? (It would be a lesson I would have to relearn years later as a director of Enron.)

In most management firms, including Equitable Capital, everyone was required to complete an annual compliance form showing all business and personal trading activities. Obviously, the Japanese portfolio manager lied on his form by not reporting the off-book trading.

I also learned that although derivatives are an essential part of the financial markets, they are inherently volatile, extremely sensitive to interest rate moves and can be illiquid, meaning not easily sold or exchanged for cash without a serious loss in its value. Because derivatives are so volatile they should only be used with the explicit approval of clients who have a sophisticated understanding of the potential downside to employing them in a portfolio.

Yet, as I watched the great meltdown of the real estate securities market in 2008 and the Madoff scandal, I saw some similarities to the Equitable Capital Japanese situation, albeit on a significantly larger scale. Dishonesty, greed, derivatives—all were found in one form or another in that crisis. We live and sometimes forget to learn.

Nonetheless, after Japan, my worldwide recognition as one of the foremost international finance businessmen deepened. I was soon elected to the Council on Foreign Relations Board of Directors and co-chaired its Membership Committee along with the Peabody Award–winning journalistic icon, Charlayne Hunter-Gault and Committee Member Ted Sorenson.

With the encouragement of the Council's then President Les Gelb, we helped to reshape and revitalize the membership of the council by attracting younger members, thus ensuring the board's future relevance. I was also elected to the board of directors of the Institute of International Finance (IIF), the preeminent association of global financial institutions in the world. As a member of that board I was to join discussions both within IIF and also with government financial officials on matters affecting global economies.

These meetings were held all over the world, including Washington, DC, London, Hong Kong, and Budapest. I also founded and chaired the IIF committee that promoted the involvement of asset management firms in the deliberations of the Institute of International Finance, expanding the role of such organizations in global financial deliberations. These affiliations catapulted me into a new level of global visibility and leadership. For me, they were the sparkle on the diamond. All of my hard work—beginning with Crossroads Africa to my work in Saudi Arabia, Liberia, and Zambia with Citibank and TAW International, as well as Europe and Asia with Equitable Capital and later with Alliance Capital—led me to a position where I was the only person of color engaged in such high-level deliberations.

These deliberations transcended not only banking or asset management, but focused on ways to enhance global financial stability and developed ways for the major private institutions and government to work hand in hand to address global financial crisis.

I felt that I had arrived at the top.

■ ■ ■

In 1993, Dick Jenrette, the then CEO of Equitable Life Assurance Society, dropped a major surprise on Equitable Capital partner John Miller and me. He had decided to merge our company into Alliance Capital, the previous investment arm of Donaldson, Lufkin & Jenrette Inc. (DLJ), which Equitable had acquired in 1985.

Alliance and Equitable Capital had thrived for years as separate entities.

But Dick thought that the combined subsidiaries of Equitable Life, the parent, would enable Equitable to increase assets under management and avoid the inevitable competition between the two companies. Furthermore, he wanted Alliance Capital to be the surviving company—not my baby, Equitable Capital.

Alliance had gone public and could, in effect, "pay" for Equitable Capital in stock, which would create a windfall for Equitable Life. The logic was compelling, but, of course, John and I did not like the idea of losing control of our company and becoming subservient to Alliance.

We objected strenuously to the merger, even going so far as to hire our own consultant to help us consider ways to buy Equitable Capital ourselves. When Dick Jenrette heard of our efforts, he became livid and immediately fired John Miller.

I was spared, but Dick had spread the world through my good Equitable friend, Darwin Davis, that I would be next if I didn't get on board with his wishes. I was torn and needed some quiet time to think. So I went to Colorado to ski for a couple of days to gain some perspective.

In the mountains, after weighing my options, I decided that I should try out the merger before making a final decision. I'd had a great career with Equitable Life so far, why not give it a chance? Furthermore, Alliance had a great reputation. So rather than just jump ship, perhaps I should stay, negotiate the best possible package, and then give it a try. If it didn't work out, I can always leave, I thought.

I sat down with Lolita and laid out my logic. I emphasized that Equitable Life wanted me to stay. That was important to me. Also, I explained that the move to go with the merger might prove to be a great opportunity for me because I would be working with some exceptional people. Additionally, I would have a real platform from which to build up international business.

Alliance Capital CEO Dave Williams wanted me to work closely with Karan Trehan, who ran the international division at Alliance. I thought Karan and I could make a good team. We could really build up this business. All things considered, Lolita agreed with my decision.

I called Dick and let him know I had decided to stay on. Next, I called Darwin at Equitable Life and told him of my decision and my conversation with Dick.

"I am so happy you did this!" he exclaimed in relief. "Dick was so close to calling you to say 'this is not going to work out, so let's talk about your severance.' I'm sure he was happy when you called him because he did not want to see you leave."

Who knows where I would be today if I had waited any longer to make that call?

Alliance was different. Although I became a member of its board, I was no longer the boss. I was not part of the inner circle of original Alliance people. I hadn't helped to build this company the way I had helped to build Equitable Capital. Yet, I became part of a strong team as chairman of Alliance Capital Management International working closely with Dave and Karan. Dave Williams was committed to expanding Alliance's global presence, so we had his total backing.

Joining Alliance started to feel right. We successfully attracted assets from all over the world and built a lucrative family of mutual funds—the Alliance 95 Fund in India, the Nile Growth Company in Egypt, and the Southern African Fund, which we built shortly after Nelson Mandela was released from prison in 1990. The Southern African fund led to my becoming a part of Thabo Mbeki's International Advisory Council.

Alliance grew to become the largest publicly traded asset management company in America, with more than $800 billion of assets under management. It had a much larger product platform than Equitable Capital ever could have built, and it boasted some of the best portfolio managers and research managers of any firm on Wall Street. Once again, I had avoided burning bridges and it paid off. Although I admittedly took a slight blow to my ego by joining Alliance in less than a high leadership position, I made it work for me. It turned out to be another case of my "snatching victory from the jaws of defeat," as my favorite former sportscaster, Jim McKay, would say.

I thought that serving as chairman of Equitable Capital was the apex of my international career and I would sail into my retirement years from that safe and secure harbor. But when the Alliance opportunity presented itself, though less than ideal, I recognized that joining the company could continue to advance my career. So, I set my sails and followed its strong current.

Back in 2000 we decided to create a $500 million African Infra-structure Fund at Alliance. But when Dave retired as CEO, his suc-cessor, Bruce Calvert, decided not to pursue the fund. Dave then suggested that I shouldn't sweat about Alliance's support of the fund and operate it myself. He suggested that I become the manager of the fund and offered to help financially if I did this. The idea intrigued me because ever since the TAW debacle in Zambia I had harbored the desire to set up my own Africa fund. But there had been a lot of water under the bridge since then and my future was taking me in another direction—retirement and the entrancing allure of my new 56-foot sailboat.

Again, I turned to Lolita.

"I have an opportunity to actually take over this fund from Alliance and go off on my own. OPIC is going to put up about two thirds of the capital in a highly attractive debt equity structure," I said, referring to the Overseas Private Investment Corporation. "I only have to raise about a third of the capital. I'm convinced that I can raise the money from the Middle East and from the U.S."

"I know how much you love Africa," Lolita said, looking deep into my eyes that spoke louder than my words. "So, I can't stop you from doing this. But you just bought this beautiful boat and you said you wanted to sail around the world. Now is probably the best time for you to do that."

She gave me a softly melting smile and said that she would support me in whatever decision I made.

I also looked to my peers for more advice. One of them was Cliff Wharton, a great old friend and confidante with common roots in SAIS at Johns Hopkins.

"You don't need to do anything else in life," he told me with a kind of concrete candor. "You've already accomplished so much. As attractive as this is, I think you should retire and enjoy your family and the rest of your life."

He pointed out that I was on many great boards and would probably be asked to do many other things to keep me busy and engaged.

He looked at me and turned very serious.

"Frank, just relax."

I considered my two options: retire and sail the world, or achieve my yet unrealized dream of returning to Africa with a major investment fund in my back pocket. I had never felt better in my life. My mind was clear and I practically vibrated with ideas. I knew, and I didn't have to look too deeply into my soul and heart to know, that I was not ready to step aside, to leave the investment world for a comfy chair in someone's boardroom or bask in sunny afternoons on the deck of my magnificent boat. I still had a lot to offer to the business world. And Africa . . . she still called me.

■ ■ ■

Everything was right; I was in very good financial shape at that time and was confident that I could assemble a crack team. More important, I believed that Africa was finally ready for this fund. A more mature political leadership was emerging on the continent. It was much more willing to work with investors like me than a previous generation of African leadership. These leaders wanted to bring Western-style development to their nations and that required Western-style infrastructure funds.

My decision was made. I was going to launch the fund.

I resigned from Alliance in August 2001 but remained on its board. The company was very supportive, letting me stay at the Alliance office until I got an office of my own. I had the two core people that I needed to get going: Leonard Murray, my trusted colleague, and Eva Evgenis, my invaluable assistant. I put together an investment team made up of three outstanding and experienced investors from MUSA Capital previously with Prince Al Waleed. I also had an outstanding legal team, Charles Hamilton and Tom Kruger from Paul Hastings.

The Overseas Private Investment Corporation fully supported my taking over the fund from Alliance Capital, especially because the former chairman and CEO of Alliance, Dave Williams, was my partner in this venture. We also had an excellent infrastructure partner. Much to our delight when we advised OPIC of the changes, it was elated because first off, its managers knew they now had my 100 percent commitment to the fund.

Everyone was happy.

I found myself back in the Africa that Madame La Savage introduced to me more than 50 years earlier by way of her exotically eclectic mix of clients and friends; I was back to the Africa I discovered in the gentle gaze of Clavender Bright, in the dream factories of Howard University, in the joyful work I did with Operation Crossroads Africa, back to the Africa I tried to defend against apartheid with TAW International Leasing.

I was ready to launch the fund under a new title: The Africa Millennium Fund.

In August 2001, it was up and running, but my sea went strangely calm before the world would change forever. My Africa dream, and the dear dreams of millions more, would be dashed that year in a seemingly relentless wave of terror, fear, deceit, and criminality: first came the September 11, 2001, attacks on the United States, and a short time later followed the Enron crisis and its assault on trust, decency, good business. And my good name.

Yet I survived it, I persevered, and I reemerged to catch the trailing edge of my destiny to steer a true course as long as there is wind in the sky and wind in my lungs.

That's the Savage Way.

Yet, before I could masterfully navigate those waves, and many others, that life washed over me, I needed to fully master one more thing: sailing.

Chapter 9

Sailing *Lolita*, Pulling It All Together

Frank Jr., you can be anything you want to be.

—*Madame La Savage*

I often wonder what my mother would have made of my life if she could have lived into her nineties like her sisters, my aunts Naomi, who is 92, and Hazel, who is 93.

Sure, she would have been proud of me as a man, a father of six wonderful children and five fantastic grandchildren. She would no doubt have celebrated my vindication in the wake of the 2001 Enron scandal, but not without worrying about me when I was first entangled in its murky mess. She would have been much pleased in the way my wife Lolita has bloomed into a family matriarch; she would have adored our homes, our way of life, and my renewed work in international finance; my mother would have also been delighted in the way I jet to Africa at a moment's notice to advise a head of state on how best to invigorate his nation's economy.

And she would have loved to sail with me.

I have always been at peace when I sail, and I know it would have been the same for my mother, Madame La Savage. I see her seated on the sunshined deck of my legendary Swan 56, *Lolita*. La Savage loved the breeze blowing through her meticulously coiffed hair when she drove her fancy Pontiac, a little too fast. I know she would have loved the sea breezes slipping over the bow of my yacht to fast dance in her hair.

I lost my mother in 1981. She lived long enough to see me scale unimaginable heights in the corporate and professional worlds. But she never got the chance to see me rise to the highest levels of sailboat racing 20 years later. Yet, her influence continued to affect every aspect of my life, including sailboat racing.

La Savage actually dissuaded me from sports during my youth, preferring that I concentrate my attention on books and studies. Somehow I know that she would not have viewed sailboat racing as just another sport. She would have smelled the challenge of it, like I do, and she would have been my greatest cheerleader to prevail over all comers. That, too, is the Savage Way.

When I was a boy, my mother always told me that I could be whatever I wanted to be in life. To my way of thinking, a championship yachtsman was simply another one of those possibilities. I had dabbled with tennis and skiing. I often played tennis with my Equitable friends and colleagues, Darwin Davis and Coy Eklund. But I had no real passion for either sport. None carried the sort of all-hands-on-deck insistence that sailing does, especially the manner in which competitive sailing demands.

When I was in my sixties and fate was showing me that life is not all ups but that it packs some plunges, too, sailing was there to enliven my spirit, clear my thoughts and heal my wounded soul. Some people live for that perfect golf swing, that 30-foot jump shot at the buzzer, that last big trade at the market's closing bell. Me? I came to live for sailing, especially ocean sailboat racing.

There were times, in the darkest days of Enron, for example, when *Lolita* literally sailed me away from islands of self-pity and deep depression. Sailing helped me reclaim my life. Own it again. Was God working in the mysterious ways that my grandmother so often said of Him? I may never know for certain, but I do know that sailing became my sanctuary just when I needed a sanctuary the most. For that, among so many blessings under the sail, I will always be grateful.

I have little doubt that some may wish to dismiss sailing, especially sailboat racing, as yet another diversion for people with too much money or too much time, or both. And to be honest, yes, sailing is a very expensive sport. But any pursuit of genuine excellence requires great sums of money or time or both. For me, sailing pulled it all together. It requires everything that I'm about—preparation, teamwork, mutual respect, discipline, and no small degree of daring to dare.

■ ■ ■

Picture *Lolita* the third sailboat I christened to honor my wife—her ivory-color hull gilding over the Caribbean's foamy, white-capped Atlantic. The sailcloth of its broad-shouldered spinnakers is fully out-stretched, catching the wind as if it is a thief. The sky is blue and rich with cottony clouds that squat on the horizon as if they have gathered to watch the grand spectacle.

It is May 2003 and it's the Antigua Race Week regatta. I've set my sights on taking home its top prize—overall fleet winner. I'm at the helm and my boat's 17-member, international crew performs flawlessly. We are ready. *Lolita* has new racing sails, new lines, a smooth bottom, perfectly tuned running and standing rigging and all winches and blocks in perfect shape.

More than 300 other sailboats from all over the world are hoping to best us. But *Lolita*, a 56-foot-long Swan wonder of Finnish engineering, is fast and smart in the water. My heart pounds and I feel myself smile as the ancient acceleration of nature and nautical machine conspire to drive us onward.

"We're going to take this," I say to myself as I survey the smattering of tall sails contrasted against the rolling, green hills of Antigua. "This regatta is ours to win."

But I knew the second those words escaped my lips that believing it and doing it are two distinctly different things. It is as if *Lolita* hears me; she quickens her pace.

I am enraptured. I loved that boat.

Frank at the helm of his sailboat, *Lolita*, in Newport, Rhode Island, in 2001

While I sold *Lolita* last spring, I remain deeply involved in the community of sailing from my membership in the New York Yacht Club and my seat on the honorary board of directors of the National Sailing Hall of Fame. And there are the many close and enduring friendships I enjoy with those I have sailed with—and against—around the world. And I have my memories.

A handmade model of *Lolita* stands in a glass case on a pedestal in the living room of my Manhattan home.

Now that I've finished one phase of my sailing career, I'm looking to get a new boat, a smaller one, a vessel I can sail closer to home, in local waters, with my friends and family.

I just saw one I liked the other day . . .

■ ■ ■

Like many things in life, my entry into sailing started in a most unlikely fashion. In the winter of 1983, Lolita and I vacationed on Caneel Bay, the stunning Rockefeller resort in St. John, U.S. Virgin Islands. Awaiting the plane home, I picked up a sailing magazine, just something to flip through. I opened it to a picture of a sailboat heeled over like a mighty living thing and heading hard into the sunset. Something about that glossy, color picture—the rusty redness of the sunset, the coral cool tones of the sea, the angle of the boat muscling under the power of the invisible wind—struck me.

Nudging Lolita, I said, "Look at this."

She took a cursory glance, engrossed in a magazine of her own.

"That really looks good to me," I said, "like something that maybe I could be interested in . . . sailing."

"Why don't you take it up?"

"Well, I just might," I replied.

Up until that point the only sailing experience I had was when I was a kid back in Washington and sailed a paper mache sailboat down a gutter after a rain.

That casual interchange was the start. The week after returning from Caneel Bay, I surprised Lolita when I enrolled in the Steve Colgate sailing class in Long Island City in New York. I was 45 years old and knew absolutely nothing about sailing; it was something I had never dreamed I would want to do.

At the time, I was serving as the pro bono chairman of Freedom National Bank, a historic black financial institution in Harlem. But my work there was like being a chariot driver with eight horses each wanting to thunder off in separate directions. I needed to find some way to relax. Jogging helped, but the thought of being on the water appealed to me more.

The first few days of the sailing course were in the classroom where I learned about the various parts of the boat, the effect of the wind, currents, tides, and safety. Near the end of the week, all the students were taken on our first sailboat ride. The boat was a 21-footer called a Soling. I felt a stir of trepidation when I boarded it. There was only a small engine and five of us on board.

The instructor was handling everything himself. He pulled off from the dock under engine power and motored toward the middle of the Long Island Sound. Before I knew it, he lifted the sails, turned off the engine, and turned the craft into the wind. The boat heeled over, gathered speed under the open palm of the wind, and then—and I cannot express what happened next in any other way—I fell in love. The feeling of the wind blowing on my face as the boat's hull angled hard to the waves on one side was incredible, one of the most incredible feelings that I've ever had.

After the course, I raved to Lolita about my newfound sport. I was enthusiastic to sail, but unfortunately, I didn't have a sailboat, yet. While attending a business reception in New York, I met someone named Tabor Bolden who worked for CBS. As we talked, we discovered that we both lived in Stamford, Connecticut. Thinking I may have found a new tennis partner, I asked Tabor if he played tennis.

His reply was short and sweetly shocking.

"No, I sail."

Boom! Tabor's words struck me like a lightning bolt.

"I just took a sailing course and I really like that sport. Where do you sail?"

"Out of the Stamford Yacht Club. I generally sail on the weekends with family and with friends. I also race."

"You *race?*" I asked in wonderment.

He explained that there was a summer series of competitive sailing there and that I should "come out some time."

Brimming with anticipation, I showed up at the dock on an early Wednesday evening. This was amateur sailing, so Tabor's crew was comprised of a great group of five to six close friends of his rather than professional sailors. He introduced me to the crew as a new sailing enthusiast and they warmly welcomed me aboard, beginning my first racing experience.

For the two or three seasons I raced with Tabor in the Stamford races. I was primarily an observer, not really playing a key role in the crew work. This team had raced together for so long that everyone knew their roles; I did not want to disrupt their system. As I watched the crew work, I learned a great deal about sailing the boat. But as skipper, Tabor had one unforgettable trait; he was a screamer.

During particularly tense races, he would scream orders.

Trim the Mainsail! Trim the Jib! Luff the Sail! Tack on!

God forbid if someone made a mistake. The crew seemed to take his ranting in stride; it had become accustomed to his style and just accepted it. Consequently, I came to think that screaming was a customary part of the sailing culture. It isn't.

Racing with Tabor introduced me to the pleasure of racing at night. My first time came on a summer night brightened by a full moon. It was one breathtaking sight to see all of the spinnaker sails hoisted, pushing all the boats downwind as the moonlight pranced on nodding waters.

It was fabulous to be a part of Tabor's team, even as an observer. There was a celebration and awards party at the close of the season. We never won a summer series but the pursuit of a win was always so much fun. I could see how the race forged bonds among everyone involved. Regardless of who won the contest, the culture of sailing built tremendous friendships. I was especially struck by the teamwork sailboat racing required.

A good crew is like a flesh-and-blood mechanism. Everyone has specific tasks that have to be performed in perfect unison. Each person intuitively knows when to move. It was a thing of beauty to witness on Tabor's boat. I also noted the preparation that was necessary in sailing. Sometimes we'd have to arrive very early, making sure the sails were in good shape and checking all the equipment, getting the craft race-ready. On the water you don't want surprises.

I never actually took the helm of Tabor's boat and sailed her, but standing on that deck, surrounded by the smooth-running hum of its crew, whipped by the wind, the water, and desire to win was greatly exciting. All of it almost made me forget that I was, in sailing jargon, the "seventh man," an observer.

■ ■ ■

In 1987, Tabor retired from CBS, sold his boat and moved farther north. Suddenly, I didn't have access to a boat. Lolita and I decided that I liked the sport enough to invest in my own vessel.

That turned out to be a 33-foot Cal that Tabor helped me pick out. I felt comfortable with that size because I had grown accustomed to Tabor's boat, which was also a 33-footer. I named my boat, which was a beauty with a lovely interior, *Lolita.* I knew my wife would love that.

But when I went to pick up *Lolita* in Long Island and sail her to her new home in Stamford trouble found us. I didn't know anything about navigation yet, so Tabor came along to sail my new boat home. My 13-year-old son Mark came for the fun of it.

Off we went, smooth sailing until *bang!* The boat hit a submerged rock, sending my brand new craft flying into the air and then crashing back onto the water. My son, who was laying on the foredeck, almost flew off the boat.

"What happened, Tabor?" I asked in a panic.

"I don't believe this," he said. "I have never done this in my entire sailing experience around Stamford!"

"Done *what?*"

"I hit the Cows," he said referring to a well-known string of rocks that stand just outside Stamford on the Island Sound approach to the city. "I didn't pay attention to the low tide and I was skirting along the boundary of the Cows."

He was terribly embarrassed and apologized profusely. Of course, I forgave him, but I was concerned about whether *Lolita* had suffered any structural damage. Her keel, which was more than 6 feet below the waterline, had smashed into those rocks. We did arrive at Stamford Landing safely and an inspection showed, despite the hard impact, no damage.

I was now officially christened a boat owner.

So now I had a boat but knew very little of the sailings fundamentals. It was like having a shiny new sports car but not knowing how
to get it in gear. Nevertheless, I was anxious to get her on the water. I
even took my whole family out for *Lolita's* maiden voyage. I motored
out to Stamford Harbor—so far so good. I made it into the Long Island
Sound—good . . . good. I was very careful to keep the harbor entrance
within sight. But once we were really underway, I made the mistake of
following Tabor's example and started screaming orders.

Trim the Mainsail! Trim the Jib! Luff the Sail! Tack on!

My kids begrudgingly did what I told them to do. We made
numerous mistakes and Lolita became visibly concerned about my
obvious lack of sailing knowledge and the risk my inexperience was
putting our family in.

Somehow, we managed to return to the harbor in a couple of
hours. We dropped the sails and turned on the motor to enter our slip.
But I couldn't slow the boat down. Then, thinking I was throwing the
boat's motor into reverse, I shifted it forward instead as *Lolita* nosed hard
for the dock. Luckily, the owner of a neighboring boat saw my dilemma
and ran to the bow of the boat to stop it, yelling "Put it in neutral!"

It was my turn to be embarrassed. *I've got to really take more classes so I
better understand what I'm doing.* At that moment I knew I was not ready
to take anyone sailing until I became more proficient. And rubbing salt
into my wounded ego, Lolita announced that the family was not going
sailing with me if "you keep screaming!"

What a bad start. I promised Lolita to never scream on my boat
again and I kept that promise, even as I began to race competitively.

I wasted no time hiring a sailing teacher named Smitty, whom I had
met through one of Tabor's crew. During the rest of the summer,
Smitty and I went out on my boat on Saturdays. He taught me all the
fundamentals. Sometimes, with only a member of Tabor's crew along,
I would take my family and friends sailing. Before the summer's end, I
had a reasonably good command of my boat, so much so that I assumed
the helm and my family was pleasantly surprised that I actually knew
what I was doing. And I did it all without ever having to raise my voice.

I soon had developed very solid core sailing skills to the point where
I could take the boat out solo. I spent countless hours on the boat

perfecting my navigational skills. I really felt great when I was accomplished enough to go deep into Long Island Sound, maneuver the boat, and bring her back without any help at all.

During those early years, sailing *Lolita* created a special bond within the family. I especially enjoyed sailing with my sons Mark and Antoine. Each of them enrolled in sailing classes. Mark loved to bring his friends along for a sail and sort of used *Lolita*, with my permission, as a party boat. All of my children were introduced to sailing on *Lolita*. Antoine and his younger brother Frankie would eventually race with me when I bought a bigger, faster more expensive boat.

Antoine was with me when I had a potentially dangerous mishap on *Lolita* in the fall of 1991. It was a beautiful, crisp October day with little wind. Antoine, who was 10 years old at the time, and I were sailing from the northern part of Long Island Sound toward Stamford to store the boat for the winter. Then, without warning, the boat abruptly stopped.

We couldn't understand why. We were under engine power and had plenty of fuel. But I soon discovered we had run over a lobster pot and the rope attached to the trap was wrapped around the boat's engine shaft.

So here I am with my little boy stuck in the middle of Long Island Sound.

I realized what I had to do.

"Antoine, I'm going to go into the water and cut the line off the engine shaft," I told him as calmly as I could. "Here's what I want you to do: Watch me as I go down and if anything happens, go to the radio, channel 16, the emergency Coast Guard channel, and say, 'Mayday! Mayday! This is the sailing boat *Lolita*.'

"Next, when they answer, say, 'My father is in the water and needs help.' Then give them our latitude, longitude location—the numbers that come up on the LORAN navigator screen."

He put on a brave face. "Okay Dad," he said as calmly as he could. "Okay Dad."

Cutting the rope off the shaft was not easy because first I had to dive under the boat, grab the shaft, and then cut off the line. I had to dive under the water several times before I freed us from the line. Antoine was nervously watching for me every time I reemerged from the bottom. When I finally climbed back into the boat, I was shivering. As Antoine wrapped me in a warming blanket, I told him he was going to have to drive the boat back to Stamford because I was too cold to do it myself. He took his place at the helm and I talked him through all the maneuvers to the harbor and into our slip. I was so impressed.

We owned *Lolita* for six years, cruising the Long Island Sound each year from May to October. Paul Wager, a good friend from Greenwich, Connecticut, was always willing to sail with me. With Paul as crew, I was able to extend *Lolita*'s travels to Stonington, Connecticut, Block Island in Rhode Island, and Cape Cod in Massachusetts.

Once, when Paul, Smitty, and I sailed to Stonington, we went to dinner on shore. Around 10 that evening we were returning to *Lolita* on her dinghy when the small boat shuddered to a stop. It was out of fuel.

It was pitch black and the harbor's current was pulling us out to sea, ebbing at about 2 knots. We began rowing to *Lolita*, but the current was pulling us out faster than we could muscle our way back to her.

We had no radio or flashlight to summon or signal anyone for help. We started yelling to try to get attention from other boats, but no one heard us. I was very concerned. Only God knows what would have happened to us if we were swept out to sea in the dead of night in an unseaworthy dinghy.

Paul, Smitty, and I finally dug deep enough into our reserves, that place where you go when there is no other place to go, and found the strength to row to the closest boat we could find. Luckily, someone was on board and offered to tow us back to *Lolita*.

The incident taught me an important lesson: Always check both the main boat and the dinghy for fuel, oars, and a flashlight. Always be prepared for the unexpected because the unexpected is always prepared to challenge you.

But none of this deterred me.

I got the urge to buy a bigger boat to better accommodate my growing family. Lolita and I had three children, Antoine, Gracie, and Frankie, in adding to the three—Eric, Brett, and Mark—I had with my first wife. All of the kids liked sailing to some degree, even Frankie, the baby, who first boarded the boat when he was only 3 months old.

I started looking at other boats in the 40-foot range. Nautor's Swan yachts were high on my list because they had a tremendous reputation for seaworthiness. If I were to go offshore, out into the ocean, I wanted a safe and fast boat. Swan had proven themselves in the Fastnet Race and the Sydney to Hobart Race, two of the most challenging and dangerous ocean sailboat races on the planet.

During my search, I met Jennifer Stewart, the Swan representative in Newport.

"Frank, I think I've found the perfect boat for you," she told me as if I had already purchased the boat. "It's a Swan 46. It has had three previous owners, but it has very low mileage and has been well maintained."

She was a good saleswoman. She was sure to tell me that this sailboat had overhead hatches. They let in a lot of light into the cabin below, something she knew Lolita would like.

I was ready to take a look at the vessel. But then Jennifer dropped the shocker.

The boat was 3,000 miles away in Newport Beach, California.

At first I had no intention of flying to California just to see a boat that I *might* buy. But after Jennifer pointed out the boat's attractive price and impeccable condition, I found myself tempted. Then I thought about Brett. My daughter had recently graduated from New York University and had been hired as a television journalist at a station in Peoria, Illinois. I had planned to accompany her on the long drive to her new home.

Maybe I can fly from the Midwest to California.

In no time, Jennifer had me booked on a direct flight from Peoria to Newport Beach. I did make that drive with Brett to Illinois. And a broker met me at the airport in California and drove me directly to the boat. When my eyes fell on this Swan 46 I really liked what I saw. Its teak deck was gorgeous and the boat was extremely clean. Below deck was full of sunlight just like Jennifer had promised.

The boat had a beautiful rear cabin; forward, in the main salon, there was a dining area and recessed into the hull was a small bunk where a child could sleep. My youngest daughter, Grace, came to fall in love with that little alcove. It was *her* bunk. And then forward from the main salon were two cabins and a separate bathroom. The Swan 46 had ample room for my children, my wife, and me.

I knew it was customary for an offer to be made before taking a boat out for a sea trial, but the owner sensed that I was a serious potential buyer so he agreed to my request for a test drive, so to speak. It was just like the first time I went sailing on that Soling. When the boat heeled over, took off through the harbor and went hungrily into the ocean, I fell in love all over again.

Oddly enough, my friend David Weaver, a Swan owner, had invited me to spend a few days sailing with him in the Florida Keys aboard his 57-foot Swan. I had taken him up on that. The extensive experience sailing on his Swan helped to convince me that I should buy the 46. So I did.

Next I sold my old *Lolita* back home to Wesley Buford, a buddy in Los Angeles. I made a deal for a truck to transport that boat to him and pick up my new boat in Newport Beach and transport it to Miami. I also arranged to have a crew there sail my new *Lolita*, which I named *Lolita Too!*, to me in Stamford.

Everything went smoothly. I even joined the delivery crew and sailed the leg from Florida to Newport News, Virginia. It was my first ocean passage, and what a thrill!

Lolita Too! was an apt name because it afforded my family larger accommodations for more comfortable cruising. But it offered me so much more than that. In moving from my old Cal 33, a small, inshore sailboat, to an ocean-capable Swan 46, I had unknowingly reached a critical juncture in my trajectory of becoming a first-class yachtsman. I had the capability to cruise *and* race my sailboat almost anywhere in the world. This boat would open up an entirely new chapter of sailing for me.

In the beginning, I tried to manage *Lolita Too!* without any professional help, the same way I had managed my Cal 33. I soon discovered that managing the Swan was a much more demanding chore. It would take a couple of hours for my sons, Mark, Antoine, and me to check all the systems and get her ready to sail. I was spending more time prepping the boat before and after cruising than I was spending actually cruising her.

I came to realize that I needed help to enjoy this boat. I asked a friend to suggest someone who could manage the boat. He referred me to the manager of a sailing club in Darien, Connecticut, who recommended a young man who worked there. Although he was an experienced sailor who had sailed since he was six or seven years old, I was disappointed to discover he had a drinking problem. I then decided against a full-time captain, opting instead to hiring crew when I needed them for cruises. I made a concerted effort to maintain my technical skills, which would prove essential as I shifted my focus from simply cruising to competitive racing.

■ ■ ■

A 1995 cruise to Maine gave rise to a pivotal experience that cemented my desire to race. I hadn't thought much about racing since my days on Tabor Bolden's boat back in the 1980s. I had planned quite a voyage starting with Stamford to Stonington, then on to Block Island to Newport and across the Bay of Maine to Penobscott, Maine. It was all to visit my friend David Weaver, who was a fellow member of the advisory board, which I chaired of the School Of Advanced International Study at Johns Hopkins University (SAIS), my alma mater.

I decided to take along quite a few passengers: close friends Wesley Buford, George Hocker, and Paul Wagner along with Antoine and two of his friends, Juan from Madrid, Spain, and Hastings Read from Stamford. While in Block Island, Jennifer Stewart called to invite me to participate in the Swan Regatta in Newport. I told her we were on a cruise to Maine and, while I appreciated her offer, I hadn't raced in years and we were not prepared to compete.

"Oh don't worry about that," she said. "We have what we call a cruising class. You can use the same sails and you won't have to change a thing. Just come and have fun."

Since we were going to Newport anyhow I figured, *why not?*

When we arrived there we discovered that there were a lot of Swans participating. I met several other Swan owners, some of whom, like John Cummings, are still my friends. Socially, it was a wonderful time. However, our racing performance was abysmal. Other than Paul and Wesley, no one on *Lolita Too!* had any meaningful racing experience.

Racing starts are a line of sight between two points, a port, which is left, and starboard side, which is the right. Racers have to factor in the wind direction to make sure that boat gets to what we call the "favored side of the line," meaning the side where there is more wind or less current and the most direct tack to the next mark.

I did my best at the helm, yet many boats maneuvered around me. Paul gave me instructions, but as much as I tried, I always got *Lolita Too!* off the starting line either too early or too late, putting her behind the fleet. Once a boat is behind it's difficult to make up the difference. With so little experience on the team, we were very reluctant to tack or maneuver the boat, so we just fell farther behind. As our distance from the fleet widened, the team lost hope and turned its attention elsewhere, like going below to have a beer or soda. We either *did not finish* (DNF) a race or we came in last.

Nevertheless, we were certainly a happy boat. Jennifer was right. We had fun! Every day after the race, we'd invite the other teams on board for cocktails and snacks. We were fully stocked with food and booze for our cruise to Maine. The other boats tended to have empty stores to stay light for racing. We had a blast and got to know everybody.

We all made light of the fact that we were so bad on the race course. But not so deep inside my distaste for losing sat like a clenched fist. I kept all of this to myself until I confided in Jennifer at the end of the regatta.

"Thank you for inviting me, but I am so embarrassed."

"Oh, Frank, don't worry about it," she told me.

"No Jennifer, I don't like to be last. I like to be a winner. I'm coming back here next year for this same regatta. And when I come back, you'll never see me in last place again. Never."

We headed on, accompanied by John Cumming's Swan to the Bay of Maine and ultimately to Penobscott Bay, but not without another test. We had sailed all night across the bay; we were all drowsy.

"Dad, dad, wake up!" I heard Antoine hollering. "I think I hear some waves breaking!"

We all woke up and ran on deck. Through a break in the fog, we saw an island right in front of us and silver-tipped waves crashing on this island's rocky shore. We immediately tacked the boat, steering it to a narrow miss and avoiding running aground. If Antoine had not been vigilant that morning, we would have smashed into those rocks. There is no telling what may have happened in those cold waters off Maine. Again, my son Antoine proved himself worthy as a sailor.

We reached Penobscot Bay, spent time with David at his home, and then sailed back to Stamford. All in all, it was a fantastic experience. But all the time we were sailing back home I permitted to think to myself, *What am I going to do to get this boat ready for racing?*

I asked Paul what I should do to improve my racing performance.

He explained that a Swan 46 is not ideal for racing because it has a shallow 5'6" keel, the part beneath the boat that extends into the water like an inverted shark's dorsal fin. He said the boat could be modified, like replacing its sails with stronger, lighter ones and installing larger winches to trim—meaning adjust or take in the sails—faster. He said I could even have the bottom of the boat sanded and waxed so it would slip more nimbly through the water.

"All of that will cost you some money," Paul warned me.

I was willing to pay the price to outfit *Lolita Too!* while I assembled a top flight team so that I would not be embarrassed again the next year.

Not much later, Paul, Antoine, and I sailed into a big sailing yard in Westbrook, Connecticut. There I met Jeremy Maxwell, a real boat man who was the number two man at the boatyard.

I amused him with the story of my poor performance in the recent Swan Regatta. But I wasted no time letting him know that I expected to bring *Lolita Too!* up to racing standards in time to return to the regatta to win.

Jeremy told me that he had some ideas, which I expected. What I didn't expect is what came next. "Maybe I can sail with you? I've done a lot of ocean racing and know a number of sailors with racing experience. Maybe we could pull together a team."

I realized right away that our chance meeting could be the answer. Jeremy quickly laid out a plan of changes to make the boat more of a racer than a cruiser. I left *Lolita Too!* in his care. I trusted him. As the work was underway, Jeremy introduced me to Tom McLaughlin, a master sailmaker, and to North Sails, the best sailmaking company in the world. It produces the racing sails for all the America's Cup teams.

As we approached the 1997 season, *Lolita Too!* was in much better shape. The 1997 Swan Regatta was held in July on the island of Nantucket, Massachusetts. Jeremy had assembled a crew of about seven sailors, some of whom, like America's Cup sailor Tom Chiginsky, will still race with me today if I get the urge.

Antoine, Wesley Buford, and a friend of his, rounded out the crew. Jennifer was delighted, but not as much as I was.

This time, I felt very confident when we approached the starting line of the first race. Sure enough, we got off to a good start on starboard tack. We were "in the hunt," in racing parlance—running third or fourth for the whole race. Our crew work caught everyone by surprise, and we finished the first day in second place.

It was an electrifying moment when Lolita and I went to the podium to receive our award. The way we rejoiced, people might have thought we had won, but for us, second place was fabulous. I now knew that I had the potential to win. I had found my sport, and I had Jeremy to thank for making it all possible. From that moment on he has been my Racing Leader and friend.

■ ■ ■

On Nantucket, I met Andy Dickinson, who was to become my longtime captain of *Lolita Too!* and also a good friend. He had just returned to the States after having served as mate aboard a sailboat in the Mediterranean. I hired Andy to deliver *Lolita Too!* back to Stamford. Before departing, he conducted a meticulous inspection of the boat.

I was greatly impressed by his thoroughness. When he arrived with *Lolita Too!* in Stamford, I asked him to be its full-time captain. He accepted.

Everything all came wonderfully together in 1998 at the Swan Regatta at Newport. This is the real deal. We had the team in place. *Lolita* Too! was in the absolute best possible racing condition. We were ready to compete.

As the regatta was about to get underway, Dr. Richie Shulman's 51-foot Swan, the winner of nearly a half-dozen straight regattas, was the odds on favorite. *Lolita Too!* was hardly mentioned in the coverage of the event. There were six races over six days. At the end of the fifth day, to everyone's surprise, Shulman and I were tied for first place The media started reporting on the tight race between Shulman and me and on how *Lolita Too!* had become such a formidable competitor. The rise of the underdog became the talk of the regatta, and I was interviewed by all of the Newport papers.

In the last race, Shulman beat us over the finish line by less than 2.5 seconds; he may have won the regatta but *Lolita Too!* was the belle of the ball. The entire fleet was abuzz with talk of how well we had done. Shulman offered me his congratulations on the progress that I had made over the last couple of years.

"I can tell that you are going to keep winning and one day beat me," he told me. "It's clear that you are motivated."

I knew full well that *Lolita Too!* could go on to win events, and she did very well. But I had started to set my ambitions a bit higher and realized that if I was really going to win I needed yet a faster sailboat.

It so happened that in 1998 the new Swan 56 was unveiled by its maker, Nautor. It was apparent that this version of vessel embodied a significant advance in design, construction, and shape. It also came in a highly versatile racer/cruiser model. The racing version had an 11-foot-2-inch regatta keel and carbon-fiber rigging, which is both strong and lightweight. The deep keel, which weighed a third of the boat, greatly increased the vessel's steadiness under sail and the righting moment. Combine that with the boat's ultralight carbon-fiber, 80-foot mast, this Swan could sail closer to the wind than my *Lolita Too!* ever could.

One writer called the Swan 56 a "street-legal Ferrari."

I had to have it.

Rob Watson, a fellow Swan owner whose boat occupied the neighboring slip to mine at Stamford Landing, purchased the first Swan 56 racer/cruiser in Long Island Sound. He invited me to race with him in a local regatta and graciously let me take the helm for a while. I was blown away by the handling and speed of the boat he called *Neva*. And it wasn't just quick, but sported a stunning interior. *Neva* was high comfort and high performance, an exemplary racer/cruiser.

I raved to Lolita about the boat. I suggested that the 56, when combined with my extraordinary crew, could be unstoppable on the race course. Plus, the interior provided us with great space and comfort for cruising anywhere in the world. Always my greatest advocate, Lolita was very encouraging.

"I can see how much fun you had on that boat," she told me. "Go ahead and buy one!"

I contacted Jennifer Stewart again and expressed my serious interest in buying a Swan 56. She suggested we visit the Swan factory in Finland to observe the construction process and consider design layouts. I was there in my head before I hung up the telephone.

Before going on the trip, Jeremy and my team helped my Captain, Andy and I scope out a preliminary racing/cruising layout for the deck and the rigging. Having already raced *Lolita Too!*, we knew exactly how we wanted the new boat to be designed. I simply followed Lolita's guidance and fine eye for decorating when it came to the new boat's interior (I also borrowed some design touches from a SWAN 100 under construction at the factory).

■ ■ ■

The Nautor's Swan plant in Finland was very impressive. In 1998, it was a highly modern facility located in the middle of the Finnish woods and a major employer in the region. It had the reputation for attracting the best of talent. Jennifer and I had the opportunity to discuss every possible aspect of my yacht with the Swan engineers and designers. On the second day, exploring the inside of a hull, Jennifer exclaimed, "I've got Lolita on the phone and she gave me strict instructions not to let you leave without buying the Swan 56 because you really want it!"

Right after that, I signed the contract for the new boat. In March 2000, *Lolita* landed in Newark, New Jersey.

I'm big on teamwork. I knew that the secret to this *Lolita*'s racing success would lie with the crew as much as with the boat. I had Jeremy, the racing boss, who had my full trust. Tomac, (he preferred one name like Prince, Cher) the master sailmaker who had worked with us from the beginning, put together our excellent racing sail inventory. He was also an America's Cup sailor. Andy, my excellent captain for many years aboard *Lolita Too!*, had raced with us since Nantucket. Tom Chiginsky—known as T.C.—my sail trimmer, was another America's Cup sailor. Two young University of Rhode Island sailors, Jon Ziskind and Jeff Ewenson, started racing with me as college students. Jon would go on to be an America's Cup sailor. That was my core team.

We already had developed an idea of exactly how we wanted the boat to be set up. It was carefully detailed . . . the number of winches, their location, what kind of lines, how to run the lines on the starboard and the port sides. We decided to get a racing keel to enhance performance although its depth would limit my access to ports and harbors that had deep water. We arranged the deck so that it was optimal for race boat handling. There were so many decisions to be made and we made them together, as a team. Lolita and I considered the team family; we enjoyed that kind of strong bond among us.

To celebrate the launching of *Lolita* we held a big party at my sailing club, Indian Harbor Yacht Club in Greenwich, Connecticut. It was attended by many of our friends, family, fellow sailors, crew, and club members. We had an awesome reggae band that had us dancing until the waning wee hours of the morning.

Lolita was officially ready to start the 2000 racing season. The first race was the Greenwich Cup, sponsored by Indian Harbor. This is a three- to four-day "round-the-buoys" race in the Long Island Sound. *Lolita* dominated from the start and went on to win the regatta. Indian Harbor was ecstatic that one of its members had won.

But the real test of *Lolita*'s capabilities came in the Storm Trysail Round Block Island Race against some of the highest caliber racing boats around. This is an overnight distance race from Stamford, around Block Island and back to Stamford. More than 100 sailboats from the United States and Europe participate; the fleet is divided into classes and uses a handicap system that adjusts each boat's performance to equalize its time over the course. Having learned several lessons in the Greenwich Cup, we took significant time making adjustments to the boat rigging and winching so she would be better equipped for our second major race.

Depending on the weather and the boat, the Block Island Race can take from 10 to 15 hours. The crew is divided up into three shifts of five to six crew members; each shift ran the boat for about four hours then took a rest. Even during off-shifts, all crew is on call in case of an emergency. As the owner, I had ultimate responsibility for the boat and crew so before starting, I had the crew conduct man-overboard drills.

These are crucial exercises. If a crewmember fell overboard, especially at night, it would be extremely difficult to retrieve him. Overboard crewmembers proved difficult to find and some had, in fact, died during this race. Although I pride myself on taking risks in finance, losing a member of the *Lolita* team was not a risk I was willing to take.

The race started downwind and I was at the helm. We had a great start and because the wind direction did not change in the first leg, we were able to sail on the same tack almost to the end of Long Island Sound without jibing, turning toward the new wind direction. It was exhilarating for me to drive the boat.

When my shift ended the next shift came on and jibed and headed through a narrow passage of water at the mouth of the Long Island Sound known as the "Race." It is where the Long Island Sound converges with the Block Island Sound. At that point, we seemed to be among the leaders. *Lolita*'s tactician and the navigators were doing an excellent job of calling the wind shifts and currents. The second shift subsequently took down the spinnaker, tacked and turned to about 120 to 150 degrees to the wind, called a broadreach, and headed toward Block Island's leeward western shore at night.

I had a bite to eat and dozed off for a couple of hours. When I woke, it was still dark and we were on the opposite windward side of Block Island. The third shift took over and sailed the boat back through the Race as daylight began to break. In the morning, my shift got up, had breakfast and prepared to sail through to the finish.

Although we were very glad to see that we were leading our class of sailboats, we did not know how the other classes in the fleet were doing.

I assumed the helm for the final beat, a 30- to 40-degree angle to the wind, and on to the finish line. *Lolita* was flying, going about eight to nine knots upwind, as smooth as could be. The cotton strings on the headsail, the telltales, were flickering in the sun, a sure sign that *Lolita* was sailing at optimal heel. All the crew was on the windward side of the boat just like the crew in the picture in that sailing magazine when the bug to sail first bit me.

We crossed the finish line at Stamford Harbor and got "the gun," a shot fired when the first boat of each class finishes. I was ecstatic!

Later in the day, we checked with the race committee and discovered that we were number one in the entire fleet. This was fantastic. *Lolita* had proven that she was capable of winning against a very competitive fleet. The next day at the award ceremony, *Lolita* was named Best in Fleet, Best Overall, and Best in Class.

Lolita's name was also embossed on the Elmira trophy, the Harry Conover Memorial Trophy and the Henry Tripp Memorial Trophy, each on permanent display at the Storm Trysail Club's headquarters in Larchmont, New York.

Aside from the honors, I was humbled when George Coutemtaris, the owner of the famous race boat, *Boomerang*, personally congratulated me and predicted that *Lolita* would go on to win many races given the boat, her crew, and our motivation.

That night, at our crew party, I congratulated everyone on an excellent race. In our first season, we had established *Lolita* as a worthy competitor, even among the best sailboats in the United States. I was touched when the crew commended me on my helmsmanship during the race. I had earned everyone's respect by stepping up and contributing to our victory rather than sitting on the sidelines, the man with the checkbook.

I have never been a sidelines kind of guy.

There would be so many races. One was a 600-mile race to Bermuda in which my son Antoine was an able crewmember. Lolita and my children, Gracie and Frankie, waited to welcome us at the finish.

At about midnight on the second night of that race, sailing at about eight knots, *Lolita* hit something hard. She rose up, shook as if she were teetering on top of something, and then fell back into the water. Everyone ran on deck and looked around the side but we could not see anything in the pitch black night. Immediately, we inspected the hull and rigging, but nothing looked damaged.

It was not until we reached Bermuda that we learned that other boats reported similar incidents. It turned out that we had all collided with a pod of whales. Some boats suffered damage, but *Lolita* came out unscathed.

We crossed the finish line in third place in the St. David Lighthouse Division. Not too bad for our first Atlantic crossing. As *Lolita*'s inaugural East Coast racing season came to an end, I could not have been happier and the crew was looking forward to racing in the Caribbean.

Lolita participated in the British Virgin Islands, Heineken St. Martin, and the Antigua Race weeks during the 2001 Caribbean season. She continued to perform exceptionally well in all of these races against very large fleets. On every occasion, she was the most outstanding Swan. One of my proudest moments came during the 2001 Rolex Regatta in

St. Maarten when we displaced the British Swan 56, *Noonmark*, as the most successful racing Swan.

Although anyone would be hard-pressed to find a more motivated sailing crew than mine, I was not above a few creative tricks and tactics to boost the morale of my guys and keep everyone striving for the highest heights of competitive excellence.

During the rare times when our performance slacked off, I was certainly not above a little theater on deck. I would pretend, with all the exaggerated gestures of a silent film star, that I was praying to the Great Yachtsman Upwind for help.

Before the start of every regatta, I started bringing along a bucket labeled "WHOOPASS!" I told the crew that it contained "goobey dust," a potent witch doctor potion that could immobilize all our competitors, but that I didn't want to use it because it was too dangerous. The crew would have to sail as best as it could to spare our opponents from the concoction's unpredictable effects.

Everyone laughed, but that didn't keep the crew from donning the T-shirts I passed out, each shirt bearing across its back a single word: WHOOPASS!

As we headed toward a race's starting line, I would scream, "Are you ready?! Are you ready?!"

"Yes! Yes!" the crew shouted in reply.

"So let's go WHOOPASS!"

My major Swan competitors were Clay Deutsche's 68-foot *Chippewa* as well as a few new TP 52s, an improved model of the Transpac 52, which had won many of the Los Angeles-to-Hawaii races. And, of course, there was the British *Noonmark*.

I particularly loved to sail against *Chippewa*, which was being built at the Swan Pietarsaari factory at the same time as *Lolita*. Clay was a super guy and hosted many dock parties at our regattas. We became great friends and my daughter Grace began dating one of his crew, Tommy Longhborough, which helped to bring us all even closer.

From the beginning of our *Lolita* sailing campaigning, Lolita and I always housed the crew in nice accommodations and hosted nightly crew dinners. These occasions fostered our team spirit and provided us the ideal setting to critique performance and plan future strategy. We formed a strong bond with our crew, which clearly built a sense of loyalty and in no small way fostered our continuing success on the racecourse.

In the fall of 2002, we took *Lolita* to Sardinia, the second-largest island in the Mediterranean. Our mission was to compete in the Swan Worlds, held at the Yacht Club Esmeraldas, one of the finest yacht clubs anywhere. This would give us a chance to show that she could win the top Swan Regatta against the best Swans from Europe, Asia, and the Americas.

Lolita and I visited Sardinia beforehand on *Lolita* to scope out the location and the course, especially the depths and rocks. Sardinia is famous for its beautiful, yet potentially dangerous rocks and outcroppings.

On the strong encouragement of Jeremy Maxwell, I promoted Kate Mardel-Ferreira, *Lolita's* former first mate, to Captain. This made her one of the first women to skipper a Swan. I also hired a new first mate, Chris Godfrey, a young Brit whom we met in St. Maarten at the 2001 Rolex Regatta. Kate and Chris prepped the boat beautifully for the Swan Worlds race.

On the first day of racing, the wind was blowing 20 to 25 knots, gusting to 30 to 35 knots and was very fickle, to the point of almost being hazardous on the downwind legs. It was a challenging race. Several of the smaller Swan 42s lost their rudders and had to retire and other boats lost their spinnaker or broached, a dangerous hard roll of the boat that led to capsizing.

At one point, *Lolita* too rolled so dangerously that its boom almost touched the water. Thanks to Jeff Ewenson's superb helmsmanship and the excellent crew handling, she survived and was well ahead of the fleet on the upwind leg as we headed for the finish line.

At one point, as we watched the trailing boats to stern, we noticed that our rival, *Noonmark*, seemed to be standing straight up in the water with her genoa, the large leading sail, down. We thought she had some sort of problem, but a short time after, her sail was back up and *Noonmark* continued to race.

We finished the race in first place and went to the committee office to check the results. A number of reporters came over to interview me about the race. Given our performance, I was confident of ultimate victory in the Swan Worlds. Then the *Noonmark* tactician appeared and I asked him what had happened to his boat on the course. He told me that they had to stop to retrieve a crew member who had fallen overboard from another boat. That was the ethical Corinthian thing to do. But sailboat racing can be tricky business.

He said he was going to appeal to the race committee to give *Noonmark* credit in the race standings to compensate for the time lost in rescuing the sailor. Okay, I thought that was a reasonable request. When the new results were posted *Lolita* was number one and *Noonmark* was number three. But then the tactician rushed off again to the committee room. When he emerged this time, the Committee placed *Noonmark* in the number one position and had put *Lolita* at number two.

I was livid that he had manipulated the committee to give his team the win. And no, I did not officially protest because under the circumstances I did not want to show bad sportsmanship. I did, however, complain bitterly to Leonard Ferragamo, the Italian businessman who, with a group of investors, controlled and managed the company that makes the Swans. Ferragamo tried to assuage my anger by reassuring me that he was sure that ultimately *Lolita* would come out on top. Unfortunately, this was not to be the case because the loss of that first race cost *Lolita* the overall championship.

We came in second in the Swan Worlds. And even with the unearned credits *Noonmark* received on the first day of the race, she came in fifth.

I felt especially bad for my crew that day because my guys had sailed *Lolita* so beautifully, and under very trying conditions, over the entire regatta. And I think my crew was equally sad for me because of the effort I had put into preparing *Lolita* to win the regatta. But that's sailboat racing. Tricky business, sometimes.

Upon her return to the United States in the spring 2002, *Lolita* won the Swan American Regatta in Newport, an event I held in the highest regard because it was on my home turf and I had just missed winning it in 1998 with *Lolita Too!*

But this *Lolita* won every single race during the six-day regatta. As the last day of the race neared, we had built up such a lead that victory was assured; we didn't have to race the last day. But in a good sportsmanship gesture, we raced anyway. That gesture went down very well with my fellow SWAN owners. *Lolita* was pictured in a *New York Times* article about the Swan regatta and she was also featured on commercial airliner television program. *Sailing World*, the leading sailing magazine, published an article labeled "The Fastest Swan on the Pond" about *Lolita*'s continuous string of victories.

The whole family celebrated the publicity.

■ ■ ■

In the winter 2002, *Lolita* returned to the Caribbean and came in third overall in fleet, and second in her class and was named the Overall Best Swan In Fleet for the second straight year at Antigua Race Week. She was getting closer and closer to being the overall winner of the Antigua Race Week regatta, a goal I had set for *Lolita*. She had everything it took to win the regatta, but no racer/cruiser had ever won it. Only the big racing boats had done that.

Then came 2003 and our return to Antigua Race Week.

The breeze was perfect for *Lolita*, running between 15 and 25 knots; she ran away with her class, placing in the top three places in every race. The crew work was near perfection. The difference between believing we had the race and winning it collapsed into a single, sugary moment of victory.

Lolita won First Overall in Fleet, and received the coveted Lord Nelson Trophy, which adorns my living room in New York to this day.

She was first in Racing Class Two, and was named the Outstanding Swan for the third consecutive year. After the race, the crew did the customary practice of throwing me in the water once we reached the dock and they all jumped in after me in a raucous celebration. We had achieved our goal, and there were no words to adequately express our joy that day.

I could not help to note, given that we were gathered on a Caribbean island, that no black person had ever won the regatta.

Our victory made the local black majority there especially proud. My Antiguan crew member, Bobby Green, was a local hero. Flying home with all my trophies, I just couldn't stop smiling. The flight's captain even announced that "Frank Savage of the sailboat *Lolita*, winner of the Antigua Race Week regatta, is on the plane."

All of the passengers applauded. I looked over to Lolita and she was clapping, too.

We had done it. And flying that high in the heavens, I knew La Savage was applauding, too.

Reflections

The winning experience on *Lolita* was a result of the convergence of many aspects of my life. I didn't plan it to happen that way. I pursued sailboat racing purely because I loved the sport, nothing else. To win, I had to draw on all the intuitive skills as well as attributes I've had to acquire to navigate the waves of life. I like the way Herb Cummings summed it up in an October 2008 article he wrote for *Sailing World* entitled "The *Lolita* Way":

> *For well known campaigner Frank Savage, the lessons and rewards in sailing, business and life are one and the same.*

What follows are among the chief components to winning that I've come to recognize whether I am driving a boat on the high seas, driving investment in the global marketplace, or simply making success a partner in my day-to-day life:

- **Self Confidence:** I had to rely on my sense of self-confidence to take on the challenge of big sailboat ocean racing, which no other African American had dared undertake. However, I never thought of myself as the only African American in the sport. Why should I? I was just as successful and motivated as all the other Swan owners. I had already broken new ground as the most prominent African American in the international financial arena around the world and served as chairman of Equitable Capital Management Corporation and Alliance Capital Management, two major financial institutions. Fortunately, because of my business success, I had the financial resources to afford the significant costs of owning and running an international ocean sailboat racing program with a 17-person race crew and a 56-foot sailboat that had to be maintained in excellent condition at all times.
- **Preparation:** I had fully prepared myself for the challenge of competitive sailboat racing. It took me 12 to 15 years of sailing experience, starting from zero to build up the preparation required to be able to handle a sophisticated, high-performance vessel like

Lolita in the competitive, and sometimes dangerous, sport of ocean sailboat racing. Most top sailors are practically born into sailing. Given my modest background, growing up black in Washington, I did not have that privilege. So I had to catch up very fast.

- **Leadership:** My mother, La Savage, taught me about leadership and motivating people to believe in themselves so they could do their best. I put those skills to work in my international work experience at Citibank, Equitable, TAW, and Alliance Capital. I knew that showing respect for people was the best way to get results. This was an essential quality in motivating the high-powered team of world-class sailors on *Lolita*. I didn't seek people to simply replicate me, but individuals with unique talents and skills that I could lead and motivate to mesh, creating an astounding whole vastly greater than its extraordinary parts.
- **Handling pressure:** Thomas A. Wood, the visionary entrepreneur who recruited me to work with him in Africa, demonstrated how important it was to remain calm under pressure. Big boat sailboat racing is by nature a high-pressure sport because things happen so fast and the potential for catastrophic accidents is so high. When accidents occur, or equipment breaks, quick action is required. Surfing down a wave at 10 to 15 knots is exhilarating, but if the crew loses concentration, bad things, potentially fatal things, can easily happen.

During the years of 2001 through 2005 when I enjoyed my greatest sailboat racing accomplishments, I was under incredible pressure dealing with a full-blown Enron crisis. My picture was often in newspapers; unions and pension funds were suing directors, including me, and executives; and the United States government, including the SEC and the U.S. Department of Labor, were threatening action against me and my fellow Enron board members. I spent countless hours with lawyers. The only time I could get Enron out of my head was when I was racing *Lolita*.

Handling the pressure and focusing on what most needed to be done are the attributes that enabled me to succeed in business and in sailboat racing. *Lolita* provided me the platform to bring all of that together and produce the best I had to give.

Yes, that, too, is the Savage Way.

Epilogue

The question of what's next for Frank Savage is never far from my thoughts.

For me and the way I live my life, I consider my sails forever unfurled. I am forever open to the wind of destiny and to the promise of distant shores and new possibilities. Sure, my hair is a little more gray than it was decades ago when I was a young man starting my voyage, but my grip on the wheel that determines where I go and what I do in this vastly fascinating world of opportunities has never been more sure and steady.

Let me assure you, I am not – literally or figuratively – the retiring type.

My work goes on in the universe of global finance, actively engaged in searching for ways to solve our current crisis. I am a proud American and I want to do all I can to help ensure that our economy strengthens and thrives – especially among minorities too long denied access to capital and fair consideration. But I am not so provincial to believe that we live and work in a vacuum. We are all connected. Good and healthy business abroad helps to ensure that we have good and healthy business at home. And vice versa.

My heart still pounds as I near the closing of a major financial transaction. After all, finance is still my profession and I shall continue to be engaged in making constructive contributions to the global financial sector. Philanthropy occupies a soft spot in my heart, and my mind still races when I think about what I can do to help others, people and nations, as they struggle to accomplish great things.

I never tire of hopping a flight to advise and assist true nation builders in creating economic opportunities for millions of its people in any corner of the world. This is still particularly so when my work and passion carries me to my dear Africa, be it advising or helping to raise capital for a food security project in one West African nation or the redevelopment of a shipping port in another. These sorts of pursuits have a salutatory benefit for the African people, and by extension, the people of the whole world. Yes, we are that interconnected today.

And surely I shall always have a close connection to my favorite support, sailing, and will continue to introduce it to the many who have never had the chance to experience the thrill and challenge of tackling the seas.

There is so much I want to continue to do, and new waters to ply to do even more.

One of my chief concerns, and one of the primary reasons I wrote this book, is passing onto new generations of business professionals and entrepreneurs the best practices and the lessons of my generation.

No, we have never been perfect, as evidenced by the long period of segregation. But, in the end even that scourge was, in many respects, wiped away by my generation, black and white, determined to live up to the principles of our nation's Constitution that so famously states, "All men are created equal." Could the drafters of this living document have ever imagined that a black man would be elected President of the United States?

If I pass on anything in these pages, I wish to pass on the gleaming importance of living a honest life, one marked by compassion for others and guided by an internal compass, or G.P.S. if you will, affixed on the priceless treasure of unshakable integrity.

My hope is that as we continue to unlock the deeper meanings of citizenship, and that 21st-century generations of Americans recommit to living a life grounded in the highest ethics, whether on Main Street or

Wall Street or no street. Families and educators must take up the calling to teach that winning at any cost is not winning at all.

My mother, La Savage, taught me that before she taught me to tie up my shoes. I have never forgotten that lesson. It is part of her legacy, and, with this book, I wish it to become part of mine.

In the meantime, I tack toward the horizons where fresh opportunities loom, entreating all to join me, in a sense, on deck. I want to share, particularly with young people around the world, the principle that Madame La Savage embedded in me when I was a youngster:

"You can be anything you want to be."

FRANK SAVAGE

Lolita with Frank at its helm racing to Bermuda, 2000

Lolita
Racing Record

2000:
    1st in Fleet, Greenwich Cup
    1st in Fleet, Block Island Race Week
    1st in Fleet, NYYC Spring Regatta
    3rd in Class, Newport Bermuda Race
2001:
    1st in Racer/Cruiser Fleet, Heineken Regatta, 1st in Class; 2nd
        Overall, Antigua Race Week, 1st Overall, Block Island Race
        Week
    1st in Fleet, Swan Americans
2002:
    2nd in Class, British Virgin Islands Spring Regatta
    2nd in Class, Antigua Race Week
    2nd in Fleet, Swan Worlds, Sardinia

2003:

    1st in Class B.V.I Spring Regatta

    1st Overall in Fleet, receiving the Lord Nelson Trophy; 1st in Racing Class 2; Winner of the Swan Challenge Trophy, Antigua Race Week

    3rd in Fleet, Swan Americans

2004:

    Antigua Race Week, 5th in Fleet, Winner of the Swan Challenge Trophy

2005:

    3rd in Class, Heineken Race Week

    Antigua Race Week, 3rd in Fleet; Winner of Swan Challenge Trophy for 3rd Consecutive Year

    3rd in Class, Swan Americans

2006:

    3rd in Class, Heineken Race Week

    5th in Class, Antigua Race Week

    1st in Class under ORR, 2nd under IRC, Newport Bermuda Race

2008:

    3rd in Class, Racing Division, Antigua Race Week

2009:

    1st in Cruising Division, Ida Lewis Distance Race

Antigua Race Week Overall
Winner International Crew, 2003

<u>Sailing team</u>

Kevin Wakalee, USA	Bow
Greg Gendell, UK	Mast
Matias Blanco, ARG	Mast b/up
Andy Dickinson, USA	Halyards/pit
Claus Graugaard, DK	Halyards/pit
Chris Godfrey, UK	Halyards/pit

Kate Mardel, UK	F/guy & T/lift
Lars Svenstrup, DEN	Grinder
Ron Brown, USA	Grinder
Rick Rasemus, USA	Grinder
Tom Chiginsky, USA	Port Tail
Jon Ziskin, USA	Stbd Tail
Tom McLaughlin, USA	Downwind trim
Jeremy Maxwell, UK	Mainsheet
Bill Biewenga, USA	Navigator
Andy Horton, USA	Tactics
Phil Garland, USA	Helmsman
Frank Savage, USA	Helmsman

Acknowledgments

My deepest gratitude goes unquestionably to my mother, Madame La Savage, the source of my strength and never-ending inspiration. She set me on the right path and was always by my side during her lifetime and even after her all-too-soon passing; she guided me through every phase of my life, good and bad, always the beacon of pure love and light.

To my darling twin sister, Frances, you have always loved and supported me, often unselfishly understating your own impressive achievements to emphasize my accomplishments. You've always pushed me to higher heights. My extended family of Grandma Hattie, aunts Hazel, Louise, and Naomi, and Uncle Thomas, provided an indispensible foundation for me while La Savage was busy working every day and night in her beauty parlor, La Savage Beauty Clinic. This strong family laid the groundwork for my life's success.

My wife Lolita. She came into my life at a coincidental point when my business associates Brian Wruble and John Miller and I had set up the Equitable subsidiary, Equitable Capital Management, and I was charged with building our international asset management business. Lolita was the perfect partner in my life. Her sparkling personality, international experience as an accomplished fine arts painter, and fluency in seven languages helped to open doors for my business as well as open new doors into my heart. I cannot imagine my history without her.

Together, we were an African-American man and a Philippine-American woman who took on the world and won. She was indispensible to my mercurial rise in the field of international finance. And, as a result, she is a major part of my story.

I have also been blessed with six wonderful children, Eric, Brett, Mark, Antoine, Grace, and Frank. They have provided me with a special peace and pride that has enabled me to pursue my career mindful that I have set them on the right path. Both Brett and Grace, English majors, performed important editing of the early draft of *The Savage Way*, and did a fabulous job of correcting my sometimes less than perfect English.

While this is my book, my story, I drew, at various junctures, on the expertise of friends who are experts in writing and publishing to get their take on this memoir. The most important was my close friend, Charlayne Hunter-Gault, a distinguished print and broadcast journalist who had been a longtime foreign correspondent in Africa for National Public Radio and CNN. She is also an excellent memoirist in her own right. Charlayne gave my manuscript a thorough read and made some excellent comments and suggestions. Most significantly, she steered me to Michel Marriott, an accomplished and experienced writer, to give the manuscript his skilled, professional touch. Michel did a fantastic job. I cannot thank him enough for his contribution to *The Savage Way*.

I must also take this opportunity to thank my agent, Faith Childs of the Faith Childs Literary Agency, for her tireless commitment to this book. In the same breath, I must also express my profound thanks to Pamela van Giessen, associate publisher for John Wiley & Sons, and her Wiley publishing team in Hoboken, N.J.

I wish to thank and acknowledge so many that there isn't the space among these pages. But you know who you are, those who have formed the strong, favorable winds that have blown at my back and helped me make my way to distant and promising ports, and always home again.

FRANK SAVAGE

Index